In Search of
Gopher Hollow

In Search of
GOPHER HOLLOW

A Life Story of Grit & Gumption
and the Grandfather Who Inspiried Me

THERESA ANTHONY

Copyright © 2023 by Theresa Anthony

ALL RIGHTS RESERVED. This book or any portion thereof may not be reproduced or used in any manner whatsoever without the express written permission of the publisher, except for the use of brief quotations in a book review.

Excerpt from *The Life I Lead* by Rory Feek Copyright © 2017 by Rory Feek

Used by permission of HarperCollins Christian Publishing. www.harpercollinschristian.com

Library of Congress Control Number: 2023919964

ISBN: 979-8-218-30210-8

Cover Design by Emma Anthony

Author's note: This is a nonfiction memoir. Names of some individuals included in the narrative have been changed.

Printed in the United States of America

First printing edition 2023

www.TheresaAnthony.com

This book is lovingly dedicated

To my grandfather, John Botehlo Sousa

My knight in shining armor

Contents

	Introduction	1
Chapter 1:	Summer 1964	5
Chapter 2:	The Family Tree	9
Chapter 3:	A Rough Start	13
Chapter 4:	Hello Gopher Hollow	25
Chapter 5:	On Our Own Again	39
Chapter 6:	Teen Times	51
Chapter 7:	High School Days	65
Chapter 8:	Time for College	75
Chapter 9:	The Self-Absorbed Twenties	81
Chapter 10:	Brian	91
Chapter 11:	Enter John	99
Chapter 12:	Marriage and Motherhood	105
Chapter 13:	Homeschooling	121
Chapter 14:	Divorce	133
Chapter 15:	Mike	143
Chapter 16:	Matthew	149
Chapter 17:	Matt and Mike	169
Chapter 18:	Tragedy	191
Chapter 19:	The Grief Journey Begins	213
Chapter 20:	Learning to Cope	225
Chapter 21:	Covid	239
Chapter 22:	Mamasita	249
Chapter 23:	Finding Gopher Hollow	261
Afterword:	The Books	285
	About the Author	295

"However, be on your guard and be very careful not to forget the things your own eyes have seen, nor let them slip from your heart as long as you live, but make them known to your children and to your children's children."

— DEUTERONOMY 4:9

Introduction

HAVE YOU EVER WONDERED why we humans tend to have certain preferences, like a favorite flower or color or genre of music? Why do we favor one style of décor over another, or gravitate toward certain people while others repel us? What prompts us to purchase a particular house or car? Why do some places elicit feelings of excitement and joy while others stoke anxiety? Where do our personal preferences come from?

In the pages that follow, I invite you to join me as I take a peek under the hood, exploring the powerful events and experiences that have shaped my life, as well as the people who have influenced me along the way. Yes, this is an intensely personal journey I am about to embark on, but it's one that I believe is highly relatable, universal even. When we take the time to really reflect on our lives, to consider the pivotal events and the special relationships that added meat to the bones, I'd bet most of us could point to one special place or person that made a meaningful impact on our lives, our decisions, and yes, in shaping our personal preferences.

In my case, it was one man, my grandfather, who wielded an outsized effect on me. As a kid fresh out of second grade, after suffering three tumultuous years in the Northwest, I suddenly found myself living with my maternal grandparents. That summer, a magical melding occurred deep in my psyche. It was the fusion between their home, called Gopher Hollow, and the love of a grandpa that would become forever imprinted on my eight-year-old soul. In ways that only God can orchestrate, the effect that this short time period had on my life has been lasting and profound.

I understand now why my heart stirs when I spot a vintage toaster in an antique store that's identical to the one at my grandparents' house. And why I reflexively close my eyes and drink in the scents of gardenia, orange blossoms, or eucalyptus, or am moved when I hear the cooing of a mourning dove. It explains why I prefer rustic décor and simplicity over fancy home furnishings and grandiosity, and why I always struggle to balance my impatient, adventurous spirit with my practical side.

Although I have faced some daunting challenges in my life, and several tragedies, God gifted me with a strong will to survive. But that isn't all I was gifted with. I was also blessed to have a role model, a grandfather, who provided me with real-world examples of fortitude, perseverance, courage, and spunk. I soaked these up like a sponge at a young age, and by God, they stuck with me and have served me well all my adult life.

I hope you will gain something of value by reading my story, some new insights into your own life, or even experience an epiphany or two. I hope to inspire you to face any trials or challenges head-on instead of running away from them, and to know that Jesus is right there beside you to help you carry your cross.

In essence, my purpose in writing my life story is twofold. First, I hope to illustrate beyond a doubt that my strong faith is what kept me

INTRODUCTION

moving forward during some very difficult times. Secondly, I wish to honor my beloved grandfather, John Sousa, whose amazing life and spirit are inseparable from that family home, Gopher Hollow, the place that I came to view as my sanctuary.

And so it is, this discovery that throughout my life, with all its twists and turns, ups and downs, joys and sorrows, I have subconsciously been on a perpetual quest, a quest driven by a wounded soul in search of healing…in search of Gopher Hollow.

CHAPTER 1

Summer 1969

I PREFER THE DEN. I scamper off, stealing away from the others who are gathered out in the living room, chatting and watching TV. Grandma likes watching her stories and game shows in her recliner, unless there's a Dodger game on, and Grandpa likes reading in the corner chair next to the bookcase. Mommy and Ann are on the couch, cracking walnuts in a dish on the copper table and enjoying the summer afternoon together here at Gopher Hollow. Me? I just want to spend some quiet time alone in the den. You might wonder what an eight-year-old girl might find so fascinating about this room. Well, what isn't fascinating about it?

There I lie on the twin bed that's nestled snugly into the corner of the room, my long, skinny legs stretched out over the tan corduroy bedspread. This room once belonged to my uncle John when he was growing up here. These days, the den serves as my grandpa's office, and so much more.

I prop myself up and rest my head back against the wall, pondering the contents of the room with a little girl's sense of awe. Just to the left of me is the door that leads to the dining room. Straight ahead is the door to the powder room, with Grandpa's VO5 hair cream out on the counter, and to the right is the glass-paned door that leads out to the brick patio. St. Francis stands right outside that patio door, a tall, sturdy statue that has held court there for many years.

My eyes travel over to the right side of the room where Grandpa's enormous wooden desk stands. I love the giant wooden paperclip on his desk, emblazoned with the gold letters "V.I.P." that holds his mail. V.I.P. stands for Very Important Person. Yes, my grandpa is a V.I.P.

On the wall behind the desk is a large ASTA banner made of blue satin. The bright yellow letters represent the American Society of Travel Advisors, a travel association of which my grandpa is the president. Adjacent to the banner is a wooden display unit with about a dozen cubbies. The cubbies hold colorful travel brochures touting the tours that Grandpa's travel business promotes. I am obsessed with the brochures. Sometimes I'll sneak over to the cabinet, select a random trifold from inside, and unfold it just to see the pictures of the places they advertise, and the small photo of my handsome grandpa on the back.

Next, my eyes travel upward, toward the highest point of the wall. Slowly, methodically, my eyes move around the perimeter of the room, taking it all in. I find the framed photographs featuring my grandpa standing next to famous people captivating. I have no idea who they are, but they all look rather important.

And then there are the artifacts, the African masks and spears and such that hang on the wall, interspersed with the photos. I'm not sure which is more intriguing, the pictures of my grandfather with celebrities, or those cool artifacts he gathered while on his travels to exotic lands.

The sound of Grandma's silver set rattling in the adjacent dining room brings me back to the present moment. Soon after I arrived at Gopher Hollow, I discovered that when you walk across the dining room floor, the sterling coffee set on the little trolley in the corner always rattles. It's my little sister, Ann, traipsing through the dining room in search of me causing the set to rattle at the moment. Oh well, so much for the quiet alone time.

Ann is six years old. We are just getting our bearings here at our grandparents' house after arriving a week ago from Washington. It was a long drive to get here, but it was pretty fun traveling back to California in our 1959 Chevy Impala convertible. It is white with a bright red interior and big wings over the taillights. Already, our mom looks like a movie star, and in fact, in our travels, lots of people think she *is* a movie star, so driving that car attracted even more attention than usual. Grandpa bought us the car last year, and I thought that was really nice of him.

My sister and I aren't really sure why we were here at Gopher Hollow, or what was going to happen next, but that's okay. We've been through a pretty scary time and feel so relieved to now be safe and sound at Grandma and Grandpa's house. Grandma gave us the front room that used to be Mommy's room growing up. It has a big bay window that looks out over the front yard. From our beds early in the morning, we can hear the mourning doves cooing, and their song soothes me. What I like most about Mommy's old room is the vanity table with the pretty flowered curtain around it and the little stool—like it belonged to a princess. Oh, and I also like the cute sticker of a mouse holding cheese that Mommy put on the maple dresser drawer when she was a young girl.

Ann and I really like it here. I don't know how long we will get to stay, but I hope it will be for a long time. We are really tired of moving all the time.

CHAPTER 2

the Family Tree

EACH OF US IS COMPOSED of a DNA sequence that provides us with our own unique biological fingerprint. My DNA happens to be made up of a long line of Catholic stock. My maternal grandmother, Teresa Mattimore, was 100 percent Irish, and my maternal grandfather, John Sousa, was 100 percent Portuguese. My paternal grandmother, Gertrude, was 100 percent Bavarian (German), and my paternal grandfather, Francis, was 100 percent Irish.

As silly as it might seem to put stock in stereotypes, I can personally attest to the accuracy of stereotypes drawn about my ancestral countries of origin. When I consider my own personality traits, I can clearly see that my need for order and organization is attributable to my German genes, that my gregarious and generous nature comes from my Irish genes, and I blame my Portuguese roots for my overly sentimental and romantic nature—which has sometimes gotten me in some trouble.

My maternal grandparents met in San Francisco at a boarding

house. My grandmother was almost thirty when they met in 1922, and my grandpa was just twenty-two. She was studying to be a kindergarten teacher, and he was attending a local business school. The day they met, Grandma was downstairs in the parlor playing the piano and singing. My grandpa was immediately smitten. He was attracted to her lovely voice and shy nature. They soon married, and Grandpa bought them their first home in Reno, Nevada when he was just twenty-four years old.

They eventually relocated to Los Angeles and settled in the South Bay in a beach town called Manhattan Beach. Grandpa worked hard building a career, dabbling in various and sundry endeavors until he found his calling in the travel business. In 1932, my mother was born, followed by the birth of her brother in 1934.

My mom's family would have been considered fairly affluent in its time. My grandfather's was a rags-to-riches story, a driven man who eventually carved out a successful career in the travel business. The travel career afforded them a comfortable life, filled with travel and parties, as well as the ability to afford military school for their son and boarding school for their daughter, which, back then, was a status symbol.

My mother was just fourteen years old when her parents enrolled her in a prestigious Los Angeles Catholic boarding school. Even though the practice of sending your children off to boarding school was common among well-to-do families in the 1940s, my mother never really forgave her parents for it. She often shared how painful it had been to be away from her family all week long. She would be so excited to come home on the weekends, only to have to leave her family again every Sunday evening. She truly never got over it.

After high school, Mom attended a private Catholic college where she majored in theatre arts while also earning her teaching credential. Back in the mid-fifties, to be unmarried at age twenty-two was a frightening prospect for a young woman, which explains why when she was introduced to a fella named George through a high school friend, she had marriage on her mind.

George was a year older than Mom and had studied engineering before being drafted to serve in Korea. He was six-foot-four and hailed from a very musical family in which he played stand-up bass. All seven children in his family were taught to play a musical instrument, so family jam sessions were a regular event in their small, modest home. George's father, Francis, was a traveling salesman who died at the age of fifty-one, about ten years before I was born. My father's mother, Gertrude, a devout Catholic and daily communicant, was hit by a car while crossing the street to go to Mass and died that day at age seventy-four. I only saw my paternal grandmother when I was very young, so I have no memories of her.

One of George's older brothers, Pat, was married to a gal named Roberta who had become a close friend of my mom. Soon after their engagement was announced, Roberta reached out to Mom. She voiced her concerns about the upcoming nuptials. She told my mom that George had shown signs of mental instability since returning from his tour in Korea, and advised her not to marry him. I guess I should be glad that my mother dismissed these warnings because if she had minded them, I would not exist, but Roberta was correct in warning her. The man who would become my father was not stable.

For a while, our family bounced around California. I was born in Santa Maria on July 13, 1956—Friday the 13th. We had landed in Santa Maria in 1956 because George, who prior to this move had been unable to secure steady employment, had found a job there. Mom also started her teaching career there in Santa Maria. But George soon lost his job, so we moved back to the Los Angeles area where at least we were close to both sets of grandparents. Subsequently, my sister Ann was born in Torrance on August 20, 1958.

Unfortunately, my dad was not only incapable of maintaining employment, but he also struggled with mental illness and would often vanish for weeks at a time. I can only imagine the angst this must have caused my mom, who now had two little daughters to care for. As would be expected under the circumstances, her parents were beside themselves with worry. As they witnessed this ongoing instability, they became very concerned about the wellbeing of their daughter and granddaughters and became vocal about their disappointment in George.

George grew resentful of the pressure my grandfather in particular was exerting, and tension grew in the marriage. He began looking for work out of state. Soon, in late 1960, when I was four and my sister was two, he announced to our mother that he'd landed a great job in the Portland, Oregon area. Mom felt relieved but also anxious about the move; relieved because it meant her husband would once again be earning an income, but anxious at the prospect of pulling up stakes and relocating a thousand miles away from everyone she knew. It was especially difficult for her to consider moving so far away from her parents, as her mother, my grandma, had just recently suffered a stroke. Still, she knew she had to put her own family first, which meant that moving was the only real option.

CHAPTER 3

A Rough Start

IT WAS THE FALL OF 1960 when we packed up the Studebaker and headed north. My dad told us about a beautiful home he had found for us, and he assured us we'd all love our new life in Oregon. Of course, my sister and I were so young we didn't really know what was happening.

Imagine our surprise when, upon arriving in Portland, we learned that our "beautiful new house" was actually a dump. Even at just four years of age, I could see that this place was awful. I have a vivid memory of the first time I entered the house. It was dark and dusty inside and there were literally holes in the floor. Catching a glimpse into the empty, blackened crevices through the floor utterly terrified me.

But that was the least of our worries. Apparently, my father had lied to my mom, as there was no job awaiting him in Portland. It was a story he'd concocted as a ploy to get her away from her family, considering their disdain for him.

At some point, we ended up renting a different place in the area, and George continued looking for work. Meanwhile, it was up to my mother to provide for us. Thankfully, she was able to land a new teaching job in the area.

The snow came, and fortunately, my parents thought to snap some photos of my sis and me that winter. In one photo, Ann and I were standing side by side in the snow, bundled up in hats, parkas, and rubber galoshes. In the other, my sister and I were seated on top of the Studebaker wearing furry hats and holding matching muffs, with big smiles on our faces.

Sadly, I have only one positive memory of my dad. One. I remember him coming home from the grocery store one day. He was really cheerful. He picked me up and held me, telling me he'd bought honey from the store. He said, "Some honey for my honey!" If I close my eyes, I can still feel the surge of joy I experienced in that moment.

Eventually, my dad was hired at an engineering firm, which was cause for celebration. In reality, however, it was too little too late. He had just returned from yet another of his long, unexplained absences. Fortunately, my mom had made a girlfriend in the area, and I remember us going to visit her. As a four-year-old kid, I witnessed my mother crying as she confided in her friend, although I didn't really understand why she was sad.

We had acquired a cute little black dog as our family pet. I can't remember his name, but he was a small dog with a white chest. I have a photo showing me sitting on the front step holding my doggie, with my sister next to us. Like most dogs, sometimes he barked, which must have annoyed our dad.

One day, I was sitting in the living room, next to the front window that faced out to the driveway and garage. As I sat there, I suddenly witnessed my dad removing my dead dog from the trunk of his car, a horrifying, traumatic moment that I wish I could forget. He had gassed the dog in the garage, killing him. In that moment, I didn't fully grasp that my dog was dead at first. I remember racing to the telephone, a red telephone, and haphazardly dialing the rotary phone and screaming into the receiver for help. I was frantic, thinking that my poor dog was sick and needed care. Sadly, in reality, he was dead. My father had killed him.

Over the Memorial Day weekend of 1961, my dad announced to my mom that he was taking my sister and me to the local park for a little while. I vividly remember climbing into the back seat of the car and being confused because in the foot space between the back seat and the front seat, there were two suitcases, one on each side. So, my sister and I had trouble getting into the car, and this definitely struck me as odd.

It turned out that we were not going to the park at all. Apparently, my father had gotten wind of my mother's upcoming plans to leave him, so he decided to kidnap us. I can only assume that he'd told us some made-up story about where we were going and why, but I don't remember. I just recall us driving for days and days, staying in cheap motels along the way.

I do have a clear memory of one particular day while staying at one of these fleabag motels. I was wearing corduroy pants, tan with small brown checks. I remember opening the screen door of the motel room and going outside to sit on the little stoop. I was crying. My dad asked me what was wrong, so I told him that I missed my mommy. Instead of displaying a little compassion toward me, a little kid in the middle of nowhere missing her mother, my dad cruelly mocked me, making fun of me by feigning exaggerated crying. I vividly remember how powerless I felt in that moment.

We eventually landed in North Dakota and were living at some orphanage, although I don't know why. I do remember it was a yellow building. I also remember being completely freaked out seeing a lady there with a cast on her leg. To a kid who had never seen a cast before, it looked so freakish and it really scared me.

When my mother had reported the kidnapping back in May, law enforcement issued a missing persons all-point bulletin (A.P.B.), but it had been two months and so far, no one had recognized us. Around this time, I became very sick with strep throat, which landed me in the hospital. Someone who worked there had seen the A.P.B. and reported the sighting to the local police.

Once our whereabouts were known, the authorities were tasked with arresting my dad. They enlisted my mom in this planning and arranged a sting operation where she would be the bait. The idea was to lure him out of hiding. The police coached my mother as to how she would pretend she was very sorry for thinking about leaving him, and to ask him to come back to her.

Well, even though my mom was a theatre major in college, she wasn't able to pull off this scheme. Yes, my dad did meet her at the appointed place in a small little town in North Dakota. With my sister and I in the back seat, he picked her up according to plan, and off we went. The plan went awry, however, when my mother apparently blew her cover. He was on to her. In a horrifying moment that traumatized me for decades to come, enraged, my father reached across to the passenger door, opened it, and as we were driving down the street, pushed my mother out of the car. I remember shrieking at the top of my lungs, "Mommy!" and bursting into tears. I had just witnessed my father throwing my mom out of a moving car like a bag of garbage.

Needless to say, the police were close behind and witnessed this heinous act. One officer stopped to assist my mother, and the other pursued my dad. He was stopped and arrested soon after.

My father was sent to jail, and then later to a psychiatric hospital. He was diagnosed with anxiety and post-traumatic stress syndrome with homicidal tendencies toward my mother and us kids. Therefore, my father was not permitted to see my sister or me again unless he was accompanied by a police officer. We saw him only one time after that.

My mom found us a place to live near the school in Portland where she was teaching. It was a duplex, gray with pink and white trim, and was right across the street from the elementary school where I would attend kindergarten and first grade. It must have been December of 1961 that my dad made arrangements to see my sister and me because he brought us each a gift. He was only there at our apartment for a short time. I cannot recall what he gave my sister, but he gave me a red metal camping-type flashlight. An odd gift for a five-year-old girl, for sure, but I loved it. Anyway, that was the last time I ever saw my dad. He never made the necessary effort to see us again.

I have some very clear memories of that period in my life, like the nice next-door neighbors who invited us to play on their swing set. I also remember leaving my brand-new Chatty Cathy doll on the floor over a heating vent one day, and by the time I returned to her that evening, her face had melted and her hair was burnt. I also remember when my little sister fell off the couch and hit her forehead on the coffee table, which left a permanent scar on her eyebrow.

I remember we had a basement where my mom stored our canned foods. She would send me down there to grab a can of Chef Boyardee ravioli or some canned hash, which was typical dinner fare in our house. Like her mother, my mom had not a domestic bone in her body. She basically didn't know how to cook, so canned foods and TV dinners were our norm. I drew the line at canned peas, though, as they literally made me gag. And to this day, I cannot even bear to look at a Chef Boyardee can.

Because my mom was a single mother with a job, she had to find a babysitter in our new neighborhood. My sister wasn't yet school-age, so she was at the sitter's house all day, while I was only there for a couple of hours after school. Our babysitter's name was Agnes. At first, I was excited about going to Agnes' house because she had a cool teepee in the backyard for us all to play in. But it turned out that Agnes was evil.

One day, I managed to slam my middle finger in the door at her house. I still remember that the door had one of those crystal-looking doorknobs you see in old homes. Within a day or two, half my fingernail had turned black. One day, Agnes asked if she could take a look at the nail. When I held my hand out for her to see it, she suddenly, without warning, yanked the fingernail right off. I screamed! Even though the nail probably needed to come off, this was shocking and cruel.

It was my poor sister, though, who bore the brunt of this woman's sadistic nature. Ann, who was four years old, still struggled with thumb-sucking and bedwetting. Looking back, I have no doubt that these issues were residual effects of the trauma she had experienced during the kidnapping period at age two when she would have otherwise become potty trained. So, because she spent long hours at Agnes' house, which included daily naps, my little sister often wet the bed there.

Two very distressing memories related to this have stuck with me ever since 1962. In Agnes' house, there was a staircase up to the attic that was accessible through a door. To punish my three-year-old sister for wetting the bed, Agnes tied her little wrists to the banister of that staircase and then closed the door, leaving her trapped there in the dark. I discovered this when I heard Ann's cries from behind the door.

Even more cruel was the time Agnes locked my sister in the shed out back. It was a large shed, with a workshop and tools inside. I happened to walk out of the house into the backyard to witness Agnes standing outside the shed making scary noises like a growling wolf, terrorizing my little sister who was screaming in fear inside the dark shed. After telling my mom about these events she quickly removed us and found a new babysitter.

That October 1962, Oregon experienced a freakish monster typhoon with the force of a Category 3 hurricane. To this day, no storm hitting the Northwest has eclipsed the sheer magnitude of this weather event. It was on a Friday afternoon, and my little sister and I were staying at our new babysitter Mrs. Cole's house after school. Mrs. Cole was an older woman who lived in the next block, right on the corner. She was very kind. I remember sitting next to her in the front room looking out the window at the treacherous winds that seemed to have come out of nowhere.

Before we knew it, the power went out. We could hear the mayhem outside of the damage occurring, but we couldn't see anything. It was really frightening and surreal. Our mom was stranded at her school, unable to get to us. She was there all night long until the storm had passed, so we spent the night at Mrs. Cole's. The next morning, we discovered that a huge tree next to the duplex where we lived had fallen over and crushed a parked car.

As sensitive and perceptive a kid as I was, there was one thing I was not aware of. My mother was pregnant. This part of the story was not revealed until I was twenty-one years old. On that day, my mother came to talk with me in my bedroom. I had just returned home from living in the Bay Area where I had been attending college, so I hadn't yet moved to my apartment. I remember thinking it was strange how she appeared in my doorway with an odd look on her face. I guess the time had come for her to tell me what had happened in Portland that year, in 1962.

She sat me down and slowly shared her story. Mom had met a man named Richard and ended up pregnant. She loved him and believed he loved her, too. Back in the sixties, a single woman becoming pregnant was scandalous, so she expected Richard to propose to her. Finally, in her sixth month of pregnancy, he asked her to marry him. They agreed on a date and made an appointment at City Hall to be married. She told me how she shopped to find a pretty dress and hat to wear, and how excited she felt that day, that we would have a new daddy.

When she arrived at the courthouse, Richard wasn't there. She waited and waited. She sat there for over an hour until she realized that Richard was not coming. He had stood her up, leaving her there, publicly humiliated, alone, and visibly with child.

So, my mother had the baby, a little boy, and felt she had no choice but to put him up for adoption. She was alone trying to support two daughters and didn't have the means to take care of another child. The nurses literally swept him away from her immediately after the delivery. Back in those days, the records were sealed, so even if he had wanted to learn who his birth mother was, he wouldn't have had access to that information.

Even after all those years had passed, the pain this had caused my mother was evident as she shared her story with me. I imagined how crestfallen she must have felt that day, waiting there at the courthouse in vain for that man.

Of course, back in 1962, I was not aware that my mom, a school-teacher, was living through such a difficult experience. The teaching staff and principal at her school were well aware that she was unmarried, so it took real courage to endure the shame and judgment that was surely directed at her.

During this period, when my mother was due to deliver the baby, my grandfather came to visit us. At the time I didn't know the purpose of the visit, but now I know it was because he was there to support her and take care of us while she was in the hospital. Grandpa showed up with a gift for his daughter, a beautiful 1959 Chevy Impala, a white convertible with a red interior. Compared to the gray Studebaker, which must have gone kaput, we felt like movie stars.

It was wonderful having our grandpa there with us. He surprised my sister and me with tickets to the Ringling Bros. and Barnum & Bailey Circus. He bought me the coolest souvenir—a wooden red, white, and blue baton with silver glitter-encrusted tips, which I just treasured.

After the baby was born, Mom must have decided it was time to make a move and start over somewhere else, so we landed in Vancouver, Washington, right next to the Columbia River. I was now seven years old, and my sister was five, so we both attended the same school, Harney Elementary School. The school was a stately two-story brick building built in 1922 with indoor corridors.

When I look back on the year we lived in Vancouver, the memories still feel fresh in my mind. Apparently, I was gifted in math, so my teacher, Mrs. Hoffman, asked me to participate in a math quiz show that would be airing on local TV. I don't remember winning any prize or anything, but it was a fun experience and an honor to be included in this event.

I also served on the Second Grade Student Council. Oh, how I cringe when I see myself in the Student Council group photo, though. My mother had decided to give me pin curls, which were those pinwheel curls affixed with bobby pins that you slept on all night. The result was a crazy bouffant hairdo that only seemed to emphasize my buck teeth.

One standout memory from early 1964 was watching The Beatles perform on the Ed Sullivan Show. I sat there transfixed, watching these four mop-topped guys singing and shaking their thick heads of hair. Of course, I immediately had a crush on Paul, who was really cute, but mostly because he held his guitar the wrong way. That seven-year-old girl's forever love for The Beatles was launched that day.

I loved music and enjoyed singing, so I participated in various musical events at school, which I loved. I was also a member of a Girl Scout troop. The best part of being in Girl Scouts was walking to the weekly meetings after school. To get there, we had to pass an ice cream shop called The Igloo, where I would routinely order licorice ice cream.

In my school records, there was a note from my teacher that I seemed very sickly and depressed. Looking back, I do remember lots of sick days spent at the house of our babysitter, Lorraine—who was very nice. Apparently, I missed a lot of school, which may have been indicative of the tumult going on in our lives over those recent months and years.

By far the most memorable event I recall while living in Vancouver was the day President John F. Kennedy was assassinated. I was old enough to understand the gravity of the tragedy, even if I didn't really know what was going on.

My memory of that day is very clear. I was sitting outside on the front stoop. The front door was open and the screen door was shut. I remember my mother abruptly opening the screen door with a strange sense of urgency. She came out to tell me the president had been shot. I remember sitting on the stoop and crying with my mom.

Mom had the news coverage playing on the TV nonstop. For the next few days, there in our tiny apartment living room, we sat there transfixed watching the sorrowful images on our little black and white television unfold in real time. The famous image of Jackie Kennedy wearing a black veil, standing next to her children in front of the flag-draped casket, affected me deeply. Loss, shock, death, mourning, grief—there was so much pain conveyed in that one captured moment.

One spring day, a man showed up at our door. I figured Mom knew him because she invited him inside. I remember that my sister and I were in the living room watching cartoons on TV when suddenly I heard Mommy shouting loudly. I turned to look in that direction just in time to see her throw a glass of water at the man's face. He left shortly after. Now, I realize that it was Richard who upset our mom so much that day. He must have hunted her down and was probably making a feeble attempt at reconciliation. Thankfully, she was having none of it.

Soon after that event, the school year ended and summer was here. The next thing I knew, we were packing up our belongings in the Chevy Impala and heading back to California. Mom told us we would be staying for a while with our grandma and grandpa at their home called Gopher Hollow.

CHAPTER 4

Hello Gopher Hollow

AFTER A TWO-DAY ROAD TRIP, my mom, sister, and I arrived in Los Angeles. It was the end of June 1964. My grandparents were out front to meet us when we pulled up, and we were all very happy to see them. We hadn't seen our grandmother in three years, so I barely recognized her. We had seen Grandpa a year or so ago when he'd come to see us in Portland. Of course, I made sure to pack the baton he'd bought me at the circus, as it had become a prized possession.

Grandma was a tiny lady, only four feet eleven inches tall, and was seventy-one years old, seven years older than Grandpa. The effects of the stroke she'd suffered the year we'd moved away, back when she was sixty-six years old, were visible in her appearance. She had some paralysis on the left side of her face, so she wasn't really able to smile anymore. She walked with a slight limp, and her left arm, which she was unable to use, was held in a semi-bent position. I don't have any memories of my grandma when she was healthy, but my mom told me she used to be really fun-loving and social; she'd loved throwing parties and celebrating the holidays before the stroke.

Grandpa was about five-foot-nine, a dashing man with silver hair and a thin mustache. He was sixty-four years old. Since he'd been born in the year 1900, it was easy for me to keep track of his age. Grandpa was the patriarch, the head of our family, which included his spouse and two children, and their children. His views on family typified the classic Portuguese patriarchal family structure in which he'd been raised.

Grandma had been a homemaker since she married Grandpa. Although trained as a teacher, she only worked as a teacher for one year, early in their marriage. She also didn't drive, after having a terrifying experience while attempting to back out of a driveway and almost going off a cliff. So, she was very dependent on Grandpa. He always took good care of her, hiring full-time help when she was raising the children, so she was fine with his desire to rule the roost.

I had been to Gopher Hollow many times in my earliest years. Grandma had hosted festive holiday gatherings, inviting our family and my uncle's family to join them in celebrating. I only knew about these parties from family photos that showed my sister and me with my cousins there as babies and toddlers. Because we'd lived out of state for three years, I had no real recollection of the house until that June day in 1964 when we arrived in California.

Gopher Hollow was the name of about an acre of property in a nice suburb near Pasadena. The nickname had been given to the property because of all the pesky gophers that were present when the house was being built. The home was modest in size, about 1,800 square feet, with a finished basement as well. The property was terraced and featured a nice patio, a detached two-car garage, a grassy yard, a full-sized barbeque area, a "summer house," and a couple of sheds. There were apple, lemon, and orange trees, and abundant eucalyptus. I remember, when I first stepped outside to survey the scene, being greeted by a medley of lovely earthy scents.

I wasted no time walking around inside the house, wanting to get a feel for the layout, checking out the living room, dining room, kitchen, two bedrooms, den, two bathrooms, and laundry room. I remember smiling when I saw the clock hanging on a wall in my grandparents' room that displayed the numbers backward, like a mirror being held to it. This clock was just one of many quirky items I would soon discover at Gopher Hollow. I also remember thinking how enormous the main bathroom was, with its pretty shell pink and black tile work and two small windows that looked out over the property. It had a separate shower and tub, which seemed so ultra-deluxe to me at the time.

I felt instantly at home there, at Gopher Hollow. I found the kitchen especially tantalizing, with a breakfast nook cozied up against the bay window. My grandma's large gardenia plant was in full bloom right outside, so the delicious scent of the blossoms filled the kitchen. Just next to the window was a curio shelf that housed my grandma's collection of whimsical salt and pepper shakers.

In the coming weeks and months, that little nook was where we'd enjoy having breakfast with Grandpa. He made us toast in a shiny 1950s stainless steel Sunbeam automatic toaster, one that didn't even have a lever. Instead, Grandpa just dropped the bread into the toaster and slowly it descended as if by magic, and reemerged when the toast was cooked to perfection. Grandpa always taught us to bite into the crust to strengthen our teeth and credited this daily habit as the reason for retaining all of his.

Fortunately for us, our grandmother had a sweet tooth. My sister and I were completely enthralled when the Helm's Bakery truck would visit the house each week. When we heard the whistle on Wednesday mornings, we'd rush out of the house to greet the Helm's

Bakery man out on the driveway. He'd proceed to unlock the back of the truck, revealing a stack of wooden drawers. He would ask us, "What'll it be today? Doughnuts, pies, bread, cookies, or muffins?" Of course, Grandma supervised our selections, should we get a little out of control, but she was very accommodating of our wishes. My favorite was the doughnut drawer. If I closed my eyes right now, I would still be able to smell the yummy aroma of the fresh-baked doughnuts.

Because we were living there at the house, we quickly became acquainted with the people who were employed by my grandparents. There was the housekeeper, Mrs. Palmer, who came three days a week to clean and cook. My grandma didn't really have many domestic tendencies, so Mrs. Palmer was a godsend. Our mom had always told us about Mrs. Palmer's amazing fudge, and that Christmas we got to finally taste it. She packed the fudge in a tin foil-lined box that kept the fudge fresh. It was just as delicious as my mom had said.

We also met the gardener, Sam, who was of Chinese ancestry. Sam was the groundskeeper who maintained the ample property, as Grandpa was still working part-time and had no inclination to spend his off hours tending to the landscaping. Sam maintained their citrus trees, their apple orchard, and a small grassy lawn area, and generally oversaw the upkeep of the expansive lot.

Something about the home décor felt so comforting and homey to me. The house had wall-to-wall carpeting, except for the linoleum in the kitchen and the tile flooring in the bathrooms. The carpet was quite unusual, but I loved it. It was multicolored rag rug type style. There were thick pumpkin-colored drapes hanging on the living room windows, with a large brick fireplace between them. The furniture was well lived in. I especially liked the hammered-copper-topped table where Grandpa kept his quirky woodpecker toothpick dispenser. That and a funny metal penny bank where you fed the pennies into a clown's mouth, pulled the lever, and down the penny would go.

Grandpa enjoyed watching golf and boxing on his TV in the bedroom, while Grandma preferred her "stories" (soap operas) and game shows. She had trouble getting around, so the beige recliner was her home base. I sometimes sat in it when she took a nap in the bedroom, trying out the various vibrations and heat settings.

To me, each day at Gopher Hollow felt like being on a perpetual treasure hunt. While the house itself was charming, it was the property on which it sat that was rife with exciting nooks and crannies to explore, and that appealed so much to my adventurous spirit. Because much of the lot was sloped, there were terraced areas that were accessible through a network of steps.

I especially enjoyed rooting around down at "the barbeque." It was a large patio, the floor painted deep red, that had an outdoor open-air oven and expansive countertop. My sister and I would mix up concoctions made of dirt and water and leaves and pretend to cook in an old pot that hung inside the oven. There was a covered area where a picnic table and a hutch were located. I would take the placemats out and place them and the deep red glassware or the frosted mugs on the table as if we were having guests.

Mom told us that back when she was a teenager, her parents threw fun parties down in the barbeque. She described how there'd be music and food, and she and her friends would dance on the makeshift dance floor. Thinking about that now, I can conjure up images of the scene. I imagined the fifties music playing loudly while my mom and her friends, with their bobby socks and oxfords and poodle skirts, danced their hearts out. But in 1964, the barbeque was just a fun place to hang out and let our imaginations run wild. Close enough to the house to feel safe, but far enough away to feel adventurous.

From the barbeque was another set of stairs that took us to the "summer house." I admit that at first, I was afraid to enter the summer house. It hadn't been accessed in years, apparently, as evidenced by the cobweb-covered windows and the ample covering of dust I could see when peeking inside. However, once I mustered the courage to open the door, I discovered my grandma's trove of festive party paraphernalia. There were stacks of decorations for every holiday you can think of, boxes for Valentine's Day, Saint Patrick's Day, Fourth of July, Easter, Thanksgiving, Christmas, and New Year's. I suddenly understood just how much my grandma had once adored entertaining, and felt sad that she couldn't do it anymore.

Meandering down the next set of steps took us down to the lowest part of the property. There was a wash that bordered the perimeter of the property, and we could look over the chicken wire fencing down below to where the water flowed. In the summertime, there wasn't any water, which almost tempted me to jump the fence and crawl down there to investigate.

Most of the land on this lower portion of the property was natural scrub, although there was a small apple orchard carved out in one section. As we walked back toward the house, I spotted a hammock strung between two large eucalyptus trees, with ivy covering the earth for a large expanse. Later, my mom told me that was the area where they had buried their two treasured family dogs, Pal and Jimmy. Her brother, John, had actually been tasked with burying Jimmy.

Clomping through the ivy toward the house, we arrived at some more steps that led us back up to the main level. I remember hopping across the concrete stepping stones near the house that featured my mom and uncle's handprints and names, along with some colorful tiles for accents. I thought those were so cool, artifacts left behind showing they'd once lived here, that Gopher Hollow had been their home. To me, a kid who had moved five times and lived in three states by the age of eight, it made me feel wistful and a little envious.

How nice it must have been to live in one house for most of their lives—to live in this house, in this beautiful place.

That summer was filled with discoveries. I remember feeling so happy there, being with my grandparents and knowing that nothing could harm us. Over the summer, I became especially close to my grandfather. One day we were outside on the driveway, his salmon-colored Lincoln parked in the garage. Grandpa loved nice cars. He'd owned a Stutz Bearcat, a Jaguar, and various Cadillacs and Lincolns.

It was trash day, so he got the stand-up dolly out to roll the cans to the curb. Then, to my joy, he told me to stand on the dolly and he rolled me all around the driveway area. It was a fun, playful moment, just a girl and her grandpa.

Grandpa must have sensed that his oldest grandchild was very receptive to learning from him. Our lifelong bond was forged that summer, right there at Gopher Hollow. He took me under his wing and showed me many of his photo albums from the travel business. I was an apt student, soaking it all in. He inspired me with his life story, which he started sharing with me in bits and pieces.

Grandpa was a self-made man, his a classic rags-to-riches story. A go-getter blessed with a stubborn independent streak, he was wired to be an entrepreneur. He was destined to be his own boss. So, he proceeded to dabble in various trades over the years until finally finding his groove in the travel business in 1930.

After his business with the Greyhound bus line survived the Great Depression, he expanded to add two more offices in Los Angeles. But it was after World War II, in 1946, that Grandpa struck oil by coming up with a novel idea for a tour. People were ready to have fun again, so he marketed the idea as the "Funtours," a round-trip party train to New Orleans for Mardi Gras. It was ingenious. For three days and nights, the train traveled from Los Angeles to New Orleans featuring non-stop entertainment. Dixieland jazz and Big Band music kept the travelers fully immersed in frivolity as they made their way across the country to Louisiana each year.

The Funtours was his ticket to hobnobbing with celebrities, achieving notoriety in the business scene, and financial success. At the apex of his career, in 1959 at the age of fifty-nine, Grandpa was voted King of the Mardi Gras for the Krewe of Iris. During our childhoods, we grandkids looked at his photographs from that era and were in awe of our grandfather. There he was, sitting up high on the back seat of a touring Cadillac, decked out in royal regalia as they cruised around New Orleans. Other pictures showed him being presented in a tuxedo and a velvet cape at the formal ball. All this pomp and ceremony made a deep impression on me, and on all of the grandchildren.

In the early sixties, Grandpa expanded the tours to Hawaii with the Hawaii Calls branch of the business and even purchased a place there on Oahu. At this point, my grandparents owned Gopher Hollow, a cabin in Big Bear, a ranch house in Lancaster, California, a condo in Waikiki, Hawaii, and would soon purchase a vacation condo in Palm Springs.

But all this success came at a price, as Grandpa, admittedly, was rarely home to spend time with his family. He was a driven workaholic, spending ridiculous amounts of time growing his business, which no doubt impacted his marriage and his children. There may have been residual friction between my grandparents in 1964, but I was more interested in exploring than thinking about any of that stuff.

One day I took the stairs down to the basement. The stairs were painted red, and this was the staircase where my grandma had fallen in 1960 when she'd suffered a massive stroke. That day, my aunt Norma had happened to stop by and discovered Grandma at the bottom of the stairs and called an ambulance.

Sadly, the stroke had left her with permanent damage that held her hostage to her recliner most of her days. During the summer, I remember us taking Grandma to her physical therapy appointments, which were in a cute little 1930s bungalow downtown, but she never seemed to get any better.

But I digress. The day that I discovered the basement is etched in my memory. When I arrived at the bottom of the red stairs, I spotted an old beige typewriter sitting on a coffee table off to the left. A piece of paper was inserted into the typewriter. When I walked over to read the paper, I was perplexed. On it were several lines of the same sentence: "Now is the time for all good men to come to the aid of their party." At the time, I remember wondering what the significance of the phrase was. I learned later that this was a common typing drill, so it appeared that Grandpa wanted to keep his typing skills up to snuff, an effort that ended up serving the whole family well.

It was on this typewriter, a 1940s Underwood, that Grandpa would eventually type his memoirs. He started the project when he was eighty years old and didn't stop typing until age ninety-one, leaving the family with sixteen scrapbooks filled with his life stories, photos, saved mementos, newspaper clippings, accounts of family drama through the years, and all the cards and letters his grandchildren had sent him. In all, he typed over five hundred single-spaced pages. It is a cherished treasure trove of family lore that will be passed down through the family for generations to come.

That day in 1964, after spotting that paper in the typewriter, I curled up on the couch in this little alcove of the basement, directly across from a rock-faced fireplace, and faced Grandpa's typewriter. I twisted the roller in order to scroll farther down on the paper, and then hen-peck typed my way through the letters of that same sentence: Now is the time for all good men to come to the aid of their party. In this cozy little retreat, at age eight, I may just have discovered my passion for writing.

I was curious to see what else lurked in the large basement, so I began walking toward the right side of the space. First, I encountered a little sewing room, where Grandma's sewing machine and all the threads were located, and I opened a cabinet in the sewing room to find my mom's old dolls from her childhood. After looking at her dolls, I decided I liked the Shirley Temple doll best.

Just beyond the sewing room was a door with a sign that read, "The Dog House." This was my grandpa's man cave, which to this day sometimes appears in my dreams. I was simply enthralled by all the career memorabilia Grandpa housed in this room. The amazement I felt when discovering the hideaway room with all the splendid contents was probably due to the nature of his business. It was the flamboyance of Mardi Gras, with its bold, brash colors and clownish artwork emblazoned on much of the signage and marketing materials that I found so mesmerizing. In the room were a slew of photo albums featuring the Mardi Gras festivities over the years, and I found the images intensely captivating. I also remember there was a bar down there, with liquor bottles and fancy glassware. It all felt so grown up and mysterious to a little girl.

That summer, my mom arranged for us to use the family cabin, so off we went to the mountains. Having never been there before, I instantly fell in love with Big Bear, California. My sister and I were giddy at the prospect of another new place to explore, this time a little cabin built in 1933. My grandparents had purchased the cabin from two spinster sisters in 1947. My mom's family spent many summer months in Big Bear carving out wonderful memories. In one of my favorite photos of my mom, circa 1950, she is seated on a rock with Big Bear Lake in the background. She has one leg outstretched, the other pulled up and embraced, and is wearing pedal pushers and saddle shoes, the look completed with an Elizabeth Taylor hairdo.

I just loved that little cabin in the pines. It had only two bedrooms, one bath, a living room, and a teeny kitchen. In fact, the refrigerator was situated in the living room. There were old wooden floors stained a deep mahogany, and a magnificent rock fireplace. Covering the floors were assorted Navajo Indian rugs that my grandparents had purchased over the years while visiting the reservations in Arizona. The rugs eventually landed at the Palm Springs condo, where the family has enjoyed them ever since.

I have precious memories of being there in Big Bear with my mom and sister. Back then, two little girls were safe walking around without an adult accompanying them. This allowed us the freedom to go on regular adventures, such as checking out the Pan Hot Springs a few blocks away, the awesome city park, the local market, and the forest that was about two blocks behind our cabin.

While my sister and I were wandering through the trees, we came upon an old treehouse that someone had built and abandoned. The treehouse was a great find, except for the challenge we faced to actually get up into it. There were rickety wooden slats nailed to the trunk that served as stairs, but they were pretty wobbly and unstable. With trepidation, we made our way up there and commenced to pretend it was our apartment. The trouble was getting back down, especially with my intense fear of heights, but gingerly, we made our way back down the makeshift steps.

The highlight of my first trip to Big Bear was discovering the Peter Pan Rancho Club. In 1964, the Peter Pan Club was in its second iteration of the venue. The original, called the Peter Pan Woodland Club, was much more luxurious but had burned to the ground in 1948. My mom's family were members of the original club and were very saddened when it was destroyed. The new version of the Peter Pan Club was not nearly as lavish, but to a soon-to-be third grader, it was amazing. My sister and I absolutely loved the pool, and especially the snack bar where we'd always get the frozen Milky Way bars.

One memory of the Peter Pan Club stands out. It was August, and we were in the swimming pool when a thunderstorm rolled through, as they often do in the mountains. We were all rushed out of the pool, lest we be struck by lightning, and herded into the clubhouse. I absolutely loved being in the clubhouse, where we waited out the storm. We hung out in the lobby area, where there was a large rock fireplace and color television—a special treat while in Big Bear, since the cabin didn't have a TV.

That August day, while we were killing time in the clubhouse, my mom sat down at the piano and started to play. She entertained everybody during the storm, and some folks even sang along to the tunes she played. I remember feeling so proud to be her daughter, and I was completely enchanted along with everyone else.

One day, during our stay in the mountains, Grandma and Grandpa drove up to join us. Grandma was also a music lover and tuned the little radio in the cabin to the Big Band station. We assembled on the front porch and took in the beautiful mountain vistas and pine-scented air with that 1940s music traveling from the living room through the screen door and out to entertain us on the porch.

I remember taking a walk through the forest with my grandpa, showing him where the treehouse was located. It was during that walk that he gave me very sound advice that served me well for many future Big Bear trips to come. He told me that if I ever got turned around and couldn't figure out how to get back to the cabin, to just look for Gold Mountain and then walk in that direction. He pointed out Gold Mountain to me, a large rock-faced mountain to the south of the cabin's location.

When my mom was growing up, she and her family spent a lot of time at the Big Bear cabin. There were plenty of tales of family lore. Once, Grandpa, her dad, was thrown off a horse and had to be transported "down the hill" for a broken back. Another drama happened when my then fourteen-year-old mother dove into the pool at Pan Hot Springs and burst her eardrum. So painful was her memory of this that she never submerged her head in water again.

My sister and I found our way to the Big Bear city park, which was located several blocks away. It had the tallest slide I had ever seen—so high we were afraid to climb up to the top and slide down. My personal favorite thing about the park was the swing set. It, too, was really tall, which meant the chains were long and you could really get some height. I just loved the way I felt on that swing set, like a free bird, my chin tilting up and the wind kissing my face.

After a week or so in Big Bear, we returned to Gopher Hollow, which had really begun to feel like home to me. I now knew every inch of the place and had not only surveyed the entire property but also the neighborhood. I loved to explore. I often took walks around the adjacent streets and can still recall the names of those streets.

I remember how much I loved it when Grandma invited my uncle John and his family over to join us for dinner. My sister and I always enjoyed seeing our two cousins, as we were all so close in age. The four of us would traipse around the property, exploring its nooks and crannies together. Then the adults would herd us into the house for dinner, which was usually delivered from Chicken Delight. What made Chicken Delight so awesome was the blueberry muffin included in the dinner box. We would gather around the huge table in the dining room, with our Chicken Delight feast awaiting us.

I remember going to Mass a couple of times that summer. Prior to moving back to California, my mom, sister, and I rarely (if ever) went to Mass. I do recall making my First Communion, but I admit I was more fixated on my shiny white patent leather shoes than on the Sacrament. Hence, my grandparents felt it was important for my sister and me to become acquainted with our Catholic faith and took us to church. I don't think my sister and I really had a clue what was going on during the Mass, but I do remember how focused my grandparents were, especially Grandma.

By this point, it was almost September. After spending almost three months there, my mom announced that she had accepted a teaching position at a school in Orange County. Of course, this was her plan all along, to find a teaching job and be able to support her two daughters on her own. Everybody was happy about this news.

I was happy too, until I discovered that Orange County was a long way from Gopher Hollow. To a kid, that hour-long drive seemed like a great distance. It was then that I realized that my mother finding a job meant we wouldn't be seeing my grandparents very much anymore, which made me sad. But the time had come to leave our beloved Gopher Hollow.

CHAPTER 5

On Our Own Again

IN THE SIXTIES, divorce was not very common. A woman with children but no husband was a rare sight indeed, so there we were, a little family missing a father. In a way, my grandfather had become my new father figure. He taught me things and made me feel safe and loved, just like a dad would. I was grateful to have such a wonderful grandfather, so it hadn't really bothered me much that I didn't have a dad in my life anymore.

Mom was able to find a small duplex to rent just two miles from her new school. Grandpa was nice enough to buy us a refrigerator since the apartment didn't have one. It was a Sears Kenmore that you had to defrost every so often.

I liked the little duplex apartment a lot, and we lived there for three whole years, the longest we had ever stayed in one place. It had two bedrooms and a bath that we all shared. I remember watching my mother, mesmerized, as she applied her cake mascara in the bathroom mirror.

My sister and I walked to school, which was about a half mile away. I remember I had a red plaid metal lunchbox with a thermos inside, but once a week, Mom would splurge and let us buy a school lunch on hamburger day. I had a great teacher named Mrs. McMahon, and she remained my favorite teacher for years to come. I enjoyed school and got good grades.

I was a dorky-looking third grader. I was very skinny, had big buck teeth, hairy legs, and a pixie haircut. My mom bought an assortment of velvet bows, from which I would select a color to match my outfits and affix it to the top of my head. I was definitely not an attractive child.

I remember there was a girl at school I'd become friends with. One day, she informed me she was no longer allowed to play with me. When I asked her why, she said that her parents didn't want her hanging around kids with divorced parents. I clearly recall how much those words stung. I realized then that my family was looked at as unacceptable to some people. She didn't mean to hurt my feelings, as she was just being honest, but it did hurt.

I was able to make friends with a few girls in my class, but my favorite friend was Cindy. Her dad was the principal of the school, which came in handy over the next few years. She was a mischievous child and I pretty much followed along with her antics. I spent a lot of time at their home and was so envious that she had her own bedroom, and even better, her own powder-blue princess telephone. Together we made many prank phone calls and laughed ourselves silly.

Cindy and I loved playing her mom's Ray Charles albums—one of them was made of red vinyl—and dancing our hearts out to them in the living room. When I'd spend the night, her mom always gave us Cocoa Krispies for breakfast, which was such a treat, especially drinking the chocolate milk left in the bowl. One day, when we were home alone there, Cindy demonstrated how she could climb up on the roof and jump off. So, of course, in monkey see, monkey do fashion, I followed her example. I, the kid who was terrified of heights, was jumping off the roof.

Cindy and I loved to imagine that we were secret agents. This was during the era of *Get Smart* and *The Man From U.N.C.L.E.* We'd skulk around the local shopping center pretending to follow people, popping into phone booths and leering at them and making notes in the notepads we each carried for this mission. We even followed people around at a local hotel where we'd walk in like we owned the place, and then ride the elevators and stop on various floors to find our newest subject of interest.

Our very favorite place to sleuth was at Disneyland. Cindy's dad had a side job working at the Flying Saucer ride in Tomorrowland. Of course, this meant we were treated to lots of trips to Disneyland. Her dad had a shoebox full of tickets in their hall closet, so we would siphon off all the "E" tickets and then spend most of our time riding the Matterhorn, over and over again. But we never missed making a trip over to Tom Sawyer's Island, where we could put our detective skills to good use. We would each choose a person to follow and hide in all the nooks and crannies around the island as we trailed them.

It was during this period of my life, the mid-sixties, when my grandfather's influence on me started to surface. I fancied myself quite the entrepreneur, just like Grandpa. I was always trying to figure out new ways to make money. The apartment had a small backyard, so because I enjoyed singing, in March I decided to host a St. Patrick's Day concert in the backyard for my friends. I literally wrote "Happy Saint Patrick's Day" in green crayon on the cinder block wall that separated our patio from the other apartment, and, of course, got in trouble for it. The clothesline, which happened to be situated parallel to the patio, provided the perfect place to hang sheets that served as stage curtains. I set up towels on the grass for friends to sit and watch this fantastic St. Patrick's Day show, and charged them twenty-five cents admission.

Another time, I decided to create a three-ringed circus. I used the garden hose to form these rings and then dragged all of my sister's and my stuffed animals out to the backyard. I placed some stuffed animals in the rings and lined up the others around the perimeter of the yard. I also charged twenty-five cents for this event, and offered Freckle-faced Strawberry Kool-Aid and cookies for refreshments. I'd initially wanted to bake a bunch of little cakes and cookies for my guests with my Easy Bake oven, but that wasn't practical, so store-bought cookies had to do.

One summer day, I thought I'd try my luck at making a sundae stand. I clearly remember spending seven dollars at Boy's Market to purchase the ice cream and toppings. I did sell several sundaes (surely to some kind neighbors who had taken pity on me), but when I tallied up my revenues, it came to just five dollars and change. This was my first experience of running a business in the red.

By far the most hair-brained idea I came up with was the motel I wanted to build on the street corner across from our duplex. I built this motel out of the cardboard boxes that I had lugged home from Boy's Market and Alpha Beta. I even made a cardboard sign for my motel, and was sure the location was excellent, being right there on the corner. I was crestfallen that no one actually came to stay at my cardboard motel.

As early as eight or nine years of age, I was regularly expected to run errands for my mom. At the time, I just did what I was told, but in hindsight, I can see where my sense of duty and responsibility, so deeply engrained in my character, originated. It was pretty darn young for a kid to have such responsibilities. My mom would often send me to pick up some items from the grocery store, or to fetch our dinners at Buddy's Burgers or the broasted chicken place. To accomplish these errands, I rode my bike, gripping the grocery sack or bag of burgers with the right handlebar. I remember once being sent to the store to get milk and feeling so crushed when the paper bag ripped as I was riding home, sending the carton of milk tumbling to the street where it exploded. I felt so bad, like I had failed my mom and wasted her money.

Speaking of money, my mom often asked me to ride to the store to cash checks for her. Back in those days, the clerk actually would cash them and hand me the money. But once, my mom sent me to a little boutique called Jaheng's, where she often shopped, to cash one of her checks. I was mortified when the saleslady refused to cash it, saying the last one didn't go through. I didn't really understand what that meant at the time, but when I returned home cashless, my mom was visibly embarrassed.

But a seed was planted in my young head that these paper checks were magically converted to cash, so a devious plan was hatched. It was the end of the school year, and my fourth-grade teacher, Mrs. Boise, had announced she would be moving away. The kids all adored her, so I got the bright idea to throw her a little going-away party. You can already guess how I financed the soiree. Yep, I forged one of my mother's checks for fifteen dollars and used that money to buy the refreshments and napkins. Well, you can imagine the trouble I got in. When the check cleared and was sent in the monthly statement, my mom spotted the odd handwriting right away. I was grounded for a long time after that little episode.

In the summer of 1965, our little family took a road trip to the Grand Canyon. I was nothing short of amazed at seeing this natural wonder. We even got up very early one morning to watch the brilliant sunrise over the canyon, and to see the group of tourists heading down into the canyon on donkeys.

Our convertible Chevy Impala had a plastic rear window, which literally burned under the hot Arizona sun. The plastic turned brown, making the car unsafe to drive, so soon after we returned from the trip, Grandpa gifted Mom with a brand-new 1965 Mustang. We were thrilled to bip around town in this snazzy new car, and to this day the '65 Mustang remains my dream car.

Music had an ever-growing influence on me and on my soul. This is directly attributable to my mom's love of music, and her filling our little apartment with the sounds of an eclectic array of genres. Her record collection included the top artists of the mid-sixties, like the Rat Pack, Englebert Humperdink, Robert Goulet, and Tom Jones. Mom really loved bossa nova, especially the music of Antonio Carlos Jobim and Brazil 66. Because of her love for musical theatre, there wasn't a soundtrack we didn't own. *The Music Man*, *The Sound of Music*, *My Fair Lady*, *Oklahoma*, and *Carousel* were just some of the records that were constantly playing in the background.

One of my favorite albums from Mom's collection was Tchaikovsky's *Swan Lake*. I was obsessed with the music and the beautiful ballerina on the album cover. I'd play this classical music and leap and twirl around the room pretending to be a prima ballerina, even down to the dramatic ending when the swan dies. I had that totally down.

I remember seeing *My Fair Lady* at the movies with my grandparents when I was nine years old. I was completely besotted with Eliza Dolittle and that beautiful white gown she wore at the ball. My mother played the My Fair Lady soundtrack album all the time, which meant I knew each and every song by heart. Inspired by the movie, I decided to entertain my fellow students in the girl's bathroom, belting out "I Could Have Danced All Night," serenading them as they came in to use the restroom. I'd hang out in the bathroom all through recess to sing this song to whoever happened to visit the restroom, and wow, the acoustics were amazing.

One of the silliest memories I have from fifth grade was actually coming to believe that I was a budding star. I guess I fancied myself quite a talented singer and just knew that I was destined for stardom. One day, sitting in Mr. Hamilton's classroom, I actually took a pen, not a pencil, and wrote the words "A star is born" right through my hair onto the scalp on the back of my head—like I was branding myself as the next big thing. Of course, my hair covered this up, but *I* knew it was there and that's all that mattered. Alas, my singing career in elementary school encompassed performing in little school plays and participating in the sixth-grade choir. Not exactly barnburner events that would launch me into stardom.

My friend Cindy and I were both huge fans of The Beatles, so when *Hard Day's Night* and *Help!* were released, we saw these movies over and over at the local theater. I think we saw *Help!* seven times in all. These silly movies only endeared us to the lads that much more, and soon we had formed a little faux Beatles band of our own. We asked the owner of the ice cream shop next to Alpha Beta if he had any large cartons to toss out, and lo and behold, he did. These became Ringo's drums, and we made cardboard cutouts of guitars to pretend we were John, Paul, and George. We then lip-synced to the Beatle's songs while strumming and pounding our pretend instruments… and we fancied ourselves pretty good, too.

I was a big reader growing up and truly enjoyed being transported to another world through books. I gobbled up all the Nancy Drew mysteries, and around fifth grade discovered the Beverly Cleary sock hop-themed books about high school teen romances. I absolutely loved how the author described the outfits the female character would select for the dances or other social events, with vivid descriptions of the skirts, sweaters, and shoes. I didn't really care about the romance storylines, which were totally G-rated, but adored getting a glimpse into teen life—even though these stories were set in the 1950s.

Because I enjoyed reading, a monthly highlight at school was Bookmobile day. This was so much fun, climbing the little steps into the large bus that had been converted into a library, and then browsing through all the books. Another nice feature offered at our elementary school was Religious Release time on Wednesdays. The kids who'd signed up for Religious Release walked across the street to a participating church to receive religious instruction. I really enjoyed these excursions and loved reading the little handouts we were given in class.

Speaking of handouts, the *Weekly Reader* was a favorite. These were eight-to-ten-page booklets that provided summaries of current events, like the space program and other interesting topics. I remember being so enthralled with a story about jet packs, and how in ten years the technology would allow us to fly around town, powered by a pack of fuel strapped to our backs. While this never came to pass, to a kid, the idea of flying from my house over to a friend's house, high above the traffic, was riveting.

It was also the Cold War era, with all the related fears of communism and nuclear bombs. Once a year, our school performed duck-and-cover drills where upon hearing the sound of a loud signal buzzing over the intercom, we'd dive under our desks. We were told that this action would save us from impending nuclear fallout.

It was also about this time in the mid-sixties that I discovered my love for fashion, which was stoked by the yearly Spiegel catalog. Mom would hand me the catalog and tell me to select two new outfits at the start of each school year. I scoured the pages of children's frocks, gravitating toward bold colors. I remember the bright-pink dress with puffy sleeves and matching plastic daisy necklace I got when I started fifth grade; I wore it in my school picture, smiling broadly with my new braces. My other selection was a deep-purple dress with hot-pink trim and some hot-pink fishnets to match. This was the

Twiggy era, with her painted-on eyelashes and mod fashions. It was a fun time for bold and sassy English-inspired trends, like white go-go boots and mini-skirts.

In fifth grade, our class was given an assignment to write a poem. I had always loved hippos, so I decided to write a poem about a hippo. It went like this:

> *I saw a hippopotamus one day among the reeds.*
> *I looked at her, she looked at me, and boy was there a sneeze!*
> *It blew away the clouds and sun, it blew away the trees.*
> *It blew away the reeds and grass, and then she was at ease.*
> *I was so scared I ran away as fast as I could go.*
> *I looked at her, she looked at me*
> *And then she blew her nose.*

Believe it or not, my teacher, Mr. Hamilton, was very impressed with my poem and sent me to the principal to recite it. Of course, I was beaming with pride.

Along with all the fun memories from that year, I recall this somber moment. One night, while lying in my little twin bed and drifting off to sleep, I suddenly had a random but disturbing thought pop into my head. I realized that someday my grandpa would die. I don't know what prompted this sad thought, unless maybe I was just becoming aware of mortality at that time. Or maybe I was simply missing him, since we didn't see our grandparents very often by then. But there I lay, weeping in the darkness, as I pondered life without my grandpa in it.

When I was in sixth grade, we moved a few blocks away to a large apartment complex. To me, this was like top-drawer living. There was even a swimming pool right across the way from our apartment. By far, though, the best thing about this new place was that I got to have my own bedroom for the first time in my life. My sister and I shared a wall, but we had very strict boundaries. She was not to enter my room without permission, and I was not to enter hers. If I so much as put a toe into her doorway, she would yell for our mom to tattle on me for trespassing.

Don't get me wrong. My sister and I were extremely close, even though as sisters we couldn't have been more different. Ann was sweet and quiet and shy, and I was sassy and loud. She was an average student in school and had just one close friend named Jenny, whereas I was a good student with several friends. She was more domestic and artistic, whereas I lacked the patience she possessed. Every year on my birthday, Ann made me a homemade birthday card. These little treasures remain in my possession to this day. Our personalities were totally different, but we adored each other. We had been through a tough early childhood together, which had definitely cemented our bond.

That year, my mom gave me her old ice skates and signed me up for ice skating lessons at Glacier Falls Ice Rink. Cindy and I were regulars there, and when we stopped at the snack bar for candy, we always bought Flicks. We also enjoyed the roller-skating rink, where we'd skate to "The Monster Mash," "Little Red Riding Hood," and other hits of that time, but I much preferred ice skating to The Beatle's "Hello, Goodbye" while practicing backward crossovers.

I found ice skating to be beautiful and romantic and graceful, so I was thrilled to finally get to take lessons. I clearly remember learning how to carve figure eights in the ice, and to shift my weight from one edge to the other. Each week, I would try to lift my leg up a little higher on the spiral, and I was thrilled when I mastered a waltz jump. Sometimes, I'd have dreams that I was skating just like Peggy Fleming. In my dreams, I could feel myself skating to the music with such passion and skill.

One day while at home upstairs in my bedroom, I opened my closet where my prized possessions were located and felt a surge of gratitude. There in the closet, I gazed upon my mom's hand-me-down skates, a badminton racket, my enormous stuffed basset hound named Morgan given to me by my grandma on my one-year birthday, and a circus-themed musical jewelry box from Bullock's that she gave me when I turned eight. There I was, an eleven-year-old girl standing in front of her bedroom closet, feeling overcome with immense appreciation for my modest little possessions.

Cindy was my very best friend, but she was a bit wild and was increasingly not a good influence on me. She was the alpha in our friendship, and I followed along like a puppy dog. I remember leaving campus at lunchtime with her, venturing down the street to a little market where we'd buy candy. When we finally got caught being off campus, we didn't really worry because her dad was the principal.

Cindy also showed me how to substitute metal slugs for nickels in pay telephones. She'd gotten ahold of about a dozen of these things, and we made the rounds inserting slugs into phone booths and making prank calls to the information lady. Cindy also instigated other assorted petty crimes. She was an adventurous spirit and fearless, and I was always her willing accomplice. I just adored her.

It was during that year, 1968, that my mom met the man who would become my stepfather. Mom dated quite a bit while I was growing up. She was a beautiful woman with a shapely figure. Mom favored the trendy styles of the era. She wore her hair high, favored bright blue eye shadow and short shorts. Even though she had no trouble finding men to date, most were not too keen on taking on two little girls, so the relationships were usually short-lived.

For a while, she dated a guy named Jack. He was an okay guy, and I do remember how happy my sister and I were when he took us all to Huntington Beach one Saturday. Jack sent me on an errand to get some milkshakes at the snack shop. However, when the shakes order came up, I quickly realized I wasn't able to transport four milkshakes across the sand on my own. As I stood there contemplating a strategy, two nice teenage boys offered to help me. I was very appreciative of this kind gesture. So, I carried two of the shakes, and one of the teens carried the other two. About halfway to the spot where my group was, I turned around, only to realize that they had taken off with our shakes. I learned that day that I was much too trusting and naïve.

Things were different with Richard. He was divorced with children, too, so he was open to dating someone with kids. He had a daughter, Elaine, who was nine months younger than me, and a son, Ricky, who was five. While they were dating, we kids got to hang out and get to know each other. I was enthralled with Elaine's baton-twirling skills while watching her perform a routine. Of course, I had to learn it, too, so she taught me. We all got along really well, and, before we knew it, my mom and their dad were headed off to be married.

What my sister and I weren't aware of was the plan they'd made to move to another city. I was devastated at the thought of leaving my friend, Cindy. Worse yet, my mom made it clear that we would not be seeing each other again. I understand why she felt it was best for the friendship to end before I went totally off the rails, but still, it was a very painful loss. We packed up and moved, becoming a new kind of family, a blended family.

CHAPTER 6

teen times

IT WAS 1968 and I had just turned twelve years old, so the spirit of rebellion was bubbling up in me. Our family became a real-life "With Six You Get Eggroll"-type blended family, and it was not an easy transition for us kids. Our parents seemed to be in a perpetual honeymoon phase and we were relegated to being background noise, four little nuisances who were not going to invade their bliss.

This whole concept of answering to a dad figure was totally foreign to me. On occasion, I tossed out the ole, "You aren't my real dad! You can't tell me what to do." After all, by the time my mom remarried, she had been single for seven years. Suddenly having a strict stepdad just didn't sit right with me. He was indeed a strict disciplinarian, and I was borderline wild, a free-wheeling preteen with no desire to conform to his rules.

In fact, we four kids bonded in our mutual misery, pretty much hanging out in our rooms and avoiding the parents as much as possible. We lived in a four-bedroom rental, with my stepsister Elaine and I sharing a room, and my stepbrother Ricky and Ann each having their own rooms. I entertained myself much of the time by playing all my Beatles albums nonstop on the record player I'd received for my twelfth birthday. I played my beloved *Hard Day's Night* album over and over; the instrumental version of "Ringo's Theme" was my favorite track. That track moved me then and it still moves me now.

I really missed my friend Cindy and begged my mom to let me visit her. She did not relent, not even allowing me to talk on the phone with her. She was determined to put an end to that friendship, and probably for good reason. Still, I missed her terribly.

That year, my siblings and I got into some mischief, with me as the ringleader. We lived two doors away from a mini-mart. After school, we would often wander over to the store and buy candy or just look through magazines. One day, I hatched a devious plan with my siblings, naming Elaine as the designated decoy. She would enter the store first and strike up a conversation with the storeowner, distracting him while the rest of us went around the store swiping stuff. We executed this strategy on a few occasions, usually taking *Tiger Beat* magazines and snacks, and these cool mystery boxes we couldn't resist that had surprise contents inside.

Well, one day our luck ran out, thankfully. My grandparents' dog, Roscoe, had been staying with us that weekend and, being a hound, sniffed out the loot we'd stashed in our closet. He wandered out to the living room with a six-pack of Hostess chocolate mini donuts in his mouth. Our parents followed the crumbs to the closet and discovered our haul inside.

The punishment was excruciating. Our dad made us walk down to the mini-mart and admit to that storeowner, who was always so nice to us, that we had been stealing from him. It was very upsetting, seeing the look of disappointment on his face. We had to mow the lawn and do a bunch of chores to earn money and repay him for the items we'd taken. It was a tough lesson, but a very effective one.

Our schools were located about eight miles away from our house. I attended seventh grade at the junior high school, and my siblings were enrolled at the adjacent elementary school. My school picture that year was nothing short of abysmal. In it, I am clad in a brown and gold jumper with a gold turtleneck—colors I should never wear. I had the same dumb pixie haircut I'd sported for most of my life, plus pale, sallow skin, and shiny silver braces. The look had "loser" written all over it.

In history class, I sat near a girl named Angela. She had curly blonde hair and thick glasses and was really nice. For geography assignments, the teacher routinely had us create maps of the various continents, and I remember hers were so much better executed than mine. We became close friends that year, and together we also befriended a girl with long brown hair named Janie. The three of us became inseparable, and to this day we remain best friends.

This was also the year that I became involved in the music program at school. I signed up for Girls Glee and sang second soprano. I loved singing in the choir! We had an excellent choral director who was passionate about music and very dedicated to teaching his students how to read music. I still remember him drawing time meters on the chalkboard and showing us the 3/4 and 4/4 meters like a conductor. He, too, was a fan of show tunes, so much of our repertoire included them. I was introduced to songs I didn't know, which was surprising given my exposure to Broadway musicals. One of these was "When You Walk Through a Storm," a song that, unbeknownst to me, would take on special meaning decades into the future.

One of the required classes was home economics, which we all loved. Mrs. Friedrickson taught us how to cook such things as custard and Béarnaise sauce, and how to sew basic patterns. I absolutely loved going to the local fabric store to select a pattern from the McCall's or Simplicity catalogs and then choose a pretty fabric. I made a lined jumper from a hot-pink fabric with a print of small white circles, and I also made a pale-yellow, dotted Swiss dress with short sleeves that I wore for my eighth-grade school picture, a huge improvement from my seventh-grade photo.

I am forever grateful for those Home Ec. classes because my mom was definitely not a cook. She had grown up with maids taking care of the cooking for her mother, so she never learned how to cook. This explained why my sister and I lived mostly on canned ravioli, canned hash, frozen TV dinners, and take-out burgers when we were little. When I was about eleven, my little sister and I couldn't resist chuckling when our mom attempted to cook pork chops. She placed on our plates the charred remains of what was once pork—hey, nothing that a blob of ketchup wouldn't fix. So, Mrs. Friedrickson's cooking classes were very helpful in teaching me the basics.

We siblings had some rough times trying to adjust to life within a blended family. We seemed to annoy each other for the most part. There were even some knock-down, drag-out fights between Elaine and me. There was a dreadful period when the orthodontist had soldered my headgear on me so I couldn't take it off. I was mortified having to wear the thing to school. During one of our wild fights, Elaine threw a pillow at me and somehow dislodged the metal connector. I was thrilled to be able to remove the hideous appliance when I was at school, unbeknownst to my parents.

And that wasn't the only sneaky maneuver I pulled off. I remember how the cool girls at school got to wear cinnamon-colored nylons held up by a garter belt, which my parents strictly forbade. So, being the sneaky kid I was, I got a pair of nylons and wore my fishnets over them. When I got to school, I removed the fishnets and stashed them in my locker until after school when it was time to board the bus back home.

We only lived at the rental house for one year. Regardless of all the trouble I caused for my new dad, he decided to legally adopt my sister and me. So, our last names were changed as we assumed this new identity.

In the summer of 1969, my parents purchased a beautiful, brand-new tri-level, four-bedroom home out in the foothills. The home was about ten miles away from the rental, in a small subdivision surrounded by orange and avocado groves. The homes were called Peralta Hills Estates, and the streets had Italian names. Ann and I thought we'd died and gone to heaven. We had lived in apartments all our lives, outside of those three months at Gopher Hollow, so living in this spacious home was a real treat.

Our parents selected orange shag carpet for the lower level and informed us that one of our chores would involve raking the carpet to keep it looking spiffy. Yes, there was a rake in the hall closet for just this purpose. My parents were so intent on protecting this shag carpet, they even added a clear plastic runner along the length of the entryway for good measure.

Our large backyard was bare, so our dad divided the space into four quadrants. Each of us was assigned a quadrant of dirt to weed on a regular basis. This was a tedious job that we all hated, so we were thrilled when they decided to landscape the yard and add a swimming pool.

Still, chores were a staple in our life. There was a chore chart posted in the laundry room, listing the days of the week and who was designated to do which chore. Tuesdays and Thursdays were vacuum and dust days, two days were assigned to doing laundry and ironing, and another day was slated for cleaning our rooms and the bathroom. My stepdad was of German descent and he ran a tight ship.

The best thing about moving to Peralta Hills Estates was that my new friend Angela lived right down the street. Much of that summer, before we started eighth grade, was spent down at her house. She had two cute brothers, which didn't hurt, and she'd also made friends with Patti, the girl who lived in her cul de sac. When I think of that fun summer, I picture all of us hanging out in the cul de sac, listening to the radio blasting Stevie Wonder's "Signed, Sealed, Delivered."

Angela's brothers were very musical and both played guitar. They would invite other kids from the neighborhood to the house and play records in their room, which was adjacent to Angela's room. Angie and I would be experimenting with her Yardley Paint Box eye shadows and dabbing Pot 'O Gloss on our lips in her light-up vanity mirror, while the sounds of Led Zeppelin, Jimi Hendrix, Black Sabbath, and Deep Purple blasted from the room next door. We would often join the guys and enjoy the hard rock right along with them. Sometimes Janie rode the bus home with us after school or had an older sibling drop her off, so she was regularly part of this scene, too. Three of the guys eventually started a band in Angie's garage. I had a crush on the drummer, who lived on my street, and Janie had a crush on Angie's brother.

Hard rock was a huge influence in my early teen years. Remember, this was during the late sixties/early seventies when the hippie era that defined a generation of young people was in full swing. As a thirteen-year-old, I often lamented that I wasn't just a few years older during this era, mostly because I was too young to attend live rock concerts.

But the signs of the era were quite evident when stepping into the bedroom I shared with Elaine. Nothing was so cool as lounging in our bright orange vinyl beanbag chair in the dark, basking in the deep-blue glow of a black light that lit up the psychedelic-themed posters on the walls. To add to the atmosphere, I'd light some patchouli incense and play Grand Funk on my little record player.

When I wasn't listening to music, I was laying on my bed

daydreaming, or else gazing down the street at my crush's house. I had a perfect line of sight to it. His family had relocated there from Gardena, and his two best friends, Gary and Bobby, regularly rode their bikes from Gardena to visit him, about a thirty-five-mile trek. These two boys assimilated into the neighborhood group of young teens, which had become quite large. My fickle heart decided that I now liked the ginger-haired boy from Gardena, Bobby, while Angie took a liking to Gary.

Although there was plenty of strife in our family, we did manage to take some cool road trips. On several occasions during my early teens, we piled into the Country Squire station wagon with its faux wood paneling and headed out on trips to the national parks, to visit my new grandparents in New Mexico, and even took a lengthy cross-country trip across the South. Of course, we kids squabbled and fought on these trips, and took turns accusing each other of passing gas, but we did manage to have a good time anyway.

My grandpa ended up deeding the Big Bear cabin over to our family, which meant we took lots of trips to the mountains. It was a bit more crowded for our family of six in that little two-bedroom, one-bath cabin, but we made it work. One time, we arrived at the cabin to find a snowpack as high as our deck, but Roscoe was with us, and he forged a tunnel right through it to the steps, powered by his short, stumpy legs. One summer, my dad decided we kids should help him paint the cabin, so we did. And keeping with the trends of the times, we gave it a bright orange front door and matching window trims. It was nice to make new memories in Big Bear with my new family.

Daily life in our blended family, however, usually left much to be desired. We kids were truly miserable. Sometimes, we would sit on the beds in Elaine's and my room and conjure up a plan to run away. We figured we could buy wigs or dye our hair to disguise our identities, and then get bus tickets to some far-off destination. Our misery was mostly due to the harsh discipline we received without there being a counterbalance of being loved by our parents. They displayed little affection toward us, and it truly felt like our parents just didn't want to be bothered with their four kids.

An example of this was the family trips we took to K-Mart when we needed new shoes or whatever. After parking the car, we'd start walking toward the store entrance, only to have our parents command that we walk a good distance behind them. To us, it felt like they were ashamed to be seen walking with us.

At home, our friends were not welcome inside the house. They were not permitted to knock on our front door or to call out to us from the driveway up toward our rooms. Although our friends were allowed to knock at the back door, we had to get parental approval before they'd be granted entry. Most of the time, our parents said no, so we hung out at our friend's houses where we always felt welcome.

Our parents made it clear, when we moved into the new house, that we were not to disclose the fact that we were a blended family to our friends. In order to perpetuate this fraud, we were faced with some rather uncomfortable moments, such as when our friends would ask us about where we grew up. We had to think fast and come up with something that would deflect from the truth, so we told our friends that two of us had grown up in California and two of us had grown up in the Southwest. Basically, we were told to lie about our upbringing and never divulge our parents' divorces and subsequent remarriage. Again, the sixties were not accepting of divorce and our parents apparently hoped to avoid any stigma.

As the oldest, I was involved in the most run-ins with our parents. My mom was very passive and aloof and didn't seem to desire a close relationship with any of us. After she married my stepdad, she even distanced herself from Ann, which must have hurt, as Ann was Mom's favorite. Mom worked full-time as a teacher and chose to spend her evenings and weekend hours with her new husband. My mom and stepdad seemed more interested in controlling their four children than engaging with us or forming any meaningful connection. There were harsh punishments for any acting out or rule-breaking, including getting the belt. I remember us four lined up bent over the bed, side by side, as our dad beat our butts with a belt. Later, the discipline of choice was long-term grounding. If we were so much as two minutes late coming in, we would be grounded for a week, and the more serious offenses, like a poor report card or blatant disobedience, warranted months-long groundings.

Even with the disappointing family life, I can say that 1969 and 1970, when I was in eighth and ninth grades, were among the most memorable years of my life. The deep bonds I forged with the neighbor kids and Janie are forever associated with the music and fads of the time. This was also a turning point in our nation's history. The Vietnam War, anti-war protests, hippies, drugs, the birth control pill, and legalized abortion were about to radically transform society. As young teens, we could sense the electrified turmoil bubbling up, even if we didn't understand it.

One of the most memorable events of that time was gathering as a family in our wood-paneled family room on July 20, 1969, to watch the broadcast of the moon landing on our walnut console TV. It filled me with such a deep sense of pride and awe to listen to the astronauts communicate with us from a quarter-million miles away, and then watch them plant the American flag in the dusty lunar surface.

There in that safe, remote little neighborhood, surrounded by orange groves, we came of age during a much simpler time. We were adolescents going through puberty, and all that really mattered to my friends and me were music, fashion, and our social life. Basically, we were mini-hedonists, which is a pretty typical mindset for that age group.

It was also a heady time. We were imbued with a potent sense of freedom and adventure as we entered our teen years. My friends and I could walk around the neighborhood at night with no fear, invigorated by the pungent scent of the orange blossoms all around us. I have powerful memories of us hanging out together under the streetlights at night; boys and girls discovering the nuances of our different sexes, things that as kids we'd never really noticed.

In that vein, the "back road" and the orange groves were our favorite hangouts. The back road was a eucalyptus-lined narrow road that separated our subdivision from the orange groves. We all took turns etching our initials into hearts on those trees, leaving the lasting mementos of first love. It was there on the back road that we experienced that exciting rush of holding hands or even a first kiss. The orange groves, where we'd enjoyed having orange fights with the boys just a year before, became the perfect setting for clandestine make-out sessions.

Occasionally, during my junior high school years, I'd shop for cool items in the Lillian Vernon catalog and ordered a little bottle of fragrance. It was called Devon Violets and came from the United Kingdom. The glass bottle was three-sided, and there was a tiny purple ribbon at the neck. That fragrance came to represent the essence and wonder of that time in my life. Believe it or not, I have kept that bottle of perfume all these years. I still occasionally take it out of my top dresser drawer to inhale the scent, remembering just how amazing it was to be a young teen at that time in history.

By 1970 a lot had transpired since my mom, sister, and I had moved from Gopher Hollow five years prior. Still, our grandparents' home remained the family hub. Even though my grandma found it increasingly difficult to get around, she somehow summoned the energy to host occasional Sunday afternoon Chicken Delight gatherings. Nut cups, little paper cups filled with mixed nuts, were her signature party favor at the dinner table. Her Christmas parties, a highlight over the years, featured eggnog, hot apple cider, and coconut-covered snowball ice cream treats from 31 Flavors that each had holly sprigs made of icing and a candle in the center. If I close my eyes, I can still see the Christmas tree shimmering with silver tinsel in the corner window of the living room, and the whole family sitting around enjoying those snowball ice cream treats. My mother carried on Grandma's tradition at our annual Christmas Eve gatherings until 31 Flavors finally stopped carrying snowball ice creams in 2016.

Despite the fact that I was now a teenager with a new stepfather, my grandpa never stopped being the number one influence in my young life. He recognized that I was wired a lot like him, so he'd share his stories with me and always emphasized that we should never give up on our dreams.

Although Grandpa retired in 1967, he was very active and spent much of his time golfing and volunteering in the community. He formed the 1900s club, which was a social club of men who were all born in 1900 like him. He also was very active in the local Veteran's chapter, eventually being named "Commander." I remember admiring him because he was always productive and moving forward toward some goal, even in retirement. It seemed the local papers were always writing little articles about Grandpa's many activities and contributions to the community.

In 1970, now fourteen years old, I was old enough to become aware of the differences between him and Grandma. She was seven years older than him and very infirm, now with diabetes on top of the effects of the stroke a decade prior. Grandpa was very fit, social, and active, and Grandma needed his assistance to get around. Soon,

Grandma learned she had breast cancer, which required a radical mastectomy.

In the early spring of 1971, when I was in ninth grade, my grandma's cancer returned with a vengeance. I remember how upset my mother was, as she was very close to her mom. I overheard some of her phone conversations with Grandpa and my uncle and heard her crying. I could tell that it was serious. When Grandma was admitted to the hospital, she and my stepdad drove out to spend time with her a few times each week.

Grandma spent about three months in the hospital before her death on May 5, 1971. We were allowed to see her one last time a week or two before her death. I remember being very surprised at how gaunt and frail she had become, how tiny she looked in that hospital bed. But she was thrilled to tell us about her visitor that week. Grandpa, against all hospital regulations, had managed to sneak Roscoe into the hospital and up to the fourth floor to say his goodbyes. My grandma was utterly delighted to see her precious basset hound.

Up until then, I had never had an encounter with death. When we attended Grandma's funeral Mass, I immediately noticed upon entering the church that her casket was open, which alarmed me. Maybe I was being overly sensitive, but seeing my lifeless grandmother in that casket traumatized me on some level. I recall the garish shade of orange lipstick the mortuary had applied to her lips, which was just all wrong and really troubled me.

The memory of my grandmother's body lying in the casket must have seared into my subconscious. Over the years, I have had recurring dreams about Gopher Hollow that feature my deceased grandmother. In these macabre dreams, after entering the house, I open the hall closet door and discover a staircase leading down to a basement. There in the basement is my grandma lying in a casket.

Soon after my grandmother's death, I graduated from junior high school. Our school district was on an unusual schedule, with junior high encompassing grades seven, eight, and nine, and high school being grades ten, eleven, and twelve. I still remember our junior high graduation day. My friends and I were dressed in cute mini skirts, with long hair flowing, and flitted around the quad asking friends to sign our class photo, a black and white glossy panoramic shot of the ninth-grade class. In the photo, I am seated in the front row near the center, wearing plaid hot pants, a knit top, a brown leather choker, and brown lace-up boots—a classic representation of 1971 style.

As a member of the choir, we performed a short program for the students and parents on the risers outside near the quad. Our choir director, Mr. Kester, chose some tunes from *The Man of the Mancha* soundtrack for the program. I remember being deeply moved while singing "The Impossible Dream," even fighting back tears. Something about that song made me think of my grandfather and how much I admired him.

During that last week of junior high, my choir director informed eight of us that he'd recommended us for a performance group at the high school we would be attending. It was a group that featured singing and dancing to contemporary tunes, accompanied by a band. Each of the three local junior high feeder schools also sent eight kids to participate in this program. I was thrilled and honored that I would be part of the group of kids chosen to join Junior Ensemble, a preparatory class that taught the choreography and repertoire for Vocal Ensemble, which was mostly limited to juniors and seniors.

So, on that sunny June day, we wished each other a "bitchen" or "far out" summer and walked away from that safe little cocoon that was junior high school. There was a sense of glee tempered by a quiet melancholy. Being on the verge of turning fifteen, with my high school years beckoning, made walking away from the school feel like I was leaving my childhood behind.

CHAPTER 7

High School Days

WHEN THE BUS DROPPED US OFF for the first day of high school, I felt completely overwhelmed. The school was impacted by a heavy student population of about 2,800 teens. The sheer number of people bustling around the campus made me feel anxious and small. I eventually found my homeroom, picked up my class schedule, located my locker, and got to my first class. Fortunately, I fell into a groove and found my footing within a couple of weeks.

I soon discovered that high school was like a foreign land, peppered with cliques that included jocks, loadies, rah-rahs, nerds, and soshes (a reference to socialites, as in stuck-up climbers). Yep, that was how people were grouped and distinguished within the high school milieu. I got along with people in all these groups and didn't really identify with any one clique. This was good because it kept me open to making a wide variety of friends.

At age fifteen, I was incredibly shallow and silly. I giggled and laughed way too much, and was much more interested in my wardrobe and boys than my schoolwork. Fashion was so fun in those high school years. Short, short skirts, platform shoes, huge bellbottoms, and long, straight hair became codified by the Baby Boomer generation. I sewed some of my own dresses, thanks to Mrs. Friedrickson's classes, which were bright neon-colored confections. One was a bright-orange dress and one was eye-blinding chartreuse, and both were very short. I wore them with a black velvet choker and platform heels. Back in our sophomore year in 1971–72, we mostly wore dresses to school, to the joy of the teenage boys who enjoyed watching us climb the outdoor stairs.

Our local mall was just a small, modest, one-story venue, anchored by Sears, Woolworth's, and The Broadway. A favorite pastime was going to the mall to check out the latest cool clothes at Judy's, Hubbub, Pigeon's, and Redeye, as well as the selection of colorful suede platforms shoes at Thom McCann. My friends and I explored make-up trends and generally became much more fashion-conscious now that we were in high school.

As far as the high school classes went, I found them boring, and school often felt like a huge waste of time. However, I did enjoy the extracurricular activities, like participating in Junior Ensemble and Drill Team. To this day, I still remember much of the choreography we learned in Ensemble, as well as our drill team routine to John Phillip Sousa's "The Stars and Stripes Forever."

As always, music was a huge part of my life. The early seventies gave us the sounds of Motown, and the *Soul Train* TV show, which I watched religiously every Saturday. Of course, at our dances we'd form our own version of a Soul Train, and take turns dancing solo down the aisle of dancing teens. Soul was by far my favorite genre in high school, but I continued to have eclectic musical tastes, including hard rock, folk, and pop genres. I loved listening to The Carpenters as much as Alice Cooper, and Marvin Gaye as much as Janis Joplin. I thoroughly enjoyed the music of my high school years, and the songs, to this day, immediately summon memories of that heady time in my life.

These were the years of raging hormones, when boys began to shave and develop muscles while girls blossomed into curvaceous young women. Truth be told, half the fun of going to school was flirting with the opposite sex. The high school years were an exhilarating time of discovery and wonder, of crushes and breakups. In a word, we felt alive.

Although it's true that my first year of high school was primarily centered on frivolous fun, that spring I was reminded of our mortality. In May of 1972, Angie, Janie, and I were devastated to learn of the death of our junior high school friend, Cathy. Apparently, she had been riding in the bed of her seventeen-year-old brother's truck, and while on a freeway onramp, he somehow hit the guardrail, catapulting Cathy from the truck bed to the busy freeway below. Just a year earlier, Cathy's mother had been tragically killed in an auto accident, which resulted in Cathy and her brothers moving to a Los Angeles suburb to live with family. Cathy died on the eve of Mother's Day, which was the only thing about this tragedy that gave us any consolation.

Soon, my first year of high school would wrap up. Both Angie and Janie had their driver's licenses by then, but my sixteenth birthday was still a month away. On the last day of school, we left the school parking lot in Angie's blue V.W. bug, blasting Alice Cooper's "School's Out" on the radio. It was the perfect song to define the defiant, rebellious stirrings that were percolating in me and in my generation at large.

As we three got our driver's licenses, we soon discovered what freedom felt like. Suddenly, we had wheels! My mom had just gotten a brand-new Ford Pinto, white with an orange vinyl top and orange upholstery, which meant her 1965 Mustang, lovingly named "Minnie," would be passed down to me. At the time, the Mustang was just a seven-year-old used car, and I actually coveted her new Pinto. Who knew that I was driving around what would eventually be considered a classic?

Along with the freedom enabled by our driver's licenses came a whole lot of mischief. One such example was the day I talked my friend Lisa into ditching school with me. The plan was to drive up the mountain to Big Bear and spend the day at the cabin. I'd envisioned a fun day of shopping and dining in the village, driving around the lake, and hanging out at the cabin where we'd bask on the front porch.

Things did not go as planned. Instead of a fun-filled day playing hooky, the Mustang broke down about halfway up the mountain. There we were, stranded on the side of the highway, two truant teenyboppers. Thanks to a Good Samaritan who stopped to help us, he was able to diagnose the problem (a couple of bad spark plugs) and then proceeded to fix the car for us. We had about ten bucks between us, so he declined our offer to pay him and bid us goodbye. All of this took a couple of hours, thwarting our plans, so once the car was fixed, we headed back home with our tail between our legs.

There was many a time when my friends and I took advantage of our newfound freedom and drove to parties after lying to our parents, telling them we were at each other's homes. Angie would say she was at my house, and I'd say I was at her house, when in reality we were at a wild open party in an abandoned warehouse about fifteen miles away. There we encountered a thick crowd of teens, most of them strangers, and plenty of mayhem, including beer bottles flying through the air right past us. Of course, it was only a half hour before the cops showed up to bust the party, so we were off like lightning. I remember sometimes driving to a pool hall where kids from our school hung out, and attending various home parties thrown by teens whose parents were out of town. Yep, we were teens in the early seventies sowing our oats and pushing boundaries.

Of course, marijuana was all around in those days, although a much weaker version compared to present times. I remember giving it a try a couple of times when I was sixteen, only to feel sleepy and hungry as a result. I never did get a buzz. I had no interest in alcohol yet, simply because I didn't like the smell of it.

Now the neighborhood guys, well, that was another story. They did drugs, lots of drugs. I actually credit that experience, watching the effects of various hard drugs like mescaline, cannabinol, and acid on these male teens as the reason I never partook. I'd see them drooling all over themselves, throwing up, falling backward in their chair, talking nonsense, and basically looking like fools, and I wanted nothing to do with that. I never tried any drugs, not even cocaine in the rockin' eighties, simply because they scared me. I didn't ever want to feel out of control like that. I finally did, however, mix vodka with some Kool-Aid-type drink at a party when I was about eighteen.

But goody two-shoes I was not, that is for sure. As seniors, my friends and I each had serious boyfriends, and, with the advent of the birth control pill, we lined up at a local free clinic to get contraception. It is hard to place the blame on any one particular reason for the teens in my generation to be so accepting of the "free love" movement. The culture in which we were coming of age was a rebellious and nonconformist one. Though my family attended Mass on Sundays, there was no attachment to Jesus or the faith expressed in my home, no signs of Catholic devotion or prayer. Therefore, it was easy to be swept up in the sex, drugs, and rock 'n roll cultural paradigm shift that was taking place in the seventies.

Our clueless parents often took off for weekend getaways, leaving us kids home alone. It still amazes me how they could have possibly thought we would sit there like perfect angels in their absence, taking care of the plants, feeding Roscoe, and dutifully completing our daily chores. Oh, heck no.

Instead, we took full advantage of being left with no supervision and threw some crazy parties. The house would be brimming with teenagers and loud music. It astounds me that the neighbors didn't call the cops on us, or at the very least, narc on us to the parentals. Once when they were gone, I decided to take my mom's Pinto out for a spin. Boy was I sneaky! I planned ahead by placing masking tape on the driveway where the wheels were so I could pull the car back into the exact position she'd left it. All that effort just to drive around for a few minutes in a Ford Pinto!

On the days that our parents were set to return from their trips, things were hectic. We'd scour the house, cleaning the kitchen, bathrooms, and vacuuming the shag carpet. We hunted around looking for beer bottles and cigarette butts that had been tossed into potted plants or around the backyard. It was always so stressful when they returned home, trying to appear as if we had been sitting there knitting all weekend, while hoping that our dad wouldn't spot a cigarette butt we'd somehow missed.

During my teen years, my friends and I hung out at Newport Beach, about a forty-five-minute drive from home. Our haunt was Seventeenth Street, where we could always count on seeing some of our high school friends. Just thinking about hanging out at the beach immediately brings back memories of each bikini I owned and the scent of Hawaiian Tropic tanning oil—*not* sunscreen, I am talking tanning oil. Back in the seventies, the goal each summer was to get the darkest tan possible. We would spend all day there at the beach baking in the sun, coated in oil. My mom used to warn me that by the age of thirty, my skin would look like shoe leather. Thank goodness, she was not right.

Speaking of bikinis, we three loved heading down to Laguna Beach to shop at all the cool bohemian stores along Coast Highway. We'd bob in and out of the shops where patchouli incense, beaded curtains, and tapestry wall coverings were du rigueur. One of our favorite stores was the Eeni Meeni Bikini shop, where you could mix and match the bathing suit bottoms and tops. We always left there with a new suit to sport on Seventeenth Street that summer. This was during that magical time in a young woman's life when the skin is taut and the bikini was designed to make the most of our new shapely figures. At that age, I remember confidently striding toward the shoreline sans bathing suit cover-up with nary a sign of self-consciousness. We were hotties and admittedly reveled in the attention we managed to attract.

High school, for me, was a disappointment. All those 1950s teen romance novels I'd read back when I was in sixth grade had set the expectation for a truly exciting high school experience. Although my first year in high school, tenth grade, was pretty fun, by my junior year, the shine was off the penny. My classes bored me silly and I soon learned I could ditch school once or twice a week and still get B's. I remember when my second quarter report card in eleventh grade arrived and recorded twenty-eight absences out of the forty-five-day quarter. My parents immediately asked me what was going on, to which I calmly replied, "Oh, that must be a typo because I only missed two days." My parents actually bought it and didn't press me further. However, now that I knew about the new school policy of including absences on the report card, I reined in my truancy behaviors.

My best friends, Angie and Janie, and I loved to come home from school, sometimes ditching last period, and pile onto Angie's family room couch to watch *Dark Shadows*, the macabre, bizarre soap opera. On sunny afternoons, you could find the three of us out in the backyard, stretched out on beach towels on the grass, soaking up the rays. We'd put aluminum foil over a double album cover and hold it up, opened, to give our baby oil-covered faces extra tanning power.

Because my parents loved to travel sans kids, they sent us to a dude ranch called the Fun Farm, located in St. Anthony, Idaho, two summers in a row. The ranch was owned and operated by a wonderful large Mormon family, the Packers, who provided us with a couple of weeks of fun and great meals, too. We stayed in the large main house, with the living room, dining room, and kitchen downstairs. The Packers always took great care of us in our parents' absence.

Looking back, I am kind of shocked that our folks put us on a Greyhound bus to travel from Southern California to East Idaho on our own. I was the oldest, at age fifteen, and hardly the most responsible kid. I remember on the journey to Idaho, we would stop in Las Vegas in the middle of the night. If memory serves, we even got off the bus to take a break, right there in Sin City. I remember that it was over a hundred degrees at midnight when we'd stop in Vegas on those trips.

While staying at the Packers' dude ranch, I became friends with one of the daughters, Diane, who was my age. We rode horses in the rain, floated down the Snake River, jumped off the bridge, and generally had a fantastic time together. We ended up becoming pen pals.

Years later in 2006, when I was on a road trip to Yellowstone with my daughter, Emma, I drove through St. Anthony, Idaho. I was able to locate the bridge and the property, but the dude ranch had been shut down.

Once I returned home from this road trip, I decided to try to locate Diane, since we had lost touch by about age eighteen or so. I did an internet search and was able to find a Dr. Packer in the nearby town of Rexburg, Idaho, so I wrote him a note asking if he could put me in touch with Diane. Several weeks later, I heard from her.

We friended each other on Facebook and started catching up. At some point, she mentioned to me that she had kept all our letters from the pen pal days and offered to mail them to me. What a joy it was to read the letters I had sent to her about thirty-five years prior! I had written them on stationary and note cards that were a perfect reflection of the seventies style, including peace signs and daisies. My sentences were stuffed with slang like "far out" and "neat," and I smiled when reading about my job that paid $1.90 per hour.

I admit the letters revealed just how shallow and self-absorbed I was at that age. I wrote to her incessantly with detailed descriptions about my new outfits, the bands I loved, and whichever boy I had a crush on at the moment. But I now consider these little time capsules to be precious, as they really do offer a glimpse into who I was in my teens, as vapid as that might have been. The letters also remind me of all the great concerts I attended, like Jeff Beck, Uriah Heep, and Deep Purple, among others.

I got my first job at age fifteen, after securing a work permit, as a burger flipper at the little hamburger stand outside Woolworths in the mall. I got very adept at timing out the burgers on the grill and keeping up with the fries. Unfortunately, I enjoyed munching on the fries a little too much and ended up with acne.

My second job, at age sixteen, was working as a cashier at the Orange Drive-In swap meet. This was a weekend job and my role was to stand in a booth and charge the visitors a small fee as they drove up to the entrance. It was a boring, brainless job, but hey, it beat flipping burgers. I remember one day on my break walking over to sit at the little playground area. While sitting there on a bench, I spotted a little boy, about four years old, sitting on a swing and using sign language to communicate with his mother. I was captivated by the sight of this young deaf child, and I suddenly realized I had tears in my eyes. I was so moved that I even had the fleeting thought that maybe I should become a teacher someday and work with deaf kids.

That job didn't end well. My supervisor, a twenty-four-year-old male, kept hitting on me. One day he actually told me I couldn't take my lunch break unless I agreed to go home with him! Even at the age of sixteen, I knew harassment when I saw it, so I reported the guy and got him fired. It was soon after this that I got my next job at Sears, working in departments 18/38 selling lingerie.

I worked at Sears from the ages of seventeen to twenty-one, and it was a great job. In my capacity as an entry-level sales associate, I spent many hours rolling bras in the trays and sorting undies by size, working side by side with my coworkers. Because this part of the job required no concentration, it allowed my coworkers and I to really get to know each other, and beautiful friendships developed as a result. Our boss was Bunny, a fifty-something woman whom we adored, and the department was staffed with a mix of old-timers like Maggie and Flo, and several young teens like me. We all got along great, truly cared for each other, and learned a lot from each other over those years. But, back to high school…

I learned during my junior year that seniors would be allowed to graduate early if we had the required credits, and I quickly made that my goal. This meant that as a senior I would be done with high school at the beginning of January instead of slogging through that second semester.

It was during the summer of 1973 that my grandpa made the decision to sell Gopher Hollow. He couldn't bear to live there alone without Grandma, and at age seventy-three, the large property was just too much to take care of. I didn't realize how much this would affect me until the day, that summer, when the family gathered at Gopher Hollow so my mom and uncle could claim mementos that were meaningful to them before Grandpa moved out. That was the sad day when we all said goodbye to our beloved Gopher Hollow. It was also the day my family inherited Roscoe Muldoon because the apartment Grandpa was moving to wouldn't allow dogs.

CHAPTER 8

Time for College

AFTER GRADUATING HIGH SCHOOL EARLY, in January of 1974, I decided not to squander that second semester and enrolled in the local community college. I also increased my hours at Sears, hoping to save up a down payment for a new car by the time I started full-time college in the fall.

I signed up for two college classes, one of them being Composition. My professor, Mr. Carr, was a far cry from the lax, undemanding teachers I'd had in high school—a startling wake-up call for me. When he assigned our first paper, I felt very confident in the work I turned in. A week later, when Mr. Carr delivered our graded papers to us, mine had a big fat "C" emblazoned on the front, and was disfigured with comments and corrections in blood-red ink that sullied my carefully typewritten prose. On the back was a snarky note, saying my writing conveyed "superficial thinking" and "a limited vocabulary." I was devastated! Humiliated. Right then, I made up my mind to show him just how wrong he was.

The next assignment I attacked with heart and soul, determined to prove my writing chops to Mr. Carr. Not only did I get an "A" on the paper, but Mr. Carr actually recommended me for a gig tutoring fellow college students. That day he sent me to the library to apply for a paid position as a student tutor. So, in the end, I earned an "A" in his class and also got some paid teaching experience—and all before my eighteenth birthday.

I had been in a relationship with the boy across the street, my first crush, for over two years when I started attending a local four-year state college that fall. My parents were very much opposed to this relationship, as they should have been. He was a ne'r-do-well who'd been kicked out of high school and was in the group of teens in the neighborhood who were experimenting with drugs. Both he and his friends were stoners who didn't seem to have much ambition beyond playing in a band. Of course, I ignored all of my parents' pleas to dump him because I loved the guy and his shoulder-length hair.

But once I got to college, the scales fell off my eyes when I noticed young men who seemed to have a lot on the ball. Where high school was just an amalgamation of various social groups and everyone was there by order of the state, kids that chose to go to college actually wanted to better their chances to succeed in the world. By the second semester of my freshman year of college, our romance was kaput. It was sad but it was a needed change. However, to be fair, a few years later, that boy did go on to put himself through school and eventually get a lucrative job as a software technician.

The college scene was very different from the high school environment, and even community college. At least for my friends and me, high school was mostly about socializing and looking cute. At college, it was the complete opposite. No one cared what you were wearing, and most students looked like slobs. I went to a commuter school just twenty minutes away from home, so it was not at all a social scene. People just arrived at the campus to attend their classes and then split, like ships passing in the night.

Because it was a commuter school, I never had that coveted "college experience" that I had read about in those Beverly Cleary novels as a girl. There were sororities and fraternities, but my only experience with them was occasionally attending frat parties with my girlfriends. I was not a club-joiner type, so I never pursued joining any of the clubs on campus. I had a few nice friends in my classes, but because we didn't live on campus, those friendships were pretty limited.

Because of my passion for music, I entered college as a music major. My instrument was my voice, which meant I sang in the college choir and took vocal training sessions. Much of the music was classical and beautiful. I found music theory to be quite challenging, though, and was soon struggling.

The fact that my first semester was a disaster was completely due to my own actions. Now that attendance was not compulsory, I abused this freedom and ditched classes way too often. In fact, some days I would enter a classroom to find they were preparing to take a big test, for which I was totally unprepared. I soon learned you couldn't fake your way through college like high school, and my report card reflected this, as I barely clung to a 2.0. This was another wake-up call. After that fiasco, I buckled down and began to take college seriously.

After my first year in college, my parents advised me to change majors. They thought I should concentrate on a major that offered better employment potential, which I had to admit made sense on a practical level. So, I decided on Human Services, as it would open the door to a teaching position or, if I chose to continue on, a job as a child psychologist. Both of these professions appealed to me.

Culturally, when entering college in 1974, hedonism, feminism, and self-actualization were all the rage in academia. I started college as a fairly naïve young adult who'd had a conservative, nominally Catholic upbringing. But just because my parents and grandparents voted Republican didn't hold much sway once I became immersed in the progressive curricula already so deeply entrenched in academia.

Because I wound up in the School of Humanities, I was inundated with the writings of Jung, Maslow, and Freud, which pretty much molded me into a young, self-centered hedonist. About ten years ago, I happened to come upon an old college spiral notebook with pockets in which I found some of the papers I'd written in a Sociology class, and I truly recoiled in embarrassment reading my words. I had become "self-actualized" right into a very self-centered person.

In my sophomore year, I decided to take a beginning tennis class as an elective and was delighted to see a tall, blond, Bjorn Borg-type guy as the teacher's assistant for the class. His name was Brian, and I immediately had a crush on him. He was a talented tennis player but also was on the fencing team and was an Art major specializing in sculpture.

Aside from his athletic build, green eyes, and pretty, blond, wavy hair, what I found so compelling about Brian was his keen intellect. This young man was immensely gifted intellectually and had depth, which I found profoundly attractive.

Before I knew it, we had become a couple. This, however, posed a problem, since I had already made plans to relocate to the Bay Area and transfer to a different school. I had made this decision at the start of my sophomore year, mostly because I wanted to move out of the house and become more independent. Because I'd felt strongly that I was in need of a change, I'd already put the plans in motion before meeting Brian.

When it came time to make the move, I was feeling quite ambivalent about leaving. Mostly, this change in heart was because I felt sad about being so far away from Brian. Still, I went forward with the plan.

While I knew I would miss Brian, I hadn't anticipated how hard it would be to live four hundred miles away from all my friends and family. I knew absolutely no one at my new school, and I missed Brian terribly. It didn't help that the surrounding area was pretty awful. It was 1976, and at that time this town was dubbed the "PCP Capital," with people regularly tripping on the hallucinogenic drug in public. This happened on the sidewalks right outside our dorms and even at the local McDonalds. If that wasn't bad enough, a police officer came to visit the dorms and counseled the girls to not leave the building alone after five p.m. because rapes were occurring almost nightly. My grades sank with my mood, and so it wasn't long before I made plans to return to Southern California. This decision to change schools added a semester to my matriculation timeline, but at least I could chalk it up as a life experience.

As a Human Services major, I signed up for some internships to hopefully help me choose a career path. I worked for one semester as a teacher's aide in a fourth-grade class, and for another school year, I worked as a counselor for disadvantaged, at-risk kids.

While I enjoyed both of these internships, it was my time as a counselor that I really loved most. The students came from poor families, most of them with no father in the picture, which I could relate to. Over the year that I worked with them, I became very attached to these children, even visiting them on weekends and taking them skating, teaching them some disco dances, and going to the movies. In the end, it became evident that I was not suited for the role of counselor because I was too sensitive and unable to remain emotionally detached. Of course, I cried on that last day of school when I had to say goodbye to the kids.

By now, I was a senior in college and just anxious to be done. I had been working in retail for several years by then and had become interested in pursuing retail management with the goal of eventually becoming a buyer. Although my degree in Human Services wasn't particularly applicable to business, it was still a bachelor's degree, which was a requisite for a career in executive retail.

I cannot even remember my college graduation ceremony. I think I attended it, but I have zero recollection. What's funny is that to this day, I occasionally have dreams that I am searching high and low for my diploma and can't find it, and I start to question whether I finished taking all the required classes. Did I really graduate? Did I forget to fill out the paperwork for withdrawing from a class and therefore get an F? Did I flunk out? This recurring anxiety dream seems to pop up during stressful times, but I always wake up reassured that, yes indeed, I did graduate from college.

CHAPTER 9

My Self-Absorbed Twenties

AFTER I GRADUATED COLLEGE, my grandfather delivered on the promise he'd made to all his grandchildren. When we were in our teens, Grandpa placed an offer out there, like a carrot, that if we graduated from college, he would gift us with an all-expenses-paid trip to Europe.

I invited my close friend, Lisa, to accompany me on the trip, and off we went. As a twenty-three-year-old, to travel through Europe and the United Kingdom was both exhilarating and informative. I am forever grateful that my grandpa provided me with such a life-enhancing gift, allowing me to experience many different cultures and landscapes at such a young age. However, as wonderful as it was in Europe, I do remember, toward the end of the trip, having a renewed appreciation for my own country and a strong desire to return home.

Once I returned home to the States, I faced a devastating blow: my parents announced to us that they were getting a divorce. My dad had been unfaithful and now wished to marry his lover. This really hit me hard, much more so than my experience with divorce as a young child when I didn't understand what was going on. In contrast, I had come to love and trust my new dad in recent years. After all the effort and time it had taken for our two families to knit into one, to witness our blended family blow up was earth-shattering.

I felt terrible for my mom, who was humiliated telling her family, fellow teachers, neighbors, and friends that her husband had left her for someone else. And I felt angry and so disappointed in my dad. I also found it destabilizing that, after surviving a very turbulent childhood and finally gaining some sense of permanence in my life, our family home was to be sold.

So, having lived in this beautiful home for ten years, my mom sold it and moved to a condo near the school where she taught kindergarten. It was a very difficult adjustment for her, and for all of us grown kids, too.

This was a good time to take stock of my life in 1979. At this time, I was living with Brian and working as a cocktail waitress at a Mexican restaurant, a job that I was very bad at. For the life of me, I could not remember the "call order" when placing my drink orders, and had endured a terrible mishap where I managed to knock over six cocktails while transporting them on a tray to the customers. Thankfully, no one got spilled on but me, but after that incident, a light bulb went off in my head. Why on earth was I schlepping cocktails as a college graduate? I wasn't using my brain or my God-given skills, so I determined it was time to seek out some new opportunities.

The calendar turned and the world welcomed the go-go eighties, an era when aspirations of financial success would pretty much define the yuppie epoch among the Boomer generation. Just like many of my peers and the culture in general, I became enamored with designer names and cool cars, credit cards, and thoughts of making money. A sign of this mentality was when I purchased a pair of Anne Klein pumps at Nordstrom that set me back $150, an exorbitant expense for a young cocktail waitress, at a time when I could barely pay the rent. I had big dreams and champagne tastes but no money, and what little money I managed to accrue I woefully squandered.

My first attempt at landing a real job after college was interviewing for a position as a sales representative for Xerox. I dressed in a nice suit, carried an important-looking leather binder that contained my resume and references, and managed to sail through the interview. A week later, I had my second interview with Xerox. During this interview, the representative outlined what the job would entail and gave me a detailed description of the typical life of a Xerox salesperson. It was intense. I walked to my car while processing all that she'd shared with me and questioning whether this type of job was the right fit for me.

Soon after that second Xerox interview, I was having my breakfast and watching the Regis and Kathy Lee Griffin morning TV show, *Good Morning L.A.* That day, there was a guest on the show named Nina Blanchard. Ms. Blanchard headed up the top modeling agency in Los Angeles, with the likes of Cheryl Tiegs and Christie Brinkley in her stable. She was on the show that day promoting her new book, *How to Break into Motion Pictures, Television Commercials, & Modeling.* During the interview, she shared with the audience what it took to become a print model and how to go about getting representation. I sat there rapt.

This became an ah-ha moment for me. By this time, I was leaning toward a career in retail, with the ultimate goal of someday owning my own shop. Of course, to accomplish this would require lots of capital, so on that day, I made a game plan. I would become a print model, make a bunch of money to sock away for my future store, and then enter a management training program at the May Company to learn the ropes.

Now that I had a plan, I went to the local bookstore and bought Nina Blanchard's book, devouring every word. At the end of her book was a list of resources for fledgling models, such as the contact information for the top modeling agencies in Los Angeles, New York, and Paris. I got out my highlighter, marked the top three agencies in L.A., and considered my next steps.

Since I needed some photos to show a prospective agent, I booked an appointment with a photographer at a local strip mall. I hired him to take several headshots and full-body shots in various outfits. I had no idea how to pose in the pictures and absolutely no concept of what caliber of photography was standard for this particular mission I was on. The results were pretty pathetic.

I headed to L.A., wearing peg-leg jeans, strappy red sandals, and a spicy red boucle knit sweater, using a Thomas Guide to navigate my way to the Nina Blanchard Modeling Agency. I headed up the elevator to the floor of the agency, gripping the photos in my hand. When I got off the elevator, I noticed a line of women all the way down the hallway. I assumed this was my destination and got in line.

While standing in line, I couldn't help but notice that all the gals down the hallway were stunning, and that each were holding a large-sized binder. I later learned that the protocol for seeking representation from an agent was to "show your book," known in the trade as a portfolio. The portfolio would contain large 11-inch by 14-inch glossy photos and tear sheets from former print gigs, along with your "card," a cardstock composite of photos and statistics about you. And there I stood, with my sad little photos from a dime store photographer.

As the line scooted closer to the office door, which was open, I noted that the would-be model candidates were approaching two long tables set across the front of the office, with four people positioned on the opposite side of these tables. To my horror, I saw that Ms. Blanchard was one of them. I had noticed during her TV interview that she was a gruff, no-nonsense type of gal who, frankly, scared me to death. I started praying that when it was my turn to show my photos, I would get anyone but her.

Of course, when I approached the doorway, I got, you guessed it, Nina Blanchard. I sat down in front of her while she surveyed my face and body. She asked my age and I lied, shaving off two years and telling her I was twenty-one. She asked to see my book, which I did not possess, so I sheepishly placed my pathetic snapshots on the table for her to review.

She said, and I shall never forget this, "First of all, you are about five years too old to start modeling. Also, you are ten pounds overweight (I weighed 124 pounds at five foot eight), and you have dark circles under your eyes. I don't see where your look would even fit, to tell you the truth. Next!"

I clumsily gathered up my pictures and slunk my way back down the hall to the elevator. When I was safely ensconced in my car, I burst into tears. In this interaction that lasted all of one minute, my self-image had been totally obliterated by this complete stranger. Somehow, I gathered my composure and as I prepared to head back to Orange County, I suddenly had a thought. Just because Nina Blanchard threw me to the curb didn't mean all the agents would have the same opinion of me. I grabbed Blanchard's book, turned to the last pages, found the second-largest modeling agency in town, Mary Webb Davis, and made my way over to La Cienega Boulevard.

Even though it wasn't this agency's open call day, I figured I would just pop in and introduce myself. So, I walked into the Mary Webb

Davis Talent Agency and was greeted by a fellow at the desk named Tom. I showed him my pictures and held my breath. He looked me over, asked me to please wait, and disappeared into the back offices. A few minutes later, he reemerged, told me I had a very wholesome, commercial look, and asked if he could sign me for both print and commercial modeling. He gave me a list of photographers who could assist me in building my portfolio, and from those photos they would order my composite.

I was beyond thrilled, so excited to begin my grand plan to do some modeling on the side that would help me save up for my future retail shop. At this time, in 1980, a print model started at $75/hour, which was big money for a twenty-three-year-old.

Well, the modeling business was, shall we say, *interesting*. I did follow through and meet with various photographers to get some nice photos for my book. The agency ordered my composite, and I started working right away. I had quite an assortment of modeling gigs. I portrayed a stewardess for United Airlines, which entailed driving to Long Beach where the photo shoot would take place inside a mock airplane cabin. I played a Mazda car saleswoman, wearing a navy-blue power suit as I showed the "customers" the cars. Most of my modeling work, however, was for large department stores where I'd appear in large newspaper ads, and also catalog work, the boring bread-and-butter work of print modeling.

My grandpa was just thrilled every time one of my full-page print ads came out in the *L.A. Times*. He would proudly tear out the ad and pin it up on his wall, after first bragging to his golf buddies that this was his granddaughter. In these ads, mostly for May Company and Robinsons, which were two separate companies at the time, I was seen modeling jeans, sweaters, pajamas, and basic "missy" ready-to-wear clothing.

One day I got a call to do a job for May Company that was for

Maidenform. Tom mentioned I'd be working with another model and assured me that it would be a very tasteful ad. "Oh, and by the way, it pays $200/hour." The shoot was scheduled for the following Monday.

All weekend I agonized about this gig. I literally made myself sick with stress over the idea of getting photographed in a bra and panties, regardless of how "tasteful" the ad would be. That Sunday night, I didn't sleep at all because I was so nervous. I showed up at the appointed time, did the shoot with a blonde gal, and breathed a sigh of relief that it was over. When the ad came out, all I could see in my face was how sick I was feeling that day. Fortunately, the ad was indeed tasteful and classy, thank goodness, and provided a nice payday.

You can only imagine my horror when it dawned on me that my eighty-year-old grandfather would be seeing this ad in the Sunday paper. Sure enough, Grandpa called to tell me he had shown the ad to his golf buddies. I was mortified, but he seemed to have no problem at all with his granddaughter standing there in her underwear in the middle of the *Los Angeles Times*.

This experience of being a print model really opened my eyes to how damaging the business was for my mental health. I remember going on a cattle call for Coca-Cola, during which I was sitting in a room with about eighty models. A cattle call is when a client calls the top agencies and asks them to deliver a specific type. In this case, the client, Coca-Cola, had requested women in their early twenties, brunette, and a "commercial" look, meaning not exotic. In all, they saw over four hundred girls that day from the various agencies.

I remember looking around the room, gazing at the models. I noted that they seemed to have a hard, surly look to them. I noticed lots of them were smokers, as they'd light up right there in the lobby (the smoking ban was not yet legislated). Regardless, in my eyes, these women were exponentially more attractive than me. Compared to them, I felt like a plain Jane bumpkin. One by one, we were called up to show our book. The client glanced through each portfolio in thirty seconds and then sent us on our way without comment. I learned to hate cattle calls because the odds of snagging the job were so slim. The takeaway that day was how substandard I viewed myself when comparing my looks to the other models. Truly, during my modeling career I had the lowest self-esteem of my life, even trumping third grade, with my buck teeth and hairy legs, so that's really saying something.

Sadly, I soon discovered there was a seedy side of L.A. and the modeling business; something a very naïve young lady from Orange County had no prior awareness of. Sometimes, when I arrived at a photographer's studio, I'd witness them transacting with cocaine with a model. I sometimes overheard conversations between models about the local party scene, photographers, and upcoming gigs, and eventually realized they would gain access to modeling jobs by cozying up to photographers at parties. Drugs and sex are currency in this industry.

The day of reckoning came about a year and a half into my modeling career. My agent was ready for me to start working in their commercial division, so he sent me out on an audition for Chemin de Fer jeans. I was given a pair of Chemin de Fer jeans and was taken into a studio where the cameraman would film me wearing the jeans. I went to the dressing room and walked to where the camera was set up. While the cameraman was filming, after asking me a few basic questions, he then asked me to slowly make a complete turn. It was humiliating, having my rear end filmed by this strange man. Of course, I reminded myself that showing a young woman wearing these jeans was the whole point of the commercial.

A couple of days later, I received a call from my agent telling me I had made the top ten and was being asked to go to a second audition. Of course, I was thrilled. I happily made the long drive from Orange

County, eventually arriving at the Beverly Hills production studio. As I was signing in at the front desk, out of my peripheral vision I spotted a model down the corridor who was standing there topless, chatting away with the cameraman. I leaned into the woman at the desk, asking if removing my top was required. She answered in the affirmative, so I walked out.

After that incident, I decided my stint in modeling was done. I drove home feeling disgusted and disappointed, but also much more informed about what it takes to make it in this business. I gave myself kudos for having had the guts to go after such a lofty goal, like approaching Nina Blanchard with those terrible pictures. My grandpa was proud of me for giving it a go and told me I had gumption. Hearing him say that made it all worthwhile.

In late 1981, I accepted an assistant manager position at the May Company and soon enrolled in the management training program with the goal of becoming a buyer. My first department manager position was at an Orange County store, overseeing a million-dollar lingerie department. The work was stressful and grueling, but I kept my eye on my goals, and this was a necessary step toward reaching them.

Later that year, I decided to create a business plan for my dream store, which I named "Panache." I had been reading books about how to go about opening a business, and drafting a business plan was one of the first steps. I followed a template in one of the books and typed up the various parts of the business plan, including one-year, five-year, and ten-year goals. I was very proud of this effort and shared it with my grandpa. His opinion meant everything to me, and I wanted to see if I was on the right track. I was twenty-five and very green and realized I could learn a lot from him.

Well, his response was not what I had hoped for. Instead of offering me encouragement, my grandpa basically put me in my place. He gave me a lecture about not rushing things, that I needed much more job experience before even considering opening a store, oh and by the way, "You try too hard."

Wow. That cut me like a knife. I try too hard? I had always assumed he expected his grandkids to give any aspirations they had their all, to make every possible effort to succeed.

My grandfather, an eighty-two-year-old man, made his way into the business world at a very different time, starting in the Depression era. His climb toward achieving success took place in the thirties, forties, and fifties, when a great idea and a little luck could launch a successful career. In the 1980s, things were much more cutthroat and unforgiving, and opportunities were few and far between.

Unless, that is, you were willing to do what it took to play the game, to climb the corporate ladder. My two-year experience in retail management post-college had already shined a light on what that looked like, and I did not like it. I discovered that climbing the corporate ladder entailed a lot of "brown-nosing" and compromising your own values to the smarmiest executives who held the key to your advancement. I was not cut out for the corporate world at all. Besides, I was cut from the same entrepreneurial cloth as my grandpa. I wanted to be self-employed.

Following my modeling experience, I continued to pursue one brainstorm idea after the other. I often said that what I had inherited from my grandfather was like a curse because my mind never rested. I was always coming up with a new idea, some new way to make it in this world outside of the established constraints of the corporate machine. There was no way I could shut it off, this constant idea factory that lived inside my head. Looking back, I realize that recognizing this "Grandpa trait" in my early twenties was quite insightful because I never was able to turn it off. Ever.

CHAPTER 10

Brian

BACK IN 1977, after returning home to Orange County after that doomed college semester up north, my boyfriend Brian and I made the decision to shack up. There was no way in heck I could tell my parents that I was "living in sin," so I just didn't tell them. The few times they came over to visit me, I simply made sure to stash any visible signs of my male roommate in the closet. I cannot believe I actually got away with this for three years.

Even though I had agreed to share an apartment with Brian, somewhere deep inside my being resided a tiny shred of the old-school, traditional morals that led me to feel unhappy about shacking up with my boyfriend. Even though living together was very commonplace by the mid-seventies, something about it just didn't sit right with me.

Brian had no issue at all with cohabitating. As an artistic intellectual, he had no desire to live a traditional, predictable life. Even though he was upfront with me about his progressive, agnostic beliefs, my discontentment grew. So, I started pushing for marriage. I was certain that someday I wanted a couple of kids, and this, to me, required marriage.

Eventually, Brian acquiesced and we started planning our wedding. He had been raised Methodist but felt no allegiance to that denomination, or to any for that matter. I surprised myself by asking him if he would entertain a wedding in a Catholic church, and was even more surprised when he said yes. Brian was a sweet person and truly loved me, as I did him, and he just wanted to make me happy.

We met with a priest and decided not to have a regular Mass, since I had not practiced my faith for about six years by then, and we were a couple from mixed religious backgrounds. I was also living with my boyfriend, so based on all these factors, we decided on a wedding ceremony that would not include the classic Catholic nuptial Mass.

I found myself very excited and engaged in the wedding planning, and Brian was involved in many of the decisions, such as the venue, the menu items, and the invitations. To give it a personal touch, I even sewed my bridesmaids' cranberry off-the-shoulder dresses.

Because we were marrying in a Catholic church, Brian and I were required to attend a premarital program for six weeks. He was very accommodating and joined me every week for the sessions. The course culminated with each partner signing the declarations, including our intent to be open to having children and to raise them in the Catholic faith. We didn't hesitate to sign the document.

Brian and I, both of us twenty-four years old, were married in a beautiful church in Newport Beach in 1980. I was very emotional walking down the aisle with my dad, as we had healed much of our strife after their divorce. I loved Brian deeply, and after being together for four years, I truly believed we were destined to have a long and fruitful marriage. Our friends and family members joined us in celebrating this special day.

Soon, we were off to Cancun for our honeymoon. Wouldn't you know it, a ferocious hurricane named Hurricane Allen roared through Haiti and traveled up the Gulf of Mexico toward southern Texas, causing massive damage to east Mexico. This, thankfully, occurred toward the end of our honeymoon because it trashed the resort we were staying at. We were awakened by a knock on the door at three a.m. and quickly loaded onto a bus that drove us inland to wait out the storm in the basement of a bank in the city. All the resort guests sat there in that basement for about ten hours, sleeping on the floor and feasting on rubber chicken.

When we returned to the resort, it was a wreck. The pools were filled with seaweed and palm tree branches, and a layer of thick mud covered everything. Looking back, maybe encountering a hurricane on one's honeymoon was a bad omen.

Over the next three years, we were both working hard trying to get our careers off the ground. Brian finished his Master's in Fine Arts, and I pursued corporate retail and the modeling stint. Brian got hired as an installation designer for art exhibits at an upscale art museum in Orange County. We were enjoying life. We got along well, had a nice group of friends, and took annual ski trips to Colorado. On the surface, it seemed everything was fine.

Except that it wasn't. Within just a few months of our wedding day, Brian began to avoid intimacy with me. At first, I chalked it up to stress or exhaustion caused by the demands of the master's program. But when the situation persisted for months on end, I became very concerned. Was he seeing someone else? Was he gay? No matter how much I pleaded, how much I tried to open a conversation so we could get to the bottom of it, he'd only become more emotionally distant. So, eventually, we evolved into platonic roommates. We were still each other's best friends, but that was all we were. Best friends and roommates, no longer lovers.

Then one day, in early 1983, I was so unhappy and angry about the state of our marriage that I totally lost it. I was yelling and flailing around in utter frustration, and then, finally, he admitted to me what was wrong. He told me that he had decided he didn't want to have kids and was afraid of me getting pregnant. He hadn't known how to break it to me that he didn't want children. Instead, for nearly three years, he'd just avoided any physical intimacy with me.

I was devastated but didn't want to give up on our marriage. With the hope of rekindling some romance, I planned a trip to Club Med in Ixtapa, Mexico, in October, thinking that might do the trick. Sadly, the whole week went by without any romance at all. Our marriage was done.

When Brian and I returned from our disappointing trip, my family immediately reached out to me. While we were in Mexico, my sister, Ann, had received devastating news. She had breast cancer.

Ann had gone to the doctor to have a lump checked, the same lump that another doctor had dismissed three months prior. But the lump had grown and become painful, so she saw the new doctor, who immediately aspirated it. That day, she was informed she had cancer and told she'd require a mastectomy the following day. Ann impressed us all by remaining stoic and strong in the face of this terrible news.

Immediately following the surgery, Ann began receiving chemotherapy. Chemo back in the mid-eighties was much more toxic than today's version. She was prescribed high doses of erythromycin and cytoxan for an entire year, which was to be followed up with daily radiation for a period of one month. The doctors were basically throwing the kitchen sink at her because her cancer was estrogen-related and she'd had three pregnancies, which had fueled it. Even though she was only twenty-five, we were told the cancer had been in her body for seven to nine years, and that cancer is more aggressive in younger patients.

The pathology report only showed four positive lymph nodes, one of them being a clavicle node. Back in the eighties, breast cancer was assigned a stage based solely on the number of lymph nodes involved, so she was diagnosed as stage II because there were only four lymph nodes involved. This gave us much hope, as back then, stage II breast cancer had a 60 percent survival rate.

Watching my sister go through this horrible chemo treatment process was heartbreaking. She had three small children, so my mom, my sister Elaine, and I took turns helping out on chemo days and for a few days after. The chemo was so harsh that she spent all night vomiting. I remember being downstairs just crying while hearing her suffering. Her youngest daughter, who was only two years old at the time, spent the days at her mother's side, keeping her company in bed. The poor little girl wasn't able to understand why her mommy was so sick. Eventually, someone provided Ann with some marijuana to help with the nausea, which had just been discovered to have anti-nausea properties, and that helped her.

In the early weeks of chemo, in anticipation of her losing her hair, I took my sister to pick out a wig at the wig store, and we actually had some fun with it. She tried on some silly wigs that made us chuckle, and then eventually settled on a wig that was a similar style and color to her natural hair. Ann amazed us, though. Even with all the poisonous drugs being pumped into her body every month, she never lost her hair. Her hair thinned, so she went to the salon to get a cute short hairstyle, but the wig was never needed.

None of us allowed ourselves to even consider the unthinkable, that Ann could actually die from the cancer. We all pitched in and helped her as much as we could with the kids and the housework, while watching in wonder as she battled so bravely through the awful effects of the chemo. Throughout this difficult time, my sister somehow maintained a positive attitude and never complained.

There were many tender moments to behold during this year of her cancer treatments. Although we were not keen on the guy she was seeing after her divorce, at least he supported her dream, along with some financial help from Grandpa, to be a stay-at-home mom for her kids. All my sister had ever wanted was to be a homemaker. She just thrived in this role, even sewing new school clothes for her children and volunteering in their classrooms, even though she was feeling rotten. She thoroughly enjoyed her role as mommy, all she ever wanted to be.

Brian and I limped through the year, trying to somehow revive our failing marriage. I didn't want to give up on it because I couldn't bear the idea of not having him in my life. I vehemently resisted the idea of our marriage ending.

But reality stared us in the face: I was not willing to forfeit having a family someday, and he didn't want to live a traditional married life with kids. So, in mid-1984, we split up. After we had packed up our condo, and every sign of a married couple having lived in it was gone, I sat down on the floor in the empty living room and sobbed. It felt to me like I had lost a limb. My best friend of almost nine years was gone.

Years later, in 1994, I happened upon his master's degree, packed away in a box out in my garage. I took a chance that he still worked at the art museum, and drove up there to drop it off. By this time, I was married with three kids and had morphed from the liberal I was during the years Brian knew me to a conservative. When I entered the museum, I was happy to recognize the receptionist, who confirmed that Brian still worked there, although he was away at lunch at the moment. So, I passed off the document to her, asking her to give it to Brian when he returned.

On my way out the door, here comes Brian up the steps. I hadn't seen him for ten years. He had a long ponytail and a full beard and was fit and tan. I couldn't help thinking how totally different he was from my current husband, who was a clean-cut type. We hugged, I told him the receptionist had his degree, and we proceeded to get caught up a bit on each other's lives. He had never remarried, although he was living with a long-term girlfriend, and had never had children. He was living the life he wanted, and so was I. We wished each other well and said goodbye.

CHAPTER 11

Enter, John

IN 1983, AFTER COMPLETING MY EXECUTIVE training with the May Company, I decided to accept a job managing and buying for a beautiful dancewear boutique. I believed this position offered me work experience more relevant to my future goal of owning and operating my own store someday. To be a buyer for a large department store required relocating to Los Angeles, which did not appeal to me.

One day in early December 1984, in the late afternoon, a male customer entered the shop with one of our 20 percent off coupons in his hand. He was looking for a Christmas gift for his sister, who was into aerobics. Aerobics and jazzercise were all the rage at this time, in the mid-eighties. I remember I was dressed casually, wearing black rip-stop nylon joggers and a cropped sweatshirt, because I had been taking inventory that day.

I showed him some gift ideas and while we were perusing the leotards and leg warmers, we got to chatting a bit. His name was John.

He was good-looking, soft-spoken, and had recently earned a degree from Cal Poly Pomona in architecture. After about fifteen minutes, he decided he should give the gift a little more thought and thanked me for my time.

About a week later, John returned to the store and purchased some leg warmers for his sister, and then confessed that he was looking for an excuse to come back and ask me out. I told him I was open to that, and he wrote down my number. In early January, he called to set up our lunch date.

On the date, I can remember struggling a bit to keep the conversation moving, but we shared a bit about our lives and I told him about my sister's battle with cancer. He seemed nice enough, but I just didn't feel a spark. I even felt a little bored and left there thinking we weren't a good fit. A week later, though, he asked me out to dinner and a movie and that night things just clicked, so we began seeing each other.

Starting a new relationship in the early months of 1985 was not ideal. It was bad enough that I wasn't even divorced yet, but I was also still learning how to navigate life as a single person after spending nine years in a committed relationship.

The other factor was that I needed to be available for my sister. Ann had completed the chemo and radiation in December, and in early 1985, she was slowly gaining her strength back. She unexpectedly became pregnant with her new husband, which posed a serious health risk because her cancer was estrogen-driven. By the spring of 1985, she was starting to show signs of distress. Sadly, when she was five months along in the pregnancy, the doctor convinced her to abort the pregnancy in an effort to save her life. It was truly tragic, and we all suffered right alongside her during this terrible loss.

In late April, Ann began complaining of back pain. This was a very troubling development, and none of us could bear to think it might be the cancer. We hoped she had pulled a muscle in her back and maybe that was the cause of the pain. However, the doctor ordered labs, which revealed very high liver counts. This led to my sister being admitted to the hospital for a liver biopsy.

I will never forget that day. It was May 31, 1985. We were in Ann's hospital room when the doctor appeared at the door. He walked over to my sister and calmly stated that the cancer had spread to the liver and the bone. This explained the excruciating pain in her back. He told us that there was nothing more they could do for her and gave her a prognosis of six months to a year to live.

There are no words to describe how devastated we all were when we received this news, which was basically a death sentence. We got her home to her kids and just prayed our hearts out for a miracle. Then one day when I was at her house, about three weeks later, my heart sank while watching her attempt to put on a pair of shorts. She wasn't able to do it. Later, she began spitting up blood, so we called the doctor and he admitted her to the hospital.

During this time period, after working for the dancewear store for over two years, I had recently started a new job. It was a very demanding, high-stress job at Bullock's Wilshire managing an enormous women's sportswear, swim, and ready-to-wear complex. I had two assistants and seventeen employees to manage, and it was a daily pressure cooker. With my sister now hospitalized and in very serious condition, I struggled to manage my emotions at work and handle the workload. My staff was very supportive, but it was a trying time for everyone.

Those final weeks were dramatic and sorrowful. All of us who loved her were on pins and needles because there were signs her organs were failing and that the bone cancer had spread. Even on a morphine drip, she was in immense pain.

I recall visiting her one day, about a week into her stay at the hospital. The elevator arrived at the fourth floor, but before the door even opened, I could hear my sister screaming out my name. It was utterly heartbreaking to hear her suffering from down the hall. My mom, Elaine, and I took turns at her side, seeing her as much as we could while navigating the visits around our work schedules. My grandpa came to see her, as did my dad. It was very hard to witness this beautiful young woman being ravaged by cancer.

This was late July, and John and I were still seeing each other, although he had never had a chance to meet my sister during the few months we'd been dating. I asked him if he would like to come to the hospital and meet her, and he said, "Yes."

I was sitting with Ann that evening when John planned to come and meet her at the hospital. My poor sister was in a terrible way. Her body was wasting, but her abdomen was extended like she was six months pregnant due to the fluid accumulating in the abdominal cavity. This is a sign of organ failure. As I sat there next to my dear sister, John arrived. He stood at the doorway. She was sleeping, so she was never able to open her eyes and see him or meet him. When I glanced over at him standing there in the doorway, I saw tears rolling down his face. He knew how much my little sister meant to me, and seeing her like that, for the first time ever, made him very sad.

Three weeks after Ann had been admitted, my mom called me at 5:30 a.m. to notify me that the hospital had just called her. They alerted my mom that Ann's organs were shutting down and that death was imminent. So, I jumped in my car and sped to the hospital, which was about thirty minutes away. When I arrived, my mom was already there, holding her hand. My sister was comatose at that point, which was a blessing. My sister Elaine arrived, then my stepdad and his wife. We all surrounded my dear sister, thinking that each breath she took might be her last.

At about ten a.m., the nurse seemed very surprised that my

sister was still hanging on. Suddenly, my uncle John appeared in the doorway of her room. No one had called him! He said he was out on a boat in the marina doing some woodwork for a client when he suddenly had a very strong impulse to drop what he was doing and get to the hospital. He and my sister had always shared a close bond.

My sister was, evidently, waiting for her uncle to show up, because just ten minutes after Uncle John arrived, with my mom holding one of her hands and me holding the other, my beloved sister took her final breath. It was July 28, 1985. She had only lived seven weeks after that liver biopsy in May.

When someone you love is burdened with significant suffering, there is a sense of relief mixed with the sorrowful feelings of loss. It had become unbearable to witness her suffering, so God took her home, putting an end to it.

The weeks that followed her death were stressful and hectic. After her burial, my mom and I both attempted to obtain custody of the children because their biological father was not mentally stable. The courts put us through the wringer, but in the end, the court awarded custody to the surviving parent, to our deep chagrin. Fortunately, he must have realized he was not fit to parent the girls, who were then three, five, and eight years old, so his parents, the paternal grandparents, stepped up and became their guardians.

Losing my sister was the most horrendous thing I had ever experienced in my life. I was completely devastated by this loss. I couldn't even talk about it with anyone for literally years. My sweet sister, my bookend, my harbor in the storm through so many trials, was gone. She was such a kind-hearted and thoughtful person who didn't deserve to die so young. After a couple of weeks, once the shock had worn off and the reality started sinking in, I began to realize that I would never talk with her on the phone again, never sing our silly songs, or receive another cute homemade birthday card from her ever again. She was really gone.

Then, about eight weeks after my sister passed away, I learned I was pregnant.

CHAPTER 12

Marriage and Motherhood

FINDING MYSELF UNMARRIED and with child was not exactly the script I had imagined for my life. I was reeling from the loss of my sister, grieving terribly. I was barely able to focus on my work; I felt like I had post-traumatic stress disorder in the weeks following her death.

One morning, about two months after Ann's death and one week after learning I was pregnant, I was on my way to work. I had been having trouble sleeping and was very anxious and jittery. As I was driving, someone swerved toward me, cutting me off and barely missing me. This really shook me up. I was shaking so bad I could barely make it to work.

I remember going to my office and suddenly realizing I simply could not stay and perform my duties; I could not handle the pressure of this high-stress job at that point in time. So, I walked to my supervisor's office and told her, didn't ask her, that I needed to take a few days off to restore my mental health. She was not happy because

I was leaving them with no preparation, and I basically had to dump my duties onto my assistant. However, as I sat there sobbing and shaking in her office, she realized I needed a short leave of absence.

I drove out to Grandpa's vacation condo in Palm Springs to try to collect myself. I remember stopping at Kentucky Fried Chicken on my way to the condo to get what seemed like my last meal. That was how depressed and scared I felt. Once I arrived at the condo, I attempted to eat some of that gawd-awful food, gave up, and immediately headed to bed where I remained for the next sixteen hours.

When I informed John that I was pregnant, he did not jump right in and talk of marriage. Marriage was the last thing on his mind. He was only twenty-seven years old and we'd only been dating for nine months at that time. So, I told him I needed to take some time to process my sister's death and to wrap my arms around the idea that I was going to be a mother, and I told him to take his time figuring things out.

He certainly didn't jump in his car to propose to me, but eventually, after several days, he drove out to the desert and proposed marriage. Obviously, neither of us would have planned for our relationship to progress this quickly, but these were the cards we were dealt.

My transition from a liberal to a conservative began the day I had my first ultrasound. Ironically, I sure didn't look like a typical conservative woman. There I was, an unwed pregnant woman not yet divorced from my first husband—hardly the stuff of high moral Christian character. Still, it was viewing that tiny little nine-and-a-half-week-old fetus, completely captivating me up on there on the monitor, that radically changed my worldview. I lay there watching in wonder as this little being flailed its arms and legs, with all twenty digits visible, as the sounds of a beating heart filled the room.

When I was four and a half months pregnant, we drove to the beautiful Santa Barbara courthouse where we were married in a civil ceremony. John was twenty-seven and I was twenty-nine when we took our vows on that stormy, rainy Valentine's Day. On the way to the courthouse, he popped in Bruce Springsteen's tune, "Little Girl I Wanna Marry You," which was really romantic. After our wedding, we drove up the coast and thoroughly enjoyed a lovely honeymoon in Carmel, California.

Once we returned to Southern California, we focused on the new little house we had just purchased. It was a darling Mediterranean-themed home on a zero-lot line. The Greece-inspired subdivision was awash in a pastel color palette, and I just loved it. In 1986, technology had not advanced yet to identify gender, so I decided on a peach and mint green motif for the nursery.

In April 1986, when I was six months pregnant, I was getting ready to go to work when the phone rang. It was a woman who said she was my aunt Bertie, who was married to my father George's brother, Pat. She very gently informed me that my father had passed away. He had died by suicide at the age of fifty-four.

I had not seen my dad since that day when I was five years old and he made the one visit to our apartment after the kidnapping, a police officer at his side. Now, almost twenty-five years later, I learned he was dead, and I admit my response surprised me a little. After thanking my aunt for informing me of his death, I hung up the phone, feeling in equal parts shocked and emotionally detached. It was strange. But then, I had some unexpected thoughts. I realized that I would never see my father again, ever, which troubled me on some deep level that I didn't really understand. But after that day, I never really thought about my dad again.

During that time, John and I were distracted with baby showers, wedding celebrations, housewarming parties, and landscaping the tiny yards. Slowly but surely, however, it became clear once we began living together that the person I'd married was not who I thought he was.

Even the highest of hopes can be undercut by the harshness of reality, as it soon became clear we had made a mistake in getting married. There is wisdom in the advice that a couple should date for at least two years before tying the knot. However, to me, it seemed like a crapshoot either way you approach it, as I had dated Brian for four years prior to marrying him. Is marriage simply a gamble, where some couples win and some couples lose?

Granted, when John and I got married, we had only known each other for a total of fourteen months. Dating revolved around fun times and frolicking; it was pure fun and games. He was funny and handsome and had a bright future ahead as a licensed architect. I soon learned, though, that what looks great on paper doesn't always pan out in reality.

To say that our marriage was difficult is a gross understatement. I soon realized that John never really wanted to get married, and because he harbored resentment toward me for becoming pregnant, he was often quite unkind. I will leave it there, as I do not intend to air all the dirty laundry of a very trying nineteen-year marriage. Instead, I'd rather share about the beauty of motherhood.

My beautiful firstborn child was a girl, and we named her Sarah. I quickly realized that my baby daughter was nothing less than a gift from God. While true that God couldn't replace my beloved sister, He could introduce me to someone new to love. I decided to give Sarah my sister's name as her middle name, and I wept when the priest spoke the name at her baptism. My sister would live on, in some small way, through my child.

There is no doubt in my mind that having a child at that time truly saved me from the depths of depression. By focusing on this new life, by caring for her and loving her, I was able to slowly heal from the grief that had plagued me for the past year.

With this new baby, a new house, and a new neighborhood came new friends. A band of us young mothers became inseparable and remain connected to this day. Park outings, beach days, and birthday parties kept us closely knit as a solid support system for each other.

I became totally immersed in my new role as a mother. I adored my beautiful baby daughter and thrived in this role, which I took very seriously. I was given a six-week maternity leave, which I soon discovered was pitifully short. I realized, during the early weeks as a mother, that my work life paled in comparison to the important job I now held.

As the weeks passed, I began to dread returning to work. I would be forced to rely on a babysitter, a stranger, to care for my daughter while I worked all day at a job forty-five minutes away. To put my return to work off a bit, I extended my leave of absence for another four weeks without pay, bringing my full maternity leave to just ten weeks. That last week, I would cry while feeding my baby, knowing I had to return to my job soon.

I will never forget those crazy, stressful mornings trying to get the bottles ready, the diaper bag packed, and the baby dressed and ready to go by about seven a.m. I realized just how unnatural it was for a mother to leave her infant at such a young age. It wasn't right, and the stress of attempting to conform to this modern paradigm was insane. I'd rush around in the mornings and finally get everything packed and ready to go, then, just as I was placing my baby in the car seat, she would have a bowel movement. Ugh. Of course, delays in the morning routine often made me late for work, which raised some eyebrows. Remember, we women were expected to "do it all."

I realized that my full-time income had been factored into our mortgage loan approval. One day, however, I had an epiphany, a moment that changed everything in an instant. I had arrived at the sitter to pick up my little baby after work. That day, when the baby-sitter greeted me at the door while holding Sarah in the carrier, she had a two-year-old little girl standing next to her. The girl was one of her other charges. As I stood there at the door, the girl turned to the babysitter, asking her for something, and called her "mommy." Well, that was it. I was not going to have my daughter calling someone else mommy. So, I met with H.R. and transferred to a part-time sales associate position. Yes, I lost income and status, but I gained something priceless: precious time with my baby girl.

When Sarah was just one year old, I learned that baby number two was on the way. We were definitely not ready for this shocker, but we quickly embraced the idea and hoped for the best. To make room for our new baby, we bought a little bed for Sarah that fit nicely along the wall next to the crib.

On February 2, 1988, arriving about five and a half weeks early, our son Matthew was born. He was swiftly whisked away to the NICU for observation and support, as there were a few preemie health concerns present. This made me very sad and also stressed me out. I shared a room with another new mother who lay there cuddling her infant, while I sat there with empty arms.

To visit my little baby boy, I had to suit up in what amounted to a hazmat suit. Seeing him lying there in the incubator, with various monitors attached to his wrinkled little body, brought tears to my eyes. But there, in the NICU, at least I was able to hold my baby, and that was all I cared about. While I was standing there holding him, I had an overwhelming sense of doom. It was like a premonition warning me that something bad might happen to my son. I remember the powerful sense I felt in that moment that I needed to protect him.

Fortunately, Matthew, whom I nicknamed Little Boy Blue, was released to go home in two days, but with the instructions that we were to move his bassinet around to the sunny windows to improve his bilirubin levels. So, we strapped our sweet little guy, who resembled a little old man at the time, into his baby carrier and headed for home. I was now the proud mother of two beautiful children.

When my son was about six months old, I accepted a part-time job right around the corner from our house. A brand-new golf course had been built, and the golf pro needed a buyer for his pro shop and had gotten my name from someone. When I met with him, I immediately felt like this job was a perfect fit for me. I could use my retail buying and management background while being surrounded by views of greenery and trees through the large pro shop windows. I worked just two days a week, a perfect schedule.

During those days in 1988, my life was in perfect balance. I was blessed to be able to spend lots of time with my two beautiful children, hanging out at the beach and the various local parks with our tribe of friends. I had just enough engagement with the adult world to satisfy my desire to stay somewhat connected to my career and to socialize with other adult humans. Despite my troubled marriage, I felt immense satisfaction in my role as a mommy.

I kept this schedule for two years until, suddenly, a Grandpa-style brainstorm hit me. That year, in 1990, our golf shop won the prestigious Golf Shop of the Year award. This recognition was not mine but for the head pro of our golf course. I was just the person who worked behind the scenes to create a really beautiful pro shop.

After working there for two years, I decided the time was right to ask for a nice raise. The club was only able to offer me a small bump in pay, which, honestly, wasn't satisfactory. So, I got creative. I hatched a plan to become a contract buyer, to do the buying and merchandising for three or four local golf shops. I had a nice business card printed up and set about drumming up some clients.

With the help of my sales reps, I told the golf pros and some of their other accounts about my buying services, and I quickly secured three accounts in addition to the club I was already working for. It worked like this: I would have the sales reps meet me at my house where I would place the orders with my kids romping about. Then, during the week, I would make the rounds to merchandise the shops.

As you might have guessed, I wound up putting in many more hours than I had initially forecast. My new contract job was further complicated when I learned that, surprise, I was expecting baby number three. So, now I was pregnant and trying to keep up with four shops and two kids.

Expecting another child also posed a quandary—where would we put her? For almost six years, our little family of four had managed to fit like a Tetris puzzle into our cozy 1,200-square-foot home. Having to yield space to all those big Fisher-Price toys, Barbie paraphernalia, trucks, and Big Wheels, it was a tight fit, but doable. However, with the new baby on the way, it was clear we had outgrown our place.

We started to look at properties for sale in our area. There had been several recent new subdivisions constructed, so we focused on those neighborhoods. Of course, the home we fell in love with was outside our budget, so I decided to sit down with my grandpa and pitch an idea.

My grandfather, who was then ninety-one, had made generous provisions in his will for his grandchildren. I informed him of my pregnancy and asked if he would consider forwarding some of my inheritance early so we could purchase this home. To my great joy and immense gratitude, he agreed to this suggestion and proceeded to do the same for his other grandkids. With Grandpa's assistance, we were able to purchase a brand-new, roomy, four-bedroom home in the foothills. How wonderful it was to invite Grandpa over to join us for dinner at our new home. His big smile when I opened the door to greet him showed how elated he was to have been able to help us in such a meaningful way.

I don't know why, but while I was pregnant, my Type A personality came roaring up big time. One of the golf pros I worked for asked if I would be interested in opening a golf shop for him in the local mall. My eyes lit up! This was right in my wheelhouse, a retail setting where I could showcase my acquired knowledge and experience in the golf apparel business. I accepted the offer.

The contract-buying business that had begun as a great adaptation to motherhood soon became a snowball going downhill. Our shop was a big success at the mall that holiday season, so the golf pro decided to acquire several more leases in other malls. I took up the challenge and quit the other shops so I could take on this mammoth project.

My role was all-encompassing. It included accompanying the golf pro during the lease negotiations, creating the floor plans and fixturing, purchasing all merchandise and supplies, hiring and training all staff, and overseeing each store's open-to-buy and other costs. My husband was hired to design the build-outs. When it was time to open a new location, I'd work all night long, setting up the store, and then return home in the early hours of the next morning. I had taken on a gargantuan task.

I continued to see the sales reps at my house, but the five stores demanded at least four long days a week to keep up with it all. When my beautiful baby daughter Emma arrived, I wondered what the heck I was thinking.

To say that I was utterly exhausted trying to keep up with all the demands of a newborn, two kids, and a crazy job is an understatement. But since I'd bit off more than I could chew, it became my cross to bear. Somehow, I still managed to get to all the Little League games, teacher conferences, and birthday parties. I look back in wonder that I was able to do all that and not drop dead.

My grandpa had agreed to move into assisted living in 1991. He'd resisted for as long as he could, but it was time. Fortunately, my mom convinced him to pick a home that was nearby so that we could visit him often. Even though my schedule was insanely busy, I managed to visit my grandpa at the assisted living home every Thursday evening for dinner.

I remember visiting him soon after he first moved into one of the little bungalows for elderly folks who were still fairly independent and mobile. I'd accompany him to dinner in the large cafeteria and just smile, watching him entertain the other people at our table. I soon noticed he was the only one smiling and telling jokes, and I became worried that this environment would eventually bring him down. After dinner, we'd take a little walk and then go back to the cottage to sip some porto (a Portuguese dessert wine) and watch the evening news. I truly looked forward to our weekly dates.

Grandpa had trouble adjusting to life in this new place. He missed his hometown and all the things that were familiar to him. One day, while I was at one of the stores working, my mom called to tell me that Grandpa had escaped. He had hired a taxi to drive him out to the desert and was currently at some senior housing complex out there.

I immediately got in my car and drove the two hours to go retrieve my grandfather before he signed some contract. When I found the place, they told me he was upstairs looking at an apartment he was interested in. When I entered the room, there he was, seated on a twin bed looking lost, lonely, and confused. I gently persuaded him to come back with me to his own place. During our drive, I explained why he was safer close by where we were able to see him all the time. As weekly visitors, my mom and I often felt sad for all the residents who had no one to visit them. So, thankfully, he acquiesced and promised never to run away again.

Soon after this episode, he was diagnosed with stomach cancer. This meant he would be transferred to the next level of care: an apartment. The cancer surgery involved removing most of his stomach, which was very hard on him. I continued to visit him every Thursday. As he gradually got stronger, we were once again able to resume our little walks. Grandpa always took me by the elbow when we crossed the street, which made me feel so safe and loved.

But soon his health began declining again, and this time there was no bouncing back. I began to dread walking into his place to fetch him for our dinners, which were now in the small dining room there at the apartment. Upon arriving, I'd find his room and his mood were dark. He barely spoke while at dinner, and the few others at our table sat slack-jawed and drooling seated in their wheelchairs. Back in his room, the nurse would stop by to dispense pills to him, although I had no idea what these medications were.

Since the time he was eighty-one, Grandpa had been typing up his memoirs and then meticulously mounting the pages and photos into albums. He continued to type until age ninety-one, filling sixteen albums with memories. These would someday become a family treasure. Now, though, his old typewriter sat in the corner on a shelf collecting dust.

About six months later, we were told his cancer had spread to the liver, and he was transferred to the hospital setting there on the grounds. He told my mom he was ready to go. For about three days, he refused any nourishment. I saw him for one last Thursday date, on February 2, 1994, as he lay dying. I told him how much I loved him and what he had meant to me throughout my whole life. I told him that all I ever cared about, while growing up, was to make him proud of me. I told him he was my knight in shining armor, kissed his cheek, and said goodbye.

That Saturday, February 4, 1994, just like my sister's final day, my uncle suddenly felt compelled to drive over to see his dad. Soon after Uncle John arrived, Grandpa passed away. He was ninety-four years old.

After the funeral and burial, we convened at my mother's home. I waited for a quiet moment and then went over to my mom's record player and got out her *Man of La Mancha* soundtrack. I placed the needle on one particular track, "The Impossible Dream." This was the song that always made me think of my grandfather, of his strength and perseverance. This was the song I sang with my choir at my ninth-grade graduation performance, with tears running down my face. Then, and now, the song will always be my Grandpa song. I sat on the blue tile steps in my mom's home and sobbed while it played.

In December of 1994, after running the five stores for the golf pro for two years, I received my annual bonus. The yearly bonus was calculated based on a percentage of net profit. I kept very thorough records of sales and expenses for each of the stores, so I knew approximately how much to expect. The envelope contained a check that was about one-fourth of what was due to me. I asked my boss to review the figures and recalculate the bonus. He flatly refused, telling me that was all he was prepared to pay me.

So, I left. I quit right there on the spot. He had allowed his greed to control his better judgment and was willing to cheat me out of what was due to me. He had no clue how to run a retail chain, as his time was spent at the golf course while I'd worked myself ragged keeping the stores going. No more.

I started a new job as the buyer for a golf course group in San Diego, doing the buying and merchandizing for three golf shops. It was a much easier job for me to manage with my kids, and I was very grateful to not be working so hard. The many sales reps I had done business with over the years provided updates on that golf pro and all his mall stores. Apparently, one by one, he closed the stores.

MARRIAGE AND MOTHERHOOD

Although I liked my new gig, after about eight months, I was bored silly. Right on schedule, a new Grandpa-type brainstorm was soon hatched. I decided to open my own store in a local mall, since I had the formula down pat. I found a great spot near Nordstrom at a high-end mall in La Jolla, quit my job, and opened Golf Gear in 1996.

I was so proud of that little store. On my opening day, my husband and the kids came down to wish me luck and to see the finished product. My oldest two children, ages eight and ten, were now attending a private Christian school, and little Emma was just barely four years old.

The store was so profitable that Christmas season that I was able to pay off my small business loan at the end of the year. Of course, that Grandpa thing was still at work in my head when I learned that the beautiful Scottsdale, Arizona, store I had run for that greedy golf pro had recently closed, the last one of the five. It was too hard to resist, so I met with the mall leasing agent and the next thing I knew, we were installing a Golf Gear sign above the space.

But trouble was brewing on the horizon. Soon after I opened that second location, the anchor store on my end of the mall, Bullock's, closed down. The mall manager assured me that Dillard's was set to take over the location and be open and running by the beginning of the "season," which in Phoenix meant October 1.

The store held its own at first, but as the months passed and no sign of Dillard's was visible in that empty anchor space, one by one, tenants on my wing started to close. Like them, being mom-and-pop operations, we didn't have the financial backing that big chains had, and I feared this same fate would befall my store.

I soon learned that owning your own business is not for the faint of heart. The stress of meeting payroll every other week, getting vendors paid on time, and keeping up with rent, utilities, and worker's compensation insurance was unrelenting. I remember sitting in my bed with the large business checkbook on my lap and a stack of bills, cranking out one check after another (by hand in those days). That month, I wrote 264 checks.

The amount of time and energy I invested in this endeavor far exceeded what I had planned for, and it took a heavy toll. As with my former job, I placed high expectations on my ability to fulfill both my parenting duties and my work duties. I'd lost weight and looked very gaunt by Christmas of 1997 due to utter exhaustion.

As the holiday season came and went, with still no sign of a new anchor store in sight, it was clear I soon had to make a hard decision. My San Diego store was carrying the water for the Arizona store, but now I was losing money.

One day in that spring of 1998, I was at work in the San Diego store when the general manager paid me a visit. He started by telling me how much he enjoyed having me as a tenant and appreciated my being on time with my rent every month. He followed that with the statement that in thirty days he was going to call my lease. Apparently, a large chain, Thomas Kinkaid Galleries, wanted my space.

This was absolutely devastating and was the death knell for my little enterprise. I had no choice but to close both stores and liquidate the inventories to pay off the vendors. It was terribly sad, and I felt like I had failed, even though the closures had nothing to do with any lack of skills or retail savvy. Both stores met their fate due to events that were outside my control.

That May of 1998, before closing the San Diego store, I walked over to the bookstore in the mall and found the section on education. I selected a book on homeschooling and made myself comfortable on the floor there to thumb through it. The reality was that I no longer had the income to support three kids' tuition at a private school. The public schools had been a huge disappointment, so no way was I going to reenroll the kids there. For these reasons, I decided to consider the idea of homeschooling.

I remember walking back to my store that day being very aware that God was redirecting me. The recent events that had obliterated my dream to someday own my own store, a dream I'd held on to since graduating college, were leading me toward something more meaningful than selling golf shirts. Still, even with this awareness, I suffered terribly when I had to pack up and close my stores. These little stores represented all I knew how to do, all that I believed I was good at, and closing them made me feel like a failure. So much of me was wrapped up in each little display and every single decision, the details that gave my shops a unique appeal and set them apart from the typical golf shops I'd become so familiar with over the past nine years.

In the movie *You've Got Mail*, Meg Ryan's character is seen closing her little bookstore for the very last time. Watching that scene always brings tears to my eyes because it so perfectly captures the essence of loss that comes with closing a business, of the end of a dream.

CHAPTER 13

Homeschooling

WHEN MY FIRST TWO CHILDREN reached school age, I didn't hesitate to enroll them in the local public school. As a kid, I had attended California public schools, which, back in the sixties, were among the best in the nation. My mother was a schoolteacher for thirty years, teaching kindergarten and first grade, and even my grandmother taught school for a short time in the 1920s. Public school was part of my family's DNA.

It was when Sarah started second grade that I became concerned about our local public school. The principal was embracing some novel teaching ideologies, such as child-directed learning and outcome-based education that did not sit right with me. She promoted creative spelling and did not believe in correcting a child's spelling. She eschewed phonics and embraced a novel concept called "whole language" for teaching children how to read. For math, the students were not encouraged to memorize basic math facts, but rather to rely on counting on a number line, their fingers, or using a calculator.

There was no grammar or cursive handwriting taught in our school, and it seemed that just about every project was a diorama revolving around environmentalism.

In May of 1996, at the end of Sarah's fourth-grade year, she had her very first western-style horseback riding lesson. Sarah wasn't really interested in team sports but loved horses, so horseback riding was a natural fit for her. When I met her instructor at the stables, I noticed that she was an older gal with a salty, rough style of speaking. Sarah was a timid, shy, quiet girl, and I was immediately concerned that this may not work out well. She taught Sarah how to mount the horse and proceeded to guide her toward the arena. I sat on the sidelines observing the lesson as it unfolded.

As I witnessed the instructor barking out orders to my daughter, I half-expected Sarah to break down in tears. Instead, she surprised me. She absorbed the firm guidance and worked hard to please her instructor. She wanted to do well, and because of that desire, she was willing to listen, learn, and make a sincere attempt to demonstrate what was being asked of her.

On the way home, I asked her what she thought about her first lesson, and she immediately expressed how much she'd enjoyed it and couldn't wait for the next one. I pondered all this, and when we got home, I sat down and typed up a short six-hundred-word essay tying Sarah's horseback riding lesson with teaching methodology, and writing about how children will step up to the plate when they are taught using direct instruction. On a fluke, I printed the essay, put it in an envelope, and mailed it off to our local newspaper called *The Orange County Register*. Imagine my surprise when I saw it in print two weeks later—my first published piece.

I became very concerned about the schools and continued to research education. The nonsensical trends I was seeing in our school were not exclusive to that school, or even our district or county, but were being promoted by the California Department of Education and the teacher's unions. I began to study the federal legislation that was behind these teaching methods and decided to take the time to really scour the textbooks.

It became clear to me that the public schools were headed down a path that was politically motivated. There appeared to be a clear agenda in the propaganda I spotted in some of the books. This prompted me to start networking with other concerned parents and to attend presentations by prominent authors of that time who were revealing the larger agenda in public education. Based on the research I was conducting, I wrote an article about the concerns I had, and it was published. Soon, I'd had a succession of columns published in *The Orange County Register*, *The Washington Post*, the *Los Angeles Times*, *The Washington Times*, and *Investor's Business Daily*.

All this research led me to one conclusion: that I should move my children out of the public school and into a private Christian school. At that time, I didn't belong to a church. I had not attended church since I was eighteen years old. But with the shift away from my liberal twenties toward embracing conservative values in my thirties also came a nagging thought that my children would benefit from some basic religious education.

I decided to enroll my two oldest kids in a Christian school. They were in third and fifth grade when I made this change. It was a nice school and the kids made plenty of new friends there. Academically, the school was what I was looking for, with a traditional curriculum and utilizing classic teaching methods. Because it was a Christian school, my ten-year-old daughter Sarah learned how to navigate the Bible, and then taught me.

By 1998, during the period when my stores were closing, I began doing some occasional church shopping. Every so many months, I would attend a service at one of the local churches in our town. This included a Presbyterian church, a Methodist church, and an evangelical church. None of them felt like a fit for me.

Finally, one Sunday, I begrudgingly took myself to the local Catholic parish called Our Lady of Fatima. I decided to sit in the very back pew because I had not attended Mass for so many years and had no clue what to do. Then, to my surprise, and I surely did not expect this—I found myself weeping. In fact, I fought tears during the entire hour of the Mass. I had one tissue in my purse that was thoroughly soaked within minutes. During this very emotional response to being there at Mass, I clearly remember feeling deep contrition for my past sins. I remember silently telling Jesus that I was so sorry for all my sins, and how I wished I could rewind the tape and live my life over in a way that was pleasing to Him. There was no denying that it was there, at the Catholic Church, where my little family and I belonged.

That summer, after chatting with some friends who were homeschooling, I decided we should give it a whirl, too. John was on board, mostly because of the end of the expensive private school tuition. At that time, I honestly did not plan on homeschooling for the long term. I figured I would get another job and be able to enroll the kids in the parish school that next school year. Enter, God.

In late July, I headed to the convention center where a homeschooling curriculum fair was being held. I will never forget the sheer joy I felt perusing the many textbooks, one long row after another. I admit I was slightly overwhelmed with all the options available, especially because I would be teaching three grade levels, a kindergartner, a fourth grader, and a sixth grader. I made sure to look for the teacher's editions, which provided the answers to assignments and tests as I shopped.

Being an old-fashioned gal (think Norman Rockwell paintings) and embracing my newfound conservatism, my selections gravitated toward traditional history books, reading primers from the 1940s and 1950s that had been reprinted, and classic authors. I placed math workbooks and science experiments in my cart and snapped up copies of the Constitution and the Bill of Rights printed on parchment paper. I added teaching modules on the great composers and artists and a flag to put up in our dining room. It was exhilarating to realize that I, as a parent, finally had some control over what my children were going to learn.

A Catholic homeschool mom steered me toward Kolbe Academy, a private school located in Napa, California. They offered a homeschool curriculum and would also keep records for the kids in the event the state of California or a future school ever requested them. Through Kolbe Academy, I found wonderful classic Catholic literature and catechetical materials. I was all set to start my new gig as a homeschool teacher.

Just as my dear grandfather had always demonstrated, I approached this new venture with sincere determination and grit. I studied books on homeschooling and picked the brains of other parents who had chosen this daunting path. Grandpa would probably tell me that I was trying too hard, a tendency of mine. But I took my responsibility for educating my children very seriously and hoped to make as few mistakes as possible.

Just prior to starting our first year of homeschooling, I made a list of goals for the school year. It would serve as a guide to keep me focused on meeting not only academic benchmarks and spiritual goals, but also to help me stay on course to achieve my vision of what school should be. The routine I planned to implement was to teach the kids their academic subjects from nine a.m. until noon, have lunch, and save the afternoons for enrichment activities. This included art projects, science projects, and free reading time. Because I had them memorize and recite poems on occasion, they could use this time to practice.

We embarked on our homeschooling and, other than a few sibling squabbles, it went well, even better than expected. Once or twice a week I made it a practice to get the kids out into the world to do some exploring. Looking back, this was the very best part of our homeschooling years—the adventures. I believe that kids learn best by seeing and doing, instead of just reading about some topic. So, off we'd go to science museums or historical sites, to visit many of the California missions, to see plays and even an opera, to aquariums, botanical gardens, and so much more. Sometimes we would skip academics altogether and take a day trip to the Getty Museum, the local mountains, or the Santa Barbara Mission that was four hours away. Homeschooling offers freedom, which to me was just so, well, *freeing*.

One of our field trips was to visit the Huntington Library and the adjacent botanical gardens, which happened to be just fifteen minutes away from Gopher Hollow. I hadn't seen Gopher Hollow in decades, but my kids had heard all about it from my stories. So, we parked across the street from the house in a spot where I could just take it in. It looked pretty rundown, sadly. The trees were overgrown, and the house needed a coat of fresh paint. Still, staring at the front porch brought back memories of me as a young girl excitedly running to the front door, to ring the doorbell and hear the bells chime, and I still remembered the tune the chimes played. I glanced to the left of the house and let my eyes wander up the narrow driveway where Grandpa would pull up his Cadillac, and off to the right where the mourning doves cooed right outside the room where my sister and I stayed that summer.

I decided to take a chance to see if the owner would allow us to peek at the house, even just the backyard. I walked up to the doorbell and rang it, smiling as the chimes still carried the same tune twenty-five years after Grandpa had sold the place. An elderly woman answered the door. I introduced myself and told her my grandparents had built the house in 1941, that it was my grandfather whom she'd purchased it from, John Sousa. I then asked her if I could show my kids a bit of the house, since they had grown up hearing about Gopher Hollow. She said, "I am so sorry, but now is not a good time. My husband is not feeling well."

So, I offered my best wishes for her husband and thanked her for her time, and off I went. When I returned to the car, the woman who lived at that house across the street from Gopher Hollow was chatting with my kids at the car. I introduced myself, and she told me she remembered me from attending one of Grandpa's Veteran's group events, and that she had attended his funeral service. I shared with her what the lady in the house had just told me and asked if she knew what ailed the husband. She looked at me in wonder saying, "Well, that's interesting because her husband passed away five years ago." Suddenly, images of Norman Bates and his mother came to mind. It was quite an interesting field trip!

Freeing our family from the constraints of regular school was such a blessing. No longer was I required to dig through backpacks and rifle through the many handouts from school. These became so cumbersome during the public school years that it came to feel like the school owned us. Homework projects and assignments had demanded constant participation from parents, who were exhausted from working eight or ten hours and just needed some rest. The school calendar no longer dictated our family vacations, freeing us to join about twelve other homeschool families in Yosemite the week before the public schools let out.

Don't get me wrong, homeschooling is hard work. Some days would be so emotionally taxing and frustrating I admit to locking myself in my bedroom and screaming into my pillow. The kids would taunt each other, quarrel, and test my patience on the daily. But for every irritating moment, there would be twenty amazing moments.

Sitting together on the couch taking turns reading the Bible; creating a school room out on the balcony on pretty days, with the dog as a fellow student; perching themselves up on top of the back fence to do their reading; and working on cool science experiments together in the kitchen. These were the stuff of great memories.

The final project each year was a hefty, multi-level project that required several weeks of planning and work. Being an entrepreneur myself, I hoped to spur this trait in my children, so I had them create a fictitious small business for their final project. This included drawing a design of the business, including the floor plan. They designed logos and business cards and created simple business plans that outlined their goals and how to reach them. One year, my youngest, Emma, created a candy store, Matthew created a baseball training center, and Sarah created a deluxe pet hotel.

I never did pursue that job hunt I had planned on undertaking after closing my stores. I quickly learned that no job could hold a candle to what I was experiencing day in and day out right there in my own home. Needless to say, one year of homeschooling turned into two, and ultimately a total of nine years for my youngest, and four for the older two children.

One of the benefits of homeschooling is the relationships you make with other families who also homeschool. Much of our socializing revolved around events like parties, church events, and even vacations. We parents were united in many the hope of raising our children to be godly, patriotic adults. We had formed a bond amongst ourselves as like-minded parents in this quest, but honored the variations in our homeschooling philosophies. We felt confident and relaxed about our kids hanging out together, knowing that the parents were basically on the same page.

I admit I was a pretty strict parent. Part of the reason is that I had to compensate for the lack of my husband's involvement in the formation of our children. He did not attend church with us and was actually quite negative about all things religious. He was much more interested in watching the kids play sports than he was in guiding their steps. So, I "wore the pants" in the family when it came to discipline and general guidance and parenting. It was exhausting.

It wasn't only my husband who enjoyed watching our kids play sports. I, too, was always cheering them on at their many sporting events. Our son was a gifted baseball player, which I attribute to his father's genes, having been a minor-league baseball player himself. John contributed countless hours teaching Matthew the fundamentals and working with him continuously. All of this paid off, as Matt was in All-Stars several times and even played with the varsity team as a freshman in high school. As a senior, he was one of just two players who made it to the "Showcase," a league event where college scouts would look for prospects. Sarah enjoyed solo sports, her favorites being horseback riding and competitions and also figure skating. Emma was a team sport girl who excelled in soccer and softball. I was proud of all their accomplishments.

I was also passionate about my faith and felt that my number one duty as a parent was to pass it on to my children. Together, we read the Bible and learned about the life of Christ. Even though I recognize I am a poor sinner who falls down daily, I did make a sincere effort to set a good example for the kids.

One Christmas, I shared with my kids about the lighted plastic Nativity scene my grandparents used to place on their front lawn during the holidays, and how much I wished we had one just like it for our yard. But at the time, eBay didn't yet exist and I never did see anything like it in the stores. Instead, I settled for a ceramic Nativity scene that I proudly displayed in our home. I also asked my husband to make a large star out of narrow wooden planks that I covered with white Christmas lights, and I hung that outside my daughter's window.

Our homeschool girls' group decided to put on a Christmas play for the local senior center one year. We had such a great time joining our creative forces building the scenery, making costumes, and writing the script. In fact, the kids were routinely involved in volunteer work through our homeschool group, which added yet another layer to the many benefits of homeschooling.

During these wonderful stay-at-home mom years, I was no longer earning a regular paycheck. To be able to contribute financially in some small way, I continued to have articles published on a regular basis. My favorite topic to write about, of course, was homeschooling, and those articles were widely published. I loved sharing with others about the many blessings of homeschooling, versus trusting a child's education to the government.

Another income stream I created during those years was a tutoring business. I posted flyers around the surrounding neighborhoods, and it wasn't long before I had several students. One of them was a ten-year-old girl named Irena, who'd been adopted from Russia. When she'd come to my house for her tutoring sessions, she'd always play my grandmother's piano, a 1934 Baldwin spinet. She played passionately from memory with no sheet music to guide her. I truly enjoyed all the kids I tutored; for some reason, it was much easier than teaching my own kids.

As the saying goes, "All good things come to an end." This beautiful nine-year chapter of my life ended in 2006. It was time to go back out in the world and work at a regular job again. But I can honestly say, when looking back on my life, it was that period of time, as a homeschooling, stay-at-home mother, that I am most proud of. Although that chapter of my life was often challenging, it was also the most fulfilling time of my life because I got to truly parent my children. Because of those years together homeschooling, my relationships with my kids became very close. My kids learned all my crazy childhood stories, about all my favorite things, all my quirks and flaws—yes, my kids truly *know* me, and I know them. All three of my children are beautiful inside and out. They are kind, funny, loving human beings, and I took such pleasure in being their mom. Being able to stay home with them, to take part in their formation and education in such a meaningful way, was a gift from God that I will cherish for the rest of my life.

CHAPTER 14

Divorce

I AM A BIG BELIEVER in the power of prayer. Where my marriage was concerned, I could not have prayed harder. I held onto the thinnest shred of hope for nearly nineteen years that eventually John would agree to join me in marriage counseling. I had begged him to go to counseling with me since our first year of marriage, when the signs of trouble were already evident. He flat-out refused.

I have never prayed so hard for any particular intention as I did during those final six years of our marriage. I filled several journals during my Adoration hour every Wednesday at church, recording my ongoing angst about our troubled marriage and lamenting that God was not hearing my prayers. An elderly priest, Monsignor Tony, would often be there in Adoration at the same time as me. He often asked me if he could pray for me, so I'd ask him to please pray for my marriage and for my husband to return to the Church.

Back in 1999 when I had just returned to the Church, I met with a priest to hopefully receive some guidance about the state of my marriage. He guided me through the annulment process, as that was the first order of business, after which we'd have our vows convalidated, since our marriage was a civil marriage and not a sacramental marriage. He believed that by normalizing our status and getting right with the Church, graces would flow and positive changes would result. Even though my husband did not participate in our religious life, he agreed to go along with this for my sake, for which I was grateful. It felt like this was my last hope of salvaging the marriage.

On October 4, 2000, the Feast Day of Saint Francis of Assisi, we joined the priest at the altar, accompanied by our children and some family members as witnesses, and there we renewed our marriage vows. I had absolute confidence that this was exactly what our struggling marriage needed all along, and was very hopeful that things would soon improve.

Without going into the gory details, suffice it to say that no amount of prayer was going to help our marriage heal. As always, I felt that my husband resented getting married and had been punishing me ever since. He loved our children but spent the vast portion of the last many years ignoring me, basically shutting me out. He was simply emotionally unavailable to me. I remember describing how this marriage felt to me, like I was a starved dog or a dying plant that desperately needed to be watered.

By 2004, it was clear that God was not going to answer my prayers. The troubles escalated to the point that I was completely depleted, depressed, weak, and hopeless. By mid-July of that year, I was on the brink of a mental breakdown, and even entertained thoughts of suicide. I sat in my mother's kitchen during a visit that month and told her I didn't think I would make it to September. That was how despondent I was.

In addition to my mother being very concerned about me, my close friends were also worried. On my birthday, a friend called to wish me a Happy Birthday at about ten a.m. and I was still in bed. I was terribly depressed, I didn't even accept her invitation to get together and celebrate my birthday. I broke down on the phone, telling her how utterly hopeless I was about my marriage.

Another friend reached out and suggested I meet with a priest from a local monastery. These were my very favorite priests, holy, brilliant, faith-filled men who took their vocations extremely seriously. She felt one of the priests at the abbey would be able to direct me and maybe refer us to a Catholic marriage counselor.

I took her up on the suggestion and made an appointment. When I met with the priest, he asked me the reason for my visit, so I shared with him the main issues I struggled with in my marriage. This was a holy Catholic priest, a monk, who followed Scripture to the "T," and he advised me to consider leaving the marriage. Yes, that was how troubled the marriage was. He could see by my physical and mental state the toll the marriage had taken on me, and after listening to my primary concerns, he believed I was not safe.

Still, the priest did send me home with the name of a good therapist, although he said he didn't hold out much hope that my husband would, or could, make the needed changes to salvage our marriage. In addition, John had yet to agree to see a therapist all these years, so my hunch was he would simply refuse to meet with this one.

As things turned out, there was a final event that occurred the first week of September that was the catalyst for me to ask him to leave the house. I was very distraught, as I had high hopes we would make some headway in therapy, but alas, we never got there. The situation had drastically deteriorated before we ever met that psychotherapist.

The very last thing in the world I wanted was to have my family break up. For me, divorce just was not an option. I wanted with all my heart for my children to have a stable, normal childhood, to have what I never had. But as the kids had grown older, they were becoming aware of the strife in their parents' relationship and could see that it was dysfunctional. For so many years, I had put on a happy face to try and keep the peace, hoping to hide our problems from them. But now that they were older, it was impossible to shield them from the marital issues.

Still, seeing their dad move out of the house was traumatizing. Emma, the youngest, was only twelve, Matt was sixteen, and Sarah had just turned eighteen. Even though they were not little kids, this was very painful for them to witness and navigate. Everything in our lives had changed in an instant.

As for me, I felt wrecked, like an utter failure. I felt that I had somehow let my children down. Along with the guilt and angst, I was also afraid. I had been a stay-at-home mom for nine years. I had abandoned my career in exchange for the amazing time I spent at home with my children, which is a noble act…until you get a divorce. Suddenly, I realized I would have to return to work and pretty much start over from scratch. I had no idea how I would manage all the financial demands to be expected with a large home and three big kids.

I was in terrible condition at that point, in the fall of 2004. I knew I needed help, but I didn't know how I could afford a therapist. Little did I know, God was already at work. In the Sunday paper that week, there was an article about a couple in a local city that had started a ministry in their church. I recognized the woman, named Terry, because we had attended the same high school in the early seventies. So, I sent Terry an email to say hello and to explain the situation I had found myself in.

Terry responded to my email within one day and invited me to connect with a therapist at their church. I was so grateful, just to have this referral from someone I knew and trusted. I set up an appointment to meet with the counselor the following week.

It's strange how certain moments stay forever etched in your memory, and meeting Colleen, the counselor, was one of those. I arrived at her office looking as bad as I felt. I was underweight, and gaunt, and wore jeans with holes at the knees and a t-shirt. She invited me into the office and handed me some paperwork to fill out as part of the intake process. I will never forget sitting there while attempting to answer the questions on the paper, with tears running down my face.

Colleen turned out to be a lifesaver, an angel sent by God. All those years, I had prayed and prayed for my marriage to be healed, only to have them fall on deaf ears. However, God does things His way. He placed the right people in my life at just the right time, starting with the priest and now this therapist, to guide me through this challenging chapter of my life.

Colleen sat me down in her office and, after a short prayer, asked me to explain what had brought me there. In response, I focused mostly on the current events surrounding the end of my marriage, and that I had just filed for divorce. But Colleen instinctively knew there were many other layers underneath the outwardly facing problem of impending divorce.

Colleen was the perfect fit for me. I have a strong personality and am also a people pleaser, two things that could create barriers in therapy. Fortunately, Colleen was just as strong. For example, if she asked me a question and wasn't satisfied with my answer, she would look straight into my eyes and say, "I will ask you again, and this time I want you to tell me the truth." She called me out when she knew I was hedging or avoiding getting in the weeds with her.

She said she liked working with me because I was willing to do the hard work involved in the rebuilding of my life. She gave me the book *Boundaries* by Dr. Henry Cloud, asking me to read it and to also complete the workbook. She'd give me other assignments, too, and I always complied, putting a lot of thought into each one.

One of the assignments was very interesting. She had me imagine myself in four different life scenarios and told me to describe what I liked about each one. I saved this paper because it contained some keen insights into who I wanted to be.

Many tears were shed and many prayers were said in that office. Colleen gave me the tools to reshape the way I related to people—ways that were unfamiliar to me. As I integrated these new concepts into my consciousness, I knew I would never allow a partner, or anyone, to ever have such a destructive effect on me again. She taught me how to value myself as a daughter of Christ, someone to be treasured and honored, not abused.

Finally, in October 2005, at the end of a full year of working together, we both knew it was time for me to fly. During that year, I had reclaimed my joyful spunky spirit, the strong, capable person I always had been before a toxic marriage basically stomped it out of me. I decided to make her a little memento to thank her for her invaluable help, and when I showed up at that last session, she, too, had a gift for me. She gave me some beautiful heart-shaped earrings along with a letter that I have kept. She wrote:

Theresa

Loyal, Honest, Compassionate, Dedicated, Competent, Reverent

As we come to the close of our time together, I can't help but reflect back on your process. Theresa, you are a different person today than you were a year ago. When you came in to see me, you were a broken, hurt, scared woman. It was a difficult time. The dreams of having a cohesive family were shattered. You came in with just pieces left, hoping to hold on to some sort of sanity, as your core was being ripped apart. The immense amount of pain and grief were almost unbearable.

It was at this point that you knew you had a choice: A choice to be consumed by this pain or to learn from it. You see, the road less traveled encourages us to reflect on the process because it is in the process that we glean the wisdom and truth to lead a truly authentic life. Theresa, you walked this road. You were willing to look at your process. Not just the current situation but rewinding back to the beginning. Oh, how difficult this was. Yet the willingness to uncover some of life's tragedies allowed you to gain perspective. I think it is perspective that you must hold on to.

Romans 8:28 says, "All things, even bad things, work together for good for those that love God, to those that are called according to His purpose." Theresa, I believe God wrote this Scripture in the Bible for you personally, and how fortunate am I to be able to witness this Scripture come to life through your story. My hope is that someday many will read your story and will be fortunate that you wrote about it to encourage them. God gave you a talent for writing, a story to write about, and a heart willing to serve Him. Amazing how that works.

Today we conclude with our time together. And sitting before me is a beautiful, talented, put-together woman of faith. You have done the hard work to rediscover yourself through this process. You have come to truth and are living that truth out. You are living a truly authentic life. Thank you for allowing me to walk this road with you. I am truly blessed to have been a part of your life. You will be in my heart and prayers.

"My hope is that someday many will read your story and will be fortunate that you wrote about it to encourage them."

All these years later, I still attribute my ability to survive difficult, even tragic, events because of her loving counsel when I needed it most. To top off this blessing, my high school friend Terry, who had arranged for the therapy, insisted that I not pay one cent for the entire year of counseling. God does answer our prayers, but sometimes our expectations and tunnel vision make it difficult to recognize it when He does.

Divorce, any way you slice it, is simply devastating to a family, and ours was no exception. Everything had changed. Holidays were never the same again. I spent some holidays all alone because it was John's turn to have the kids. One such Thanksgiving, I volunteered to work in a soup kitchen, figuring I could at least do something productive with my day. Another Thanksgiving, I remember sitting through back-to-back movies in the theater to kill time until my kids came home. Of course, on alternate holidays, John suffered, too. We all suffered.

After a couple of years, I realized I was pretty lonely and that maybe it was time to venture out into the dating world. Since my friends were all happily married, I was always the fifth wheel, never having a plus one at the events I'd be invited to. I hoped to find a nice guy.

I'll admit that I was very naïve wandering back into dating after twenty-two years. For the past nine years, living as a Catholic mother and homemaker, I was sheltered. Now, as a divorced woman working outside the home, I had left that cocoon of protection and was more susceptible to the temptations of the world. I found myself bouncing between holiness and worldliness, and many times, unfortunately, choosing worldliness.

This was the backdrop in 2007 when I embarked on the online dating experience. After joining Match.com, I met a smattering of guys at those awkward meet-and-greets, when more often than not they looked absolutely nothing like their profile photo. A couple of the guys were nice enough, but I found them either boring or I felt no connection. I entertained my coworkers with the many horror stories of online dating.

I was also introduced to something known as "ghosting," a new addition to the dating vernacular for Boomers. I learned that ghosting refers to what happens when someone you are dating just—poof—disappears without explanation, not even a flimsy excuse. This rude behavior stung and made me realize that I didn't have a thick enough skin for online dating.

In 2008, I realized I was probably going about the dating thing all wrong. Instead of wasting money and time on dating platforms, I should be leaving the job up to God. So, in March of 2008, I created a list on a sticky note of the attributes I was seeking in a man. I dated it and attached it to a framed picture of Saint Anthony. Everyone knows St. Anthony finds things, so surely, he could find me a man. This was my list:

He will love God
He will have a great smile
He will have beautiful, soulful eyes
He will be thoughtful
He will be generous
He will be passionate
He will be kind
He will be a Catholic
He will be a man of character
He will be ethical
He will be fun/active/fit
He will enjoy my kids
He will treasure me
Who is he???

I hung this list attached to the St. Anthony picture inside my bedroom closet and pretty much forgot it was there.

I was apparently a sucker for punishment because I continued trying online dating off and on for the next couple of years. Finally, it was the last two guys that I met, within weeks of each other in the spring of 2011, that ended up being the last straw. These guys both turned out to be dishonest people, which I thankfully was able to discern early on so I never invested my time. I remember, after the second disastrous date, driving home while vowing to spend the rest of my Friday nights in my flannel pajamas with my dogs, which I found preferable to going on any more awful dates.

Enter Mike.

CHAPTER 15

Mike

I BELIEVE, AS WE SCURRY THROUGH OUR DAYS, working, parenting, going to the dentist, paying the bills, and running errands, that our lives are actually being carefully ordered from above. Daily life might feel like utter chaos when you're in it, but in hindsight, you recognize how perfectly the puzzle pieces of your life were being placed.

It was 2010. My daughter Sarah had just graduated from college and looked forward to fulfilling her calling as a teacher. Emma had just graduated from high school and would be starting college in the fall. My son was a new father to a beautiful baby girl, my first grandchild, named Grace. Life was pretty good.

At the time, I was working for an optometry group, a job I had held for about four years by then. As the frame buyer, my main job was meeting with sales reps, viewing the various lines, and placing orders for eyewear for the dispensary. I enjoyed my job. I was able to use my retail background to thoughtfully manage the open-to-buy budget and keep track of the inventory, and the reps were a lot of fun to work with. More than this, I absolutely adored the team of coworkers that I spent my days with. It was like a family there. As my first job after returning back to work post-divorce, it provided a good start.

Oakley was by far our best-selling line for several years running. On occasion, Oakley would host fun corporate events for their key accounts, and that August, I was invited to attend one of them. In classic Oakley form, the event was held at a deluxe bowling alley. Some of my coworkers met me there at the venue, and as we entered and signed in, there he was standing behind the reception desk. He was tall, athletic, and handsome. I'll admit that I felt my heart flutter a bit when I saw him.

As I approached the table he manned, Mike introduced himself to me with a big smile. Just as I went to add my email to the list as requested, I spotted a wedding band on his left hand. Dang! It's true—all the good ones were taken. So, off I went to join my group inside the venue where the meeting would be held.

Mike led the meeting, which was informative and fun. He used a game show-like format to teach us facts about the company and the special features of the Oakley lenses. During this little contest, someone was taking pictures and snapped a photo of me while I was answering a question. There I sat in my cute little summer frock, looking besotted with animated eyes and a sheepish, girly expression on my face. Little did I know that day that the die had been cast.

About four months after this event, my Oakley rep, Tiffany, stopped by the office to let me know that the territory was being reworked and she would no longer be my rep going forward. She told me that starting in January 2011, I would be working with her boss, Mike. At first, I didn't put two and two together, so she said, "You know, you met him at the bowling event in August." Oh, *that* Mike.

In early 2011, Mike called to set up our first appointment for March. Because he had been with Oakley for well over twenty years by then, it was customary for most of his accounts to just let him place the orders for them. The poor guy had no idea that he would be doing the whole dog and pony show when he came to work with me. I had him schlep in all his cases to show me tray after tray of frames. Having been a ready-to-wear buyer for years, I would have never trusted my sales rep to book an order for me. So, Mike accommodated my requests without complaint, and we actually had a lot of fun working together. We chatted about our kids, our dogs, and this and that, and although I found him immensely charming, I was keenly aware of his marital status.

About a week or two after this appointment, I heard from Tiffany, who told me that Mike had reached out to her and asked about me. He wondered if I was seeing anyone. I immediately thought, "Ewwww, what a cad!" and recoiled in disgust that a married man would be inquiring about me.

Tiffany instantly cleared things up. Apparently, he and his wife had separated the prior summer and, after six months of separation, were about to file for divorce. I wasn't sure I wanted to get tangled up in that situation, so I just told her I'd wait a bit to see what would unfold.

On May 13, 2011, our office hosted an Oakley trunk show. It was a big event, basically a party, where we invited all our patients to come out and see the entire Oakley line. We had refreshments and prizes and had two doctors booked solid that day.

In addition to Mike and Tiffany, Oakley sent a couple of people from corporate to spend the afternoon at the trunk show. During the day, I caught Mike glancing my way more than a few times, and I remember feeling like a schoolgirl with my heart all aflutter. I even remember exactly what I was wearing: a belted chambray shirtdress and tan heels.

At the end of the day, after the patients had left, we opticians were buried in orders. Mike approached the counter where I was sitting and told me they, the Oakley group, were heading across the street for dinner, and asked if I'd like to join them. I assumed he had invited the others, too, but I declined the offer, saying I had a ton of work left to do. So, off they went.

About thirty minutes later, I was heading to my car, totally worn out, when suddenly God turned me around. That's right, God did it. I was almost to my car when I turned a one-eighty and began walking in the opposite direction toward the restaurant. I reasoned it would be good for me to network with the Oakley group.

When I approached the table, there was one empty seat, right next to Mike. As I negotiated the tight space, I leaned over to him and asked if he would mind moving a bit away from me. I was worried it would seem inappropriate to be sitting so close to this man who was, after all, technically married. And, with a smile on his face, he happily accommodated me and scooted a bit over to the left. As I sat down, the waitress was delivering their dinners. Mike asked the waitress to take my order, and then he proceeded to sit there and not touch his meal until she had brought mine. Wow. He was a gentleman.

One by one, the others peeled off and left us sitting there alone together. We spent the next hour chatting and sharing our stories. He explained the marital situation and that they had just filed for divorce. His marriage sounded just as difficult as mine, so we recognized each other as kindred spirits, that we had somehow survived.

When he walked me to my car, he asked if I would be interested in having lunch someday. Even though I wanted to play it cool, I blurted out, "Sure!" At my car, he took my number, wrapped his strong arms around me…and on an impulse, I kissed him. Yep, *I* kissed *him*.

On my way home, I felt like I had been gob-smacked, like a meteor had landed on me. Once home, I sent him a text asking, *What the heck just happened?*

He replied, *I was about to send you the exact same question.*

About a week later, we went on our first date. We met at Panera Grill and spent about three hours talking outside on the patio. This was followed by a couple more marathon dates, and then one day, I allowed him to pick me up at my house. I had never let any of the buffoons I'd met on Match.com ever come near my family home. But I trusted Mike.

I will never forget the way I felt the first time I got into the car with him. I immediately felt safe. *Safe.* I knew in my gut that this man would never hurt me. By now, having spent many hours talking in person and on the phone, I knew without a doubt that this person was a quality man, a man of integrity. He was smart, honest, and a little old-fashioned, which I loved.

Thus began an amazing romance with the man I would soon realize was the love of my life. We saw in each other wounded souls, having each suffered tremendously in our respective marriages. For this reason, we treasured each other, treating each other with the kindness and care we had always deserved.

As someone who identified as a practicing Catholic, I suddenly found myself to be your classic cafeteria Catholic...selecting this teaching but passing on that one. After only about eight weeks, Mike and I were becoming serious. We were ready to take our relationship to the next level.

We decided to spend a weekend in Old Town in San Diego. Old Town is a historic center that features quaint shops filled with Mexican folk art, Mexican restaurants, and other touristy attractions. Our weekend in Old Town was romantic and passionate. Our room had a large window that faced an acacia tree that was in full bloom, covered with bright yellow flowers. We hung out at the pool and then headed over to the Mexican restaurant for a delicious dinner. This weekend proved to be a turning point for us. Even though we had only been dating for two months, it was evident we were falling in love.

Two things stood in our way. First, Mike and his wife had only recently filed for divorce. Even if everything went smoothly, it would be at least a year before he would be free. One of my concerns was his status as a married man, so I asked him if they were married in a church or in a civil ceremony. Thankfully, they were married in a civil ceremony. This meant in the eyes of the church, the marriage, albeit a legal union, was not a valid sacrament. Knowing this helped me justify dating him. To complicate matters, however, his wife soon learned that Mike was dating me. She decided to make it her sole mission not to cooperate with the divorce procedure in any way. She routinely canceled any meetings arranged between the two attorneys at the last minute. Every time she canceled, it set the process back by several months.

The other thing that prevented our relationship from growing was his demanding job. He worked about seventy hours per week as a sales rep for Oakley. It was an intense and exhausting schedule, which left little room for spending much time with me. So, for about eight months, we saw each other only two times a week. These limitations, I admit, upset me at times. However, there were only so many hours in a week, and his job and other commitments consumed the majority of them.

But it wasn't only Mike who had impediments that prevented our relationship from flourishing. My son, Matthew, was very sick, suffering from both depression and alcoholism, and as they say, "Alcoholism is a family disease."

CHAPTER 16

Matthew

THERE IS NOTHING SO EXCRUCIATING as witnessing your grown child's world falling apart in real time. My son was afflicted by the dual demons of alcoholism and depression, and his life was now spiraling out of control. Back when he was about eighteen and a half years old, this beautiful young man—handsome, sensitive, athletic, smart, funny—who had never caused his parents a minute of trouble suddenly changed. That was in the fall of 2006.

At that time, Matt was a freshman in college, majoring in engineering. His first semester didn't start off well. At first he complained about ongoing insomnia, and soon after, he contracted mononucleosis. Due to the effects of the virus and the lack of sleep, Matt was missing classes, causing his grades to suffer.

It was during his visit home for Thanksgiving, however, that I realized something more serious was going on. One night during the holiday week, he woke me up at one a.m. and asked if I could talk with him. I switched on the light and sat up in my bed, not really sure what was going on. Matt sat on the end of my bed and started crying. He sobbed. He was very sad that he hadn't heard from his dad at all during his first three months at college. He was sad that he was no longer playing baseball. He hated the engineering classes. He was miserable.

I sat there incredulous, wondering, *Who is this person?* Matt had always been happy and upbeat, just a really positive guy. Seeing my beautiful son in such a profound state of despair was nothing less than alarming to me. All I could do in the moment was console him. I couldn't, and wouldn't, offer any excuses for his dad's lack of interest in his life. As for baseball, he had made the decision at the end of his high school baseball career not to pursue college ball. When he told us this news at the end of his senior year, I was really sad, and even offered to assist him financially with expenses. But he was firm, saying he was done playing baseball. As far as not really liking his major, I encouraged him to give it a fair chance and to work on bringing his grades up. By the end of our conversation, he seemed calmer, but in my gut, I felt that something was just not right.

Matt started drinking, which is not unusual in a college setting, especially during freshman year when there is such an emphasis on partying. He lived with seven other guys in a suite, and alcohol was ever-present. The problem for Matt was that he was using alcohol to numb the uncomfortable symptoms of depression. He also had a high tolerance for alcohol, so he drank more than the other guys just to get the same effects.

At the end of the second semester, Matt decided to change majors and reclaim his boyhood dream of becoming a firefighter. I totally supported this decision as he was a perfect candidate for the job. He was caring, big, and strong, and would do whatever it took to save someone's life.

This had been demonstrated recently when he was on a short

cruise to Mexico after graduation, accompanied by some close friends and a set of parents. One night, after an evening of partying on the upper deck, the boys were heading to their rooms. Matt spotted a young woman who was apparently preparing to jump off the side of the ship. He ran over to her, convinced her to return back to the deck, and pulled her back over the railing. He had a heart for saving people.

He moved back home that summer in 2007 and planned to start at the fire academy in the fall. Over the summer, his drinking habit worsened. He was hanging out with a friend who also liked to party, which was the last thing Matt needed. Meanwhile, his mental health was becoming concerning. He seemed unstable. I made an appointment for him to see the doctor and get bloodwork done, hoping there would be no signs of drug abuse revealed. Although he tested negative for all substances, his liver counts were high, which indicated alcohol abuse.

I convinced him to see a therapist about his depression, and he complied. However, according to Matt, the therapist only talked about himself so he got nothing out of it, and that was the end of that.

During the summer, his behaviors and drinking were increasingly concerning to me. We had a big fight over it and Matt took off in his car. We didn't hear from him for a few days, so I was extremely worried about his wellbeing. He wasn't right.

Finally, a few days later, he called to say he was okay and was in Colorado with a friend from high school. It was during this conversation that my son first alluded to having suicidal thoughts. He was just nineteen years old. He told me he didn't want to live anymore, that he was so unhappy all the time. Hearing him say this, I literally dropped to the floor. My daughter Sarah joined me sitting there on the floor in the upstairs hallway while I continued to listen.

He was crying so hard I could barely understand what he was

saying, but I realized he was telling me he wanted to die. I begged him to hang on and told him that I would fly out the next day and we could drive home together. By the end of our conversation, though, he had regained composure and assured me he would not harm himself and would start his journey back to California the next day.

Matt made it home safely. It was now the end of August and he was supposed to start classes at the fire academy in a couple of weeks. But with all the turmoil he was feeling at the time, he announced he would instead spend a semester in Hawaii, joining a friend from high school at his place on Oahu. I was disappointed about the delay in starting school, but I kept it to myself. On some level, I instinctively knew that this was exactly what my son needed.

When he returned home at Christmas, he looked amazing. He was tan, fit, and happy. He had plenty of funny stories to share with us; clearly, his stay in paradise had been one big adventure. Seeing him so healthy and happy gave me great hope. Now he was ready to buckle down and start his classes.

Unfortunately, Matt continued to party with his local friends. Still, he managed to pass his first semester of classes and also worked at a local sporting goods store. Later in 2008, he landed a great job at a private golf club working carts. This provided him with free golf and lots of cash tips from the members he assisted.

During the fall semester, I became concerned about his drinking. I could tell he was hung over many days, and signs of the depression had started creeping back. He volunteered at a local firehouse and went out with a couple of the guys for drinks after the shift. When he emerged from the bar, he was still holding a beer, and a cop was right there to cite him. This was the last thing he needed, a black mark on his record. Getting hired as a firefighter was a rigorous process, and candidates are closely screened for any past offenses.

During this latter part of 2008, Matt was also becoming

increasingly irresponsible. He would get parking tickets and then ignore them, which caused them to end up costing hundreds of dollars. Guess who ended up paying them.

In early 2009, Matt met a cute girl named Amanda at a friend's party, and it was love at first sight. The next day, he couldn't stop talking about the amazing girl he'd met. He said theirs was an instant connection, and they were already planning to go on their first date. I was thrilled to see him so happy. I knew he had been lonely.

Over the next weeks and months, Matt and Amanda were attached at the hip. She also was dealing with some mental health issues, but substance abuse wasn't one of them. However, while hanging out with Matt, Amanda began to drink more. This went both ways because Amanda was a smoker, and soon Matt was smoking, too.

Matt was drinking heavily, which impacted his studies. His weekly tests at the fire program were getting harder for him to pass. The threshold was a score of seventy-five, and he was barely scraping by. Then, things started spinning out of control.

He walked off his job after a disagreement with his manager, a job that was a perfect fit for him during college. I was really upset. The country was in the midst of the Great Recession, so losing a job at this particular time was not good. He was obsessed with hanging out with Amanda, and nothing else seemed to matter. She, too, was unemployed.

A month later, they managed to get in a car accident, which was determined to be his fault by the insurance company. They immediately dropped him from my policy. Some unpaid tickets he'd racked up had fallen into my lap to pay at a cost of hundreds of dollars. I paid them only because I was so worried about his future prospects of getting a job with a fire department being harmed by these unpaid tickets.

Basically, the two of them had become little hedonists, living for nothing but themselves. Now that he was unemployed, the cost of feeding my son, who still lived at home, was becoming a real strain. I knew I was being taken advantage of.

The biggest blow to date that year came when he failed to pass the finals and would have to retake the entire semester. I was very disappointed and angry, especially knowing he wasn't studying like he should have been. After discussing all of this with my coworkers, I decided it was time for some tough love.

It was early August and I approached Matt to let him know he had three weeks to find someplace to stay. I was all done paying his expenses while he partied. He nodded and then told me that he and Amanda had something to tell me. Amanda was pregnant.

Needless to say, I lost it. These two irresponsible kids, both unemployed, now had a baby on the way. As a Catholic, the only thing that kept me somewhat in control of my temper was the fact that they intended to get married and have the baby. After I calmed down, what else could I do but be supportive of their decision?

Matt needed a job. At the time, the only job he could find was working the graveyard shift at a luxury hotel in the security department. This spelled the end of his fire academy tenure because he would not be able to continue classes while working all night. This made me terribly sad, but I held out hope that my son would straighten out now that he had a family to care for and that hopefully at a future date, he could reenroll in school.

Matt and Amanda married in November. He was twenty-one and she was twenty-two. All their family members and friends were present to wish them well on this new adventure. I had absorbed the shock and shifted toward great anticipation of my first grandchild, due to arrive in March of 2010.

Right on time, their beautiful baby daughter, Grace, entered the world. I was very honored to be able to be present, along with

Amanda's mom and grandmother, at the birth of this precious little girl. I was very proud of my son calmly encouraging Amanda through the labor. Holding his baby girl, he radiated pure joy.

Matt's alcohol abuse continued. The graveyard shift was also taking its toll on his mental health and overall wellness. Now, with the added stress of a newborn, I could see him gradually deteriorating. He requested a transfer to a daytime shift, but so far there were no openings. By the fall, it was clear there was trouble in the marriage. Matt's drinking was the main problem.

In October, Amanda asked him to leave. He came home to stay with us, and he and Amanda took turns having Grace. My son was deeply depressed. One night, after she came to pick up Grace, as he headed up the stairs I could hear him crying.

While he was staying at the house, I decided to open up a conversation about his drinking. This was met with an angry, "I am not going there!" so I backed off. I knew he had to figure it out on his own, but it was nearly unbearable to see him so sad. It was up to him to take the necessary steps to confront his problem, but he was still in denial.

He had been at the house for about four weeks when he and Amanda decided to reunite. This was the best Christmas present ever, and we all had high hopes for their future together. Soon after they reunited, Matt announced he'd been offered a great opportunity to work for Vail Resorts in Colorado, and that he had accepted it. Amanda was also on board, as she loved snowboarding and was excited for them to make a fresh start in brand-new surroundings.

Of course, both sets of Gracie's grandparents were thoroughly devastated. We had grown very attached to her and were crushed to imagine life without her. Still, we knew we needed to be supportive of their decision and happy for my son's new job. They moved to Colorado in early January of 2011.

For a few months, life in Colorado appeared to be going well for their little family. Matt kept in touch regularly with updates and photos of Gracie. By now I was dating Mike, and I was madly in love. In sharing about my life with Mike, I realized I had to tell him about my son's struggles. Mike was very kind and nonjudgmental as I tearfully told him how afraid I was about the drinking.

I made plans to visit them in July for my birthday, and was really looking forward to witnessing firsthand their gorgeous new life in the mountain resort. But just a couple of weeks before I was to make the road trip, my son reached out asking me to reconsider coming out. He said he and Amanda had separated, and he was in a bad place. With his history of depression, it was all the more reason for me to make the trek to see him, so I did.

When I arrived in Colorado after a two-day road trip, I happened to drive up right as Amanda was handing off Gracie to him in the parking lot. He looked very, very sad and barely managed a smile when he saw me. Matt was devastated when she left him. His sweet little girl was the one bright spot in his life. Despite my son's troubles, he was a very loving, doting father. This was indisputable. Over the prior few weeks, he and Amanda were able to work out an arrangement to split the parenting duties. Amanda was dating, but Matt wasn't interested in dating. He loved his wife.

Fortunately, Matt really liked his job at Vail Resorts. He worked mountain security at the ski resort and enjoyed it very much. As he showed me around, I could tell how proud he was of his accomplishments at work. Still, I sensed a deep melancholy in him.

Matt agreed to meet with an addiction counselor at the local behavioral health center where he would be evaluated. Grace and I dropped him off and then tooled around town for a couple of hours. When he emerged from the treatment center, he had some paperwork in his hand consisting of recommendations. The clinician he'd seen had suggested he just join an Alcoholics Anonymous group and attend some outpatient therapy sessions. Even though I was still learning about alcoholism, these recommendations from a professional appeared to be grossly inadequate. My son was very sick.

Over the next couple of days, Matt drove us all around his new stomping grounds, including on a short road trip down the mountain to an old mining town called Georgetown. He chose this destination because of its many quaint old buildings, and because he knew how much I loved taking photos with my 35mm camera. He patiently accommodated me as I asked him to stop the car about every other block so I could snap a picture. We found a park there, and he and Gracie had a lot of fun playing together on the equipment.

That night, we had a nice dinner at a lakeside restaurant, and he did not order a drink. He was attempting to just stop drinking on his own, since the clinician he'd seen had made no mention of undergoing a medical detox. Looking back, that was basically malpractice. Still, he seemed to be doing okay, and he really did enjoy the dinner with Grace and me. At one point, I asked him if I could take their picture. He leaned over toward his beautiful daughter and she reached out her little hand to gently touch his face with a look of pure love and devotion. What a treasure that picture is.

Even though we had enjoyed such a lovely day and evening together, my heart was deeply troubled. I felt a growing sense of urgency about the gravity of my son's problems. So much so that, once back at my hotel room, I walked over to the window that overlooked the picturesque mountain scenery and knelt down in front of it. While staring up at a black sky with thousands of twinkling stars, I prayed to God with all my heart that my son would not die alone here.

I left Colorado feeling hopeful that Matt would follow through and take the actions the clinician at the behavioral health center suggested. Matt promised me he would. But within a week or two, he called and admitted that he was not able to control his urge to drink. He said that the therapy sessions only made him want to go out and drink, and A.A. meetings had the same effect. This was evidence that the guy who had evaluated him was woefully inept, as my son was a full-blown alcoholic and could not just stop all by himself.

Matt felt so dejected, so sad about what he had done to his life, and he took full responsibility for it. It really worried me when he mentioned that his tremors had gotten so bad that he was afraid to drive the truck at work. He had been asking his coworker to drive because he was very fearful he might have a seizure while at the wheel.

It was about this time that I reached out to my uncle John, my mother's brother, who was in recovery with over twenty years of sobriety. I was so grateful that he was willing to call Matt and attempt to encourage him. My uncle said they spent a half hour on the phone, and that my son was very receptive. Soon after this, Amanda's uncle, who was also in recovery, reached out to talk to Matt as well. We were all so worried about him, and hopeful that he would follow the suggestions that people were giving him.

Matt and Gracie came home to CA to visit us in the fall. His sisters noticed how bloated his face was, and knew the goatee he now sported was grown to hopefully camouflage the problem. He had clearly been unable to stop drinking, and as his mom, I felt helpless. My son was slowly killing himself with alcohol and I was powerless to help him.

In August of 2012, Matt came for another visit. This time, I barely recognized my son as he walked toward me at the airport, Gracie at his side. At age twenty-four, he looked worn out and dejected. His belly and face were terribly bloated, and his hands shook as he stood in front of me. His once-gorgeous brown eyes were now red, glassy, and squinty. Seeing my boy like this frightened me to my core.

Still, I was determined to enjoy our time with Matt and Grace in the four days we had together. I threw a big party so the family could spend some quality time with him and Grace, but was dismayed to see him drinking so much at the gathering. One evening, Matt, Mike, my daughter Emma, and I attended a concert together. Another day, Matt, his friend, Mike, and I enjoyed front-row tickets at an Angels' baseball game. Throughout his visit, I tried my hardest to remain positive, wanting it to be a bright spot for him in the darkness.

One day, soon after he returned to Colorado, I was overcome with fear. A deep, guttural, ominous fear. I could feel in my bones that my son was in terrible condition, and that he needed help as soon as possible. However, as I learned about the disease of alcoholism, I noticed a common theme in the literature—that until the alcoholic hits bottom, they won't be open to getting help.

It just so happened that that week, right after my son flew back to Colorado, I had read something totally different, something that immediately struck a chord in me. This passage was from a book called *How to Help the One You Love* by Brad Lamm:

> *"The idea that we are powerless, that we should just watch*
> *and wait until someone hits bottom, is dangerous.*
> *You watch and wait and pray and hope*
> *and you end up with a dead spouse..."*

I sent my son a text, telling him I was very concerned about his health and wanted him to know that I was available to come out there and help with Grace when he was ready to seek treatment. He responded immediately, saying he needed help, that he even believed he was dying. He told me there was blood appearing in his urine. My heart broke reading this.

So, I replied, telling him I was willing to take a leave of absence to come to Colorado, but that he would have to give me adequate notice so I could arrange the leave with my work. I suggested that when he felt he was ready to go to rehab, to meet with the H.R. department and begin the paperwork process for taking a medical leave of absence. He agreed to this plan and was very appreciative of my offer to help out.

Within a few weeks, my son called, crying on the phone, telling me I needed to come right away because he wasn't going to make it. I told him I couldn't just leave on a dime without giving my employer any notice, but that I'd check in the morning to see when they'd be able to let me leave. He sounded desperate, and I was alarmed. However, it was obvious he was very intoxicated, so I tried to get some sleep and deal with this the next day.

I am forever grateful to my employer, who was willing to grant me a leave of absence so I could travel to Colorado and help my son check into rehab. I would be staying at his apartment in Vail while he was in treatment down in Denver, and I would take care of Gracie on the days he normally would have.

The two-day drive to Colorado was steeped in emotion. I made voice recordings of my thoughts and feelings as I drove out to help my son. My son was worth every effort I had made and would make. He was a kind person, blessed with the biggest, most loving heart. His was a life worth saving.

When I arrived in Colorado, Matt had been feverishly trying for hours to find a bed in a rehab center but was having no luck. He had spent the prior night in a "drunk tank" trying to detox under some form of supervision, but once out, he succumbed and started drinking again. I felt a sense of urgency to get him placed as soon as possible.

The two of us plowed through a list of rehabs until we finally found a bed in a Denver suburb. The woman on the phone told us another person also wanted the bed, so it would go to whoever claimed it first. He packed a backpack and we threw some snacks into a bag, and we were off. We just had one stop to make before heading down the hill.

Matt wanted to stop and say goodbye to his daughter, who was at the babysitter's house. Watching Matt pick her up and hold her close, as he promised little Gracie, "Daddy is going to get healthy" and "Daddy won't be fat anymore," had both the babysitter and me in tears. Gracie was just two and a half at the time and of course had no idea what was going on. As we left, she said, "I wuv you, Daddy."

Matt was mostly quiet during the two-hour drive down the mountain. He wasn't feeling well because he hadn't had a drink for several hours now. As we drove along, I noticed him staring out the passenger window with tears trickling down his face. When I asked him what was wrong, he said, "I just look forward to the day when I can look in the mirror again and not be disgusted by what I have become." It broke my heart.

Fortunately, we arrived at the rehab center first and Matt was given their only bed. When I left there that night, totally exhausted from a nine-hour drive from Utah, plus another two-hour drive to Denver, I felt filled to the brim with something I had not felt for several years: hope.

During the time Matt was in rehab, I immersed myself in that lovely mountain setting. The days and nights I spent with Gracie are still like little postcards in my memory. Our time spent hiking, going to the playground, shopping in Frisco, and just sitting on the floor playing with Legos was so precious. One photo, taken by Amanda on a hike we all took together, summed up this time with Gracie. We hiked to a pretty lake, and Grace and I were sitting side by side gazing out at the water. Amanda took the photo from behind, a grandmother with her little granddaughter.

I was very active in the family program at the rehab, understanding that my presence there would be helpful to Matt's recovery. Family support is a vital aspect of rehabilitation because it demonstrates your willingness to devote time and effort to the healing process. It also helped heal the wounds between us. I brought Grace to see him every Friday, which he looked forward to all week long. She was truly the only thing he lived for and was what kept him moving forward in treatment.

Without more funds, the rehab said they would have to release him after only one month. No way was that enough time, but Matt was chomping at the bit anyway. He missed Grace and wanted to get back to work. He truly believed he was good to go.

When we drove down the mountain to pick him up that day, we were thrilled to bring him home. The addiction counselor didn't really offer me any guidance, only handed me some paperwork that mentioned the medication, Lexipro, he had been placed on for depression. Looking back, it is utterly disgraceful that a rehab center would discharge a patient to the family without explaining the risks of relapse. The counselor knew Matt was depressed, that his marriage was over, that his wife was now living with another man, and that he lived alone. In hindsight, he should have warned me that the risk of relapse is high for someone with no one living with him. If he had told me this, even though I was ready to get back to California and my job, I would never have left him at that early juncture.

So, three days after Matt returned home and had located an A.A. group and set up an appointment for outpatient therapy, I headed home. Saying goodbye to not only Matt and Grace but also to that beautiful mountain resort, was very painful. But my daughter Emma, then twenty years old, had been holding down the fort for over a month while trying to keep up with her college classes, a job, and two dogs. So, off I went, gazing as long as I could in my rearview mirror at father and daughter behind me in the distance.

Five days after I returned home, I received a devastating phone call. The caller was a sheriff informing me that my son had attempted to kill himself by jumping off the fourth-floor balcony of his apartment complex. He had landed on the concrete steps, hitting the steel handrail on his way down. The officer told me that Matt was being airlifted down the mountain to a Level One trauma center in Denver. He also told me that Gracie was left sleeping in her bed, alone in the apartment, which triggered the involvement of Child Protective Services.

No mother is ever prepared for something this horrifying. I dropped to the bedroom floor as the sheriff spoke. I could barely breathe. That beautiful month of hope I'd experienced in Colorado became null and void in an instant. All I could think was, *My son, my precious son, what have you done?*

I had endured many difficult events in my life up to that point, but learning that my son had attempted suicide, and was now badly injured, was the most traumatizing to date. After the call, my daughters had to assume the role of mother. They picked me up off the ground, forced me to breathe and take some sips of water while trying to process their own sense of shock and sorrow.

I called Matt's father, John, to inform him of what had happened, and he made immediate arrangements to leave for Colorado. I was supposed to go back to work the next day, so I managed to text a message to the office manager, telling her what had happened in misspelled gibberish. Over the next several hours, all through the night, Amanda and I were in contact via text. She was traumatized too, and upset that Matt had left Gracie alone in the apartment. The police called her to the scene to gather Grace.

I also reached out to my best friend, Francesca, whom I call Franny, who'd been such a source of support during these tumultuous last few years, especially while I was alone in the mountains. She literally reached out to me every single day to check on me when I was staying in Vail. Finally, at about four a.m., I fell asleep.

When I woke up the next morning, I tried to convince myself that what had happened was nothing more than a nightmare, that it couldn't be real. Ah, but it was. I reached out to the hospital to get an update on Matt's condition. The representative told me he had been tended to in T-10, which is the high-tech operating room reserved for the worst trauma injuries, and it was believed he would survive his injuries. He was then transferred to the psychiatric intensive care unit.

John arrived in Colorado later that day and called with an update. He is not prone to hyperbole, so when he told me it was a good thing I was not seeing my son at this juncture, I knew it was bad. Matt had twenty-five staples in his scalp to close a gash that had resulted from hitting the steel handrail. He had six broken ribs and a broken clavicle. His left leg bore the worst of the injuries, with huge lacerations on his shin and upper thigh. In fact, the leg injuries were the reason for requiring T-10.

As the full impact of what had transpired sank in, I started to lose it. That night, I found myself inside my walk-in closet, frantically searching for photos of my son in the tubs of mementos I stored in there. With photos of my son splayed in front of me, I wailed, loudly, "What happened to my son? What happened to my beautiful son?" just like an animal. I instinctively reached out to Franny, who was out on a date with her boyfriend. She turned the driving over to him when she realized the gravity of my mental state in order to stay connected with me. For an hour, she soothed me with Scripture verses that she swore came straight from God through her fingers to my phone. I was so shaken that I wasn't able to talk on the phone with anyone, other than my mother, so texting had become my lifeline.

John and I arranged to split a hotel room that was close to the hospital. He would be there for five days, and then I would relieve him and stay the next five days. The day I arrived, John was at Matt's bedside, where he had spent the majority of his time over those five days, and there our son lay broken to bits. I tried not to let Matt see the shock in my face or the sorrow in my eyes when I greeted him. He tried not to let me see the shame he felt.

The first week was very distressing. We had to let Matt know that he had lost parental rights because of leaving little Gracie alone in the apartment the night he attempted suicide. He was devastated. I also had to witness Matt receive a phone call from his boss, informing him that his job with Vail Resorts was terminated and that he had to vacate his employee housing within one week. As his mother, I was heartbroken watching the tears slide down his face at this news. Everything he truly loved was lost in an instant.

It fell on me to return to the apartment in Vail. I was going to have to pack it up and put his belongings in storage, because at that time he was unable to even walk. Entering his apartment and seeing on a chair the blood-drenched clothing that the first responders had cut off my son was completely traumatizing. Seeing the exact spot where he had landed was also very upsetting. In fact, one of the grounds-keepers stopped by the apartment as I was packing up and said he had witnessed the scene and described it as the most horrific thing he'd ever seen.

In all, I spent ten days there in Denver with Matt this time around. Six of those days, Matt spent in the psych ICU. It was a very trying time in every way. The healing process was slow, and his mental health was poor. After a couple more days in a regular hospital room, he was ready for discharge. Upon discharge, he was transferred to a horrible psychiatric institution. This was a humiliating and disturbing turn of events, but thankfully, after the doctor there conducted a thorough evaluation, Matt was released after just thirty hours.

During those two weeks, my son suffered severe pain from a large hematoma on his left upper thigh, which had to be drained multiple times. He was attempting to wean himself off the pain medications so that he could enter sober living. But because he was in so much pain, so bad that he couldn't even walk, this process dragged on.

Meanwhile, we shared a hotel room. What made this so very unpleasant was the liquor store across the street beckoning him. I felt like I had to babysit him as if he were a two-year-old child, just to prevent him from relapsing again. Matt became very angry and resentful toward me because I would not leave him alone.

As the reality began to set in of what all he had lost when he'd relapsed and attempted suicide, my son became hostile and angry. I honestly couldn't stand to be around him while he was in this state. I did join him at an A.A. meeting, which helped a bit. But he was unable to move forward and enter sober living due to the hematoma and had become very frustrated. It was a catch-22.

Finally, John arrived in Denver to relieve me of this torture. He would be in charge of moving Matt into a sober living home in a nearby town. Now I could return home, back to my job and to Mike, whom I missed terribly. Meanwhile, all I could do was pray for my son, that he would stay strong and resolute in his newfound sobriety. He had a formidable road ahead, that much was certain.

In a couple of weeks, after Matt was safely ensconced in a sober living home in Aurora, Colorado, John felt it was safe to return back to California. Our son was to live in a safe, substance-free home with a house manager on site. His first goal was to find employment, which would allow him to contribute to the care of his daughter and eventually earn his parental rights back.

Because Matt was still unable to walk, he was stuck inside the house and had to search for work online. The other housemates had jobs, which meant he was really feeling the brunt of homesickness now that both of his parents had returned home. At one point, he was taken to the emergency room because the hematoma had again become so painful and engorged. The doctors were concerned that his leg was infected, which scared me so much. I worried about him losing the leg; it had already been considered at one point.

The impact of loneliness on Matt intensified as the holidays neared. On Thanksgiving, he called both John and me and wept while on the phone. He missed his daughter terribly and felt so alone there in Colorado. Since he was not yet permitted to see her, we convinced Matt to return to California. Thankfully, Matt agreed. Because John and I both worked full-time, we agreed Matt would live at a sober home near both of us, as we couldn't take the risk of him relapsing again.

This plan was put into action in early December. The whole family was happy, and very relieved, to know that Matt was going to be living close by. All of us could be sources of support for him and would surround him with love. Thus, the roller-coaster ride that was the year 2012 had come to a close.

CHAPTER 17

Matt and Mike

IN EARLY 2013, things were looking up. Matt was thriving in his new sober life. He liked the guys he roomed with at the sober living home, and he always had funny stories to share. He joined a local gym and started working out daily, in addition to taking several hikes a week. He shed all the weight that he'd put on the last few years, and by Easter, all the injuries were healed. He had found a full-time job via a referral from a friend, and this kept him busy and productive. He was tan, trim, and healthy-looking for the first time since 2009.

I was happy to accompany Matt on a couple of his hikes in the beautiful foothills near my house. We had always had a close, open relationship, so hiking the trails gave us plenty of time for some interesting conversations. One day, I asked him if he still missed playing baseball, and he admitted that he did. I suggested he find a recreational baseball league to join, especially now that he was back in excellent physical shape. I even shared a story about a professional baseball player who had also battled alcoholism and managed to make a comeback. He pretty much laughed that off, telling me at age twenty-five he was too old. Still, as we chatted about baseball, I detected a hint of the joyful spirit that had been absent for years now. That little spark was in his eyes again, something that had been missing, even in sobriety.

Just when I started to finally relax a little, Matt disappeared from the sober home. He had run off on a bender. By the state he was in when we finally located him, it was obvious he was attempting to drink himself to death. This was a huge setback, and we were heartsick over it.

Fortunately, the manager of the house really liked Matt. He felt Matt was a good influence on the housemates, and so he decided to override the house policy and allow him a second chance. I was so relieved that he wasn't getting kicked out of the house, and so was he. At this point, all I could do was pray that my son would be able to hang on to his sobriety, and move ahead with my own life.

Mike was an amazing person to have in my life. We enjoyed our time together and deeply loved each other. I wasn't open to "shacking up," so we maintained separate residences. Unfortunately, even in 2013, he was still enmeshed in a very contentious divorce, so living apart was the appropriate decision for us. Oh, but how we looked forward to the day when we would be able to marry and finally begin our life together as man and wife.

Mike was an athletic man. He was trim and muscular and had a passion for mountain bike racing. I regularly joined him at these races so I could cheer him on from the sidelines and snap cool photos of him on his bike. In April 2013, Mike invited me to join him in Santa Barbara, California, for a mountain bike competition. The course was situated in particularly rugged terrain, but Mike had trained diligently for the race.

As usual, I set up my base right there at the starting gate. During many of the races, I would walk around the course to watch him pass by, but this course was not accessible, so there I sat waiting for him to cross the finish line.

An hour or so later, I noted that some of the guys from his heat had already come in, and I expected to see Mike at any minute. He didn't appear. After some riders from the heat that followed his began approaching the finish line, I began to panic. My worry was that he had fallen and sustained an injury, which would explain why he hadn't yet finished the race.

Another half hour passed before I finally saw Mike coasting toward the finish line. He dropped the bike and sat down on the ground looking utterly defeated. He said he'd had to stop riding halfway through the race. After resting, he could only walk the bike for much of the remaining distance. He seemed mystified about the sudden loss of stamina and just figured he hadn't consumed enough nutrition for the grueling race.

That evening, as planned, we went out to dinner in the nearby town of Solvang. While we were nearing the end of the meal, he told me he really needed to lie down as soon as possible. So, we returned to the hotel room where he then collapsed into bed. The next day, after about ten hours of sleep, he felt a little better, but I still offered to drive us home.

Over the next few days, Mike attempted to visit his accounts as usual in San Diego. He really struggled, though, and even had to cancel some appointments. He figured he had been hit with a nasty flu bug. However, on Thursday evening, his roommate reached out to me to tell me he was worried about Mike. He said Mike had a strange rash on his face and also had a fever, and that he had just gone to the local urgent care center to be seen by a doctor.

I immediately called Mike, who had just been seen by the doctor. He said the doctor was sending him over to the hospital. Apparently, the results from the urinalysis and blood work indicated something concerning. It appeared he had pretty severe anemia, which indicated possible internal bleeding.

The hospital ran some tests and had him do an internal imaging procedure called capsule endoscopy that involved swallowing a tiny camera device. The hope was that the images would reveal the source of the bleeding.

After the thousands of images had been analyzed a few days later, the doctor reported that the camera had not detected any internal bleeding. This prompted him to admit Mike back into the hospital for more extensive testing. That evening at dinner, Mike admitted to me, with tears in his eyes, that he was scared. I tried to keep a positive front for his sake, but honestly, I was scared, too.

It took about a week for us to get back all of the testing results, which included growing specimens in a petri dish at a lab. On May 13, 2013, exactly two years to the day from that first date after the Oakley trunk show, we were informed that Mike had a very rare form of leukemia called chronic myelomonocytic leukemia (CMML). We were all utterly devastated.

The next day, my daughter Sarah called to tell me what else had occurred on May 13. Matt had been admitted to a mental hospital. She knew I was with Mike at the hospital when this happened, and was worried sick about the diagnosis we had received for Mike, so she wanted to spare me from this news until the next day.

About two weeks prior, my son had decided to go live with his dad in order to save the money he was spending on the sober living home. I wasn't thrilled about this, but Matt assured me he was in a good place now. Well, it turns out that was not the case. Apparently, a few days after moving in with John, Matt started drinking. This led to a crisis event on May 13 when Matt first passed out on the front porch and then ended up out in the street yelling at the top of his lungs that he was going to kill himself. John called Sarah, and she arrived to find Matt running down the street drunk out of his mind. They feared for his safety, so they called the police. Matt was picked up on a Code 5150, which was an involuntary seventy-two-hour hold at a mental hospital.

Learning my son had relapsed and was suicidal again, and was now being held in a psychiatric ward, was too much for me to handle. I literally had to put it in a compartment in my mind so I could focus on my beautiful man at his time of need. I would deal with my son later.

None of us had the slightest idea what CMML was. Apparently, that extra "M" in the CMML is what made this type of leukemia very rare, as CML is a more common and highly treatable version of leukemia. Unfortunately, there were no local hematologists who had ever treated a patient with CMML, so I began the mad search for a doctor who had. I was able to locate one such doctor at UC San Francisco, and another doctor at Stanford. I called them both and was able to get an appointment at Stanford on May 28.

I felt terrible to do this to my employer, especially after they had been so accommodating back in the fall of 2012 during my son's problems, but I had to drive Mike up to Stanford to see this specialist. This caused issues at work since my shifts needed to be covered with zero notice. I just didn't know what else I could do.

Mike and I took the fastest route via the grapevine (I-5) and made it to Stanford in less than seven hours. During the final two hours, Mike spiked a fever and acquired a strange rash around his midsection. Of course, I was stressed out, but I tried to remain calm for his sake.

We arrived in Palo Alto and checked into the hotel. Mike was not feeling well at all, so we really looked forward to our four-hour appointment at the Stanford Cancer Clinic the next day.

The following day, a team of leukemia specialists at Stanford met with us, and a dermatologist was summoned to look at the rash. Samples were taken and blood was drawn. The next thing we knew, based on the results of these tests, Mike was being admitted to the hospital there at Stanford. Our appointment with the clinical team to discuss his illness had to be postponed until the infection was under control.

For two days, Mike was pumped full of antibiotics. That first night, I wandered into the little gift shop downstairs and found the perfect card for him, with the lyrics "You Are My Sunshine, My Only Sunshine" emblazoned across the front. He truly was. Finally, after a few days, he was well enough to be released from the hospital, and we headed back to SoCal.

All of this was very emotional for both of us. Over the last week or so, there were many tearful moments sharing feelings, fears, and hopes. We didn't know what had hit us. It was upsetting and frustrating that our trip to Stanford was a bust. Now, back home, all we could do was await the report from Stanford after they'd completed analyzing the bone marrow slides. In the meantime, Mike had a six-hour blood transfusion to boost his hemoglobin back to safe levels.

We received a call from the Stanford team stating that his blood did not show any leukemia, which was a cause for celebration. We gave all props to God, that He had given us our miracle. Instead of CMML, his updated diagnosis was myelodysplastic syndrome, or MDS, a bone marrow disorder. From here on out, a local hematologist would care for him with weekly labs, Procrit shots, and transfusions if or when warranted. We were ecstatic. The CMML prognosis was extremely grim, but an MDS diagnosis offered us an excellent outlook.

Now, back to my son. After the three-day stint at the psych ward, my son was released to us. It was recommended that he reenter a rehabilitation program as soon as possible. He was very ashamed that he had caused us all this added stress and was genuinely remorseful. Now that I was much more educated on the disease of alcoholism, I understood how the cravings can overcome the person and overtake their will. Matt felt so badly for Mike and offered to help in any way he could. I told him the best thing he could do for himself and for all of us was to enter rehab. Fortunately, he agreed.

The problem for our family was the cost of treatment. It was outrageous, and we were still in debt from the last rehab stint in September of 2012. Someone suggested The Salvation Army, saying they offered free treatment and room and board in exchange for labor. John and I checked it out and it sounded great. It was a six-month program, which is how long it takes for someone with severe alcohol use disorder, like my son, to have a chance at a sustained recovery.

During the six-month stay, Matt would be expected to work about six hours a day in the warehouse, sorting donated items for the various Salvation Army retail stores. Not very inspiring work, but I appreciated the idea that he wouldn't be playing ping-pong and pool all day like he did at the last rehab center. This program expected the clients to be productive and earn their keep. So, as soon as the Valium—the benzodiazepine that was given at the hospital to prevent seizures related to alcohol withdrawal—was out of his system, he was able to enter treatment. This offered me a great sense of relief, just knowing my son would be safe and unable to access alcohol.

Along with other basic clothing items, Matt was instructed to pack a button-down shirt and a Bible, as The Salvation Army is a Christian organization that requires its clients to attend church services once a week. It was also suggested to Matt that he bring along some stationary and stamps to be able to write his loved ones, as he would have no access to a phone for the first month.

His dad and I were invited to attend a class every Wednesday evening there at the campus, where we would learn more about addiction and how to offer emotional support to our loved one in recovery. We were instructed not to make contact with our son should we see him while we were there at the treatment center. One Wednesday, while being given a tour of the facility, we spotted Matt walking across the cafeteria, dressed in his button-down shirt. He looked so great, so healthy. He glanced our way, smiled at us, and we made a little clandestine gesture acknowledging him. It was so hard not to walk over and hug him.

We were also taught the wily ways the disease of addiction works in the victim's mind. This was very helpful information, in light of all the drama that had unfolded in May. In fact, the instructor told the group that if our loved one suddenly appeared at our door, they were likely to tell us they'd been "kicked out" of the program. If this should happen, he told us, we shouldn't fall for it. The Salvation Army rarely kicked anyone out of the program, other than due to a violent offense. He was very clear that if they should appear at the door, we should *not* allow them in. We were advised to not provide them with a "soft landing," but to instead persuade them to return to the program where they have a comfortable room and three meals a day.

During the month of July, Matt wrote his dad three letters, me just one, but most importantly, he wrote his precious little girl three letters, which her mommy read to her. He sounded so good, so upbeat, in all the letters. We were so encouraged that he would be able to stay the course and do what it takes to beat the demon of addiction.

The revised diagnosis for Mike was also a huge boon for us all. Since I was to be his primary caregiver post-stem cell transplant, I had him move in with me when his lease was up. Meanwhile, my employer had no option but to replace me, due to my sporadic need to run Mike to the E.R. when troubles flared up, which still occurred on occasion. Leaving my job of six years was messy and hard to accept, but necessary. In turn, I devoted my time to helping Mike on the road as he slowly returned to making his sales calls. I took care of inventories, returns, cleaning shelves, and schlepping the large, heavy sample bags from the van so he could concentrate on his clients. We were a great team.

After only four weeks, Matt showed up at my daughter Sarah's door. We had all been schooled about how to handle this situation and were on the same page—we would not allow him to stay with us. Poor Sarah was his first stop, and she felt really bad having to turn him away. Of course, he lied and said he had been kicked out for "not keeping his room tidy," which of course was a flimsy excuse he'd concocted for actually having left the program of his own volition.

After Matt left his sister's house, he called his dad to see if he was cool with letting him stay there at his house. John stood firm and told him no, and pleaded with him to go back to The Salvation Army. Matt told him, "No, Dad, I can do this on my own. Grace is coming to town next week and I couldn't stand the thought of not seeing her."

Matt had approached his family members in the order he felt he would have the best chances of persuading us. Now, it was my turn. I had already been forewarned that Matt was out and looking for a place to stay, so I was prepared mentally to refuse his request, although emotionally, not so much. Telling my son that he was not welcome to stay at his family home was one of the hardest things I have ever had to do. Like Sarah and John, I also told him he needed to get back into treatment. He was very polite but reiterated what he'd told his dad, that he could do it on his own. After we said goodbye, I put my head in my hands and sobbed. I realized there was a very good chance he would become homeless.

When we didn't hear from Matt for a couple of weeks, I became increasingly worried about his safety and well-being. I wondered if he was living under a freeway underpass, or whether he was alive at all. I knew that whenever he relapsed, he became suicidal, so that was my number one worry—that he would relapse.

Finally, in mid-August, I heard from my son. I broke down in tears just hearing his voice on the other end of the phone, so relieved was I. He told me that he was doing fine. He was living out of his car in a nearby town where he had found an A.A. community of mostly older men who had basically taken him under their wings. He said he attended the seven a.m. meeting every day, and sometimes multiple meetings a day. The guys would bring him sandwiches and water.

The reason for his call was to ask for a blanket, specifically, the royal blue twin comforter that was his bedspread as a child. I still had it, so I offered to bring it to him. I also asked if he needed a toothbrush, and he did, so I stopped to get him a toothbrush and toothpaste, trying not to imagine how poor his dental hygiene must be after weeks on his own.

I drove to the community center where he was located, and as I turned into the parking lot, I spotted my boy right away, riding around on his skateboard. I know my kid, and I could tell right off that he was still sober. He was lean and tan and beamed a big smile my way.

I looked over at his Jeep and died a little inside seeing the newspaper taped up on his windows. My son was homeless. This was very difficult to process and filled me with sorrow. However, after hugging and chatting for a bit, I realized that this was his choice. He had chosen to leave treatment to "do it on his own," knowing there was a good chance he would end up living in his car.

He told me all about the men who had befriended him and their generosity. It was clear that he was extremely grateful for their support and friendship. His goal was to find a job as soon as possible. I asked if he had any gas in the car so he'd be able to get to a job interview. He said no, not really. So, I offered to buy him one gallon of gas

($3.50 at that time), and he said, "Thanks, Mom, but I want to do this on my own," and politely refused my offer. I hugged my beautiful son and told him I was praying for him. I handed him a blessed Miraculous Medal and asked him to put it inside his wallet, which he did right then and there. Then, we said goodbye.

Despite my son leaving rehab and ending up homeless, Mike and I managed to enjoy our summer together. We were just so relieved that his condition had improved. We caught the annual classic car show and some beautiful sunsets at the beach, spent a ton of time with friends—backyard barbeques, dinners at restaurants, and gatherings at our house—and Mike even felt well enough to golf and participate in a bike race.

It was near the end of August when I received a call from my son, telling me that he had found a new job, but that it was a graveyard shift working security. Not this again! But at the time, he had no other offers and wanted to start providing child support for Grace, so he took the job. A few days later, he reached out to tell me he was cited for vagrancy for sleeping in his car during the day in a public space. I felt so badly for him that I asked Mike if it would be okay if Matt came by during the afternoons to get some sleep in his old room, which was now a guest room. Without the ability to get some solid sleep, there was no way he could keep this job. Mike said, "Are you kidding, just tell him to stay with us until he gets back on his feet." So, Blue moved back home that week under a list of conditions: he had to continue to attend the daily A.A. meetings and remain sober. If he relapsed, he would be asked to leave. He happily agreed.

Having Matt with us was a blessing. He helped out with chores and with the dogs, things that Mike and I were having trouble keeping up with. Mike was very limited as to what he could do, so my son happily pitched in.

Mike and I topped off our fun summer with a Heart concert at an outdoor venue in San Diego. It was Friday, August 26. As we were enjoying the concert, Mike happened to turn to me and there it was, that familiar rash emerging on his face. In utter dismay, I mentioned the rash to him. He was in denial, saying he was probably just breaking out. Except, Mike never broke out, ever. I honestly could not believe what I was seeing.

The following Monday, we saw the hematologist, who was concerned about the rash and also his bloodwork. We told the doctor about our plans to go to Palm Springs for the upcoming Labor Day weekend and were hoping we could still go. The doctor helped us achieve this goal by giving him the weekly Procrit shot and also putting him on a heavy antibiotic called Cipro. As we left his office, he instructed us to immediately take him to the E.R. if he spiked a fever.

To be on the safe side, I had made arrangements with Matt's dad for him to stay those three days with him. I didn't feel comfortable leaving Matt alone at the house. This is how it is when you have an alcoholic child. You never stop worrying. You are always trying to stay two steps ahead, just to limit any possible scenarios that could enable a relapse.

Another tactic I had learned was to wait until the very last minute to let him know we were leaving town, as the more time he had to think about it, the more opportunity the disease had to flare up in his mind. So, as we were about to leave, I told Matt that he would be staying at his dad's over the three-day weekend. He said that was fine since he had to work all three days anyway.

So, off Mike and I went to Palm Springs. I was concerned about him, but he really looked forward to playing some golf. As it turned out, we had to cut our trip to Palm Springs short. On that Sunday, Mike complained that his tongue was swelling and he was having trouble swallowing. While we were at church that morning, I was concerned enough to leave him there in the pew so I could walk out front to put a call into the hospital back home. They said his symptoms were indicative of an allergy reaction to the Cipro that could become severe, so they suggested we head back. During the two-hour car ride, Mike started showing signs of illness.

When we arrived back home Sunday evening, a day earlier than planned, my son's car was parked on the driveway. This was strange because he was supposed to be staying at his dad's house. I figured he must have stopped by to pick up some clothes or something as I helped Mike up the stairs and into bed. I took Mike's temperature to find he was running a slight fever. Just as I was about to call the triage nurse at the hospital to get guidance, I received a text from my son asking if I would go to his room. *What? Why doesn't he just come down to my room?* I wondered. Suddenly, the alarm bells started going off.

As I entered Matt's room, I found him lying on his bed in the fetal position, deeply intoxicated and sobbing. He said he was afraid, that he had been drinking for two days straight. He was clearly very close to alcohol poisoning. He kept apologizing, saying how ashamed he was, but most of his words were incoherent. I was furious and terribly disappointed in him. Here Mike was in bed sick, and yet my drunk son was now demanding my attention.

My gut feeling was that my son was in a very bad state and needed to receive emergency care. I decided to take him to the hospital myself. The problem was, he weighed over two hundred pounds. I managed to turn him around so his legs were at the side of the bed and then launch him to a standing position, and then I basically dragged him to the staircase.

Taking one stair at a time, and then pausing to steady the two of us before attempting the next step, was tricky. He could easily have toppled over, taking both of us down. But somehow I managed to get him down the stairs and into the garage. His mood vacillated between highly agitated one moment and gentle the next.

Trying to negotiate this large deadweight into the passenger side of my car proved to be quite challenging. He had little control over his movements, so it was hard to position him in such a way that he could sit down in the car. Finally, I succeeded in getting him seated, closed the door, and started to back out of the garage.

As my car slowly backed down the driveway, Matt suddenly opened his door and threw himself out of the car, rolling down the driveway to the curb. I could not believe it, after all the effort it had taken for me to get him from his room into the car. I was pissed. I pulled back into the garage and looked at him, lying in a heap on the sidewalk like a drunken bum, feeling utter disgust. I yelled, "I am so over this!" and marched inside the house. I was totally spent, emotionally and physically.

I went upstairs to check on Mike and called the triage nurse as I had attempted to do twenty minutes prior. She guided me, telling me that if his temperature reached 101, I would need to bring Mike to the hospital. After placing a fresh cold washcloth on Mike's forehead, I decided to check on my son.

I stood upstairs at the front window and saw Matt sitting out on the curb. He was holding his head in his hands and crying. This sight made me very sad, seeing what had become of my boy. He was pitiful, sitting there. He was filled with remorse, especially knowing that he would be asked to move out of the house now that he'd relapsed.

I resisted the urge to go talk to him. I had to give him the space to deal with the repercussions of his actions, to process the gravity of it all. I checked on Mike again, who remained stable. Then, after a few more minutes, I walked back to the window to check on Matt. He was gone.

I called his cell phone and he answered. I asked if he would still like me to take him to the hospital, and he said he had already called the police, and they were on the way to come get him. I asked where he was, and he told me he was at the nearby elementary school, so I drove over there.

When I arrived, the police were already there talking to Matt. I told the officer that Matt was my son and asked what the plan was. He said, "Ma'am, your son is gentle as a lamb, but obviously very sick. He is very cooperative, so I suggest you allow us to transport him to the hospital."

I agreed that it was safer for the police to drive Matt to the hospital, based on what had happened earlier at the house. He then warned me that they would have to put him in handcuffs, which might be difficult for me to witness. And it was. Tears ran down my face while I watched my son being cuffed and placed into the back seat of a police car. This was his second 5150 in three months' time. He would be transported to a behavioral health hospital for a mandatory three-day hold.

When I returned home, I checked in on Mike, who now had a fever of 102. I packed him up and off we went to the E.R. He was immediately admitted to the hospital and placed in isolation. I had to wear a gown, a mask, and rubber gloves to be allowed in his room. Something about this recent development gave me a deep sense of foreboding.

His team of doctors was hard at work trying to make some sense out of this latest speed bump. Apparently, the infection was not responding to antibiotics, so the Stanford doctor ordered a new bone marrow biopsy. From these results came the bombshell news—his condition had evolved from MDS to the deadly acute myelogenous leukemia or AML.

He was transported by ambulance to the City of Hope, a top-tier clinical research hospital located about an hour and fifteen minutes away from home, where he would reside for the next few months. Things had taken a very serious turn for the worst.

Once we were situated at the City of Hope, he was assigned a team of doctors who would work in tandem with the Stanford team. He was in excellent hands. The doctor was very upfront with us, saying that once the AML was confirmed via pathology, they would move swiftly to get him into remission. It was sobering to learn that, without this aggressive intervention, Mike would be gone in two weeks. The plan was to bombard him with chemo for a solid week to destroy all the leukemic cells, and then prepare him for a stem cell transplant, which was his only hope of survival. Even so, the doctors were clear that a stem cell transplant only gave him a 10 percent chance of surviving to the five-year mark. This news was absolutely devastating, but Mike wanted to fight for his life, so he gave them the go-ahead.

My son was released from the mental hospital the same week that all this was going on with Mike. He got a ride from the hospital and as soon as he arrived home, he immediately began packing up his stuff. He knew he had breached the agreement and assumed responsibility. He expressed deep remorse for having disappointed me and asked for my forgiveness. He also told me that, because of the bender over Labor Day weekend, he had been terminated from his job of only three weeks.

I don't know what exactly came over me in that moment, other than pure motherly love and forgiveness and some heavenly guidance, but I walked to his car and began removing his belongings to bring them back inside. He asked me what I was doing, and I said I was giving him another chance. He sat on the bottom step and started weeping, telling me he didn't deserve another chance. He thanked me for still believing in him. I sat down next to him and told him, "Blue, I will never give up on you, ever. As long as I live, I will love you and be your biggest fan."

Later, we sat down to discuss the way forward. This was his recovery, so the plan had to be his. He realized his first order of business was to find a new job. I suggested the best way to improve the chances of his former employer giving him a good reference was to go and see him and apologize face-to-face. No, it wouldn't get him his job back, but it demonstrated integrity. So, he took my advice and drove to the resort where he offered his apology to the man who had taken a chance with him, and whom he had let down.

The disease of alcoholism is very sad. It is such a powerful force that, no matter how determined a person might be to remain sober, the cravings can overwhelm their own convictions. Matt had surely needed all six months in treatment to truly gain a foothold over this monster, but he thought he could do it on his own. Now he realized that no matter how much he wanted to be free from it, he was not strong enough to throttle it on his own.

I told him my expectations, and that he would have to show me proof of his job-hunting activities. I suggested he go out to look for work, i.e. pound the pavement, three days per week. To bring home the applications and show them to me when he had completed each one, and then take them back to each business. On alternate days, he was to look for work online, and prior to submitting an application, he'd have me witness him press the send button. This was reminiscent of managing a young adolescent, but these firm boundaries were mandatory under the circumstances.

He already knew he had to return to his A.A. group and confess about his relapse, and once again proclaim himself a newcomer. Having to admit this, and then start all over, is a very humbling experience for someone in recovery. Matt wasted no time in fulfilling these items. He was diligent about his job search, returned to the daily meetings, and also started back at the gym.

I involved Mike in this whole process, needing him to partner with me in allowing Matt this second chance. Thankfully, he, too, believed in Matt and was willing to give him one more shot. At that point, of course, neither of us knew just how much my son would be needed in the coming weeks.

Once Mike's AML had been confirmed and chemotherapy was started, it was time to look for a stem cell donor. As fate would have it, his only living sibling, his brother, was a perfect match. This was actually a very rare occurrence, as sometimes there would be multiple siblings and not a single bone marrow match. Mike felt immensely blessed that it was his beloved brother who would be his donor.

The next few weeks were very difficult for Mike, as the chemo caused sores in his throat and up and down the esophagus, making it hard to eat. Frequent visits from his friends, coworkers, and family members kept him in a positive frame of mind. For his daughter, his brother, and I, who took turns spending our days at his side, it was sometimes exhausting. The sheer energy it took to remain upbeat and positive while watching him waste away in front of our eyes was significant. By mid-October 2013, Mike had shed thirty-six pounds.

During this period, I would return home late at night after spending upwards of ten hours at the hospital before facing a long commute. My son would cook us meals for the week, clean the house, do the laundry, give the dogs baths, work in the yard, and complete various other chores. This took such a huge burden off of my shoulders at a time when I had very little energy.

One night, after a particularly difficult day at the hospital, I came home feeling very depressed and worried. Mike was so weak and frail and was still unable to eat. Matt was still up when I got home, so I filled him in on Mike's condition. Then I told my son that I would really just like to sit with him and watch skate videos together like we did back when he was fourteen. Matt's eyes lit up. He grabbed his laptop and there we sat on the couch, side by side, watching his favorite skaters performing various tricks, and just enjoying each other's company.

My son was very lonely. He missed his daughter terribly, as she still lived in Colorado with her mom. I even made him a wall calendar using a Walmart app that featured a beautiful photo of him and Gracie together for each month, hoping this would keep him motivated in his sobriety. I added an inspiring A.A. slogan to each of these images. The calendar hung on his bedroom wall, where he was systematically crossing off the days until October 29, when Grace was due to come for a visit.

As he awaited his daughter's visit, Matt kept himself busy with his job search, and also by spending time with his friends. He met up with his old baseball friends to hit balls, played an occasional round of golf, hit some tennis balls, and just threw a football around at the beach. These activities, in addition to his A.A. meetings, kept him distracted from the mighty foe: the demon of alcoholism.

I also realized, during these final weeks of September, that I had made the right decision allowing my son to redeem himself. Knowing how much he was missing Gracie, and how many empty hours there were now that he was unemployed, the scene was ripe for depression to take hold again. By living at home again, he not only felt somewhat accountable to me, but he also truly aimed to be of help to me during a very trying time.

Mike was the kind of person that everyone adored and respected. There are countless examples of the outpouring of love and support shown to him during this phase of his health crisis. Friends organized blood donations and plasma donations. His work buddies sent a trove of Get Well cards that his brother lovingly arranged on the wall of his hospital room. One friend had a giant poster made of Mike riding his mountain bike. Twenty guys and one gal from Oakley shaved their heads in solidarity with Mike's bald head. A steady stream of visitors did their best to keep his spirits up during those harrowing weeks of September 2013.

Mike received the excellent news that he would be discharged for three weeks in order to put on some much-needed weight before returning to the hospital to face the stem cell transplant on November 20. It was a glorious day, October 18, when his brother brought him home to me. I had hung a big Welcome Home banner across the garage and was sitting on the driveway holding a Welcome Home balloon when they arrived. We intended to make the most of the three weeks ahead.

Over the weekend the three of us, Mike, Matt, and I, enjoyed watching the baseball playoffs and also some football games. I cooked and cooked, determined to put some pounds on my guy. Matt split his time during the baseball playoffs, watching the games with us, his dad, and his friend Kevin. October was always centered around baseball in our house.

That weekend, when I unpacked Mike's bag from the hospital, I noticed that the wooden cross I had hung on his wall in the hospital room was missing. Mike asked his brother if he had removed the cross from the wall, but he was sad to say he hadn't. So, I called the hospital, told them we had just checked out the day before, and asked if the Crucifix was still in the room. The nurse checked the room and told me that it was apparently discarded by the cleaning crew.

I was really sad about this, as it had sentimental value. It was a First Communion gift to Matt and had hung in his bedroom since he was ten. She suggested I call the lost and found, but they had no sign of it either. Oh well. I was sad, but at least I had Mike home safe and sound.

That Monday, I took Mike on a day trip to Julian, a small town in east San Diego that is known for its apple pies. I always loved going to Julian with my kids in October, as it is the apple-picking season and a perfect way to kick off the fall season. We had a wonderful day, and Mike consumed huge quantities of calories, which was the goal.

Wednesday, October 23, was going to be a workday. Meaning, Mike had a whole day of tests, including a new bone marrow biopsy, in preparation for his stem cell transplant planning. We also had some classes to attend that would help prepare me for the post-transplant caregiving that lay ahead. Because we would be gone all day, I waited until that morning to inform Matt about our plans. He was getting ready to leave for his regular morning meeting, dressed as usual in his gym clothes because he hit the gym immediately following the A.A. meeting. As we crossed in the hall, he asked where we were off to, so I told him we had some appointments at the hospital. He asked me where I kept the tennis racquets because he and his friend Kevin had made plans to play. He also told us that Sarah had asked him to babysit my grandson Jake that afternoon, and he was happy that she'd even offered to pay him. I asked about his job search for the day, and he had it scheduled after the gym and before the tennis. So, we all had a very busy day planned. As we headed out the door, Mike turned to Matt and said, "Matt, you are doing great. Keep it up."

CHAPTER 18

Tragedy

I TRULY BELIEVE THAT MOTHERS are hardwired in such a way that they can literally feel their child's pain. Never was this more evident than the morning of October 23, 2013. As Mike and I were awaiting his second appointment at the hospital that day, I suddenly experienced, out of the blue, what can only be described as a panic attack.

As we entered the lobby area at about 10:15 a.m., I started trembling. Soon, I was hyperventilating and felt a terrible headache coming on. A moment later, I was in tears. Mike got me seated and went off to get me some hot tea, hoping that would help. When he appeared with the tea and handed it to me, I dropped it, spilling the tea all over the floor. I sat there shaking and crying but had no idea what had overcome me.

Finally, I settled down and his name was called for the next doctor's appointment. After that one was finished, we ambled back to the lobby to sit and plan what to do about lunch. It was about eleven a.m. I realized I hadn't checked my phone since we got there, and the ringer was off, so I dug it out of my purse to find just one text message. It was from my daughter-in-law Amanda, sent from Colorado. She texted, *I think something is up with Matt.*

I immediately called Matt, fearing that he had relapsed again, but he did not pick up so I sent him a text asking him to call me. After getting no response, I called Amanda asking her what was going on. She forwarded the text he had sent her at 10:11 a.m. It was a cryptic message. Basically, he was saying goodbye to their daughter, Grace.

I was instantly panicked and knew I had to get home as soon as possible. Amanda offered to call in a citizen check from Colorado to our home in California. I called John, who worked about thirty minutes away from the house, knowing I had a minimum drive of an hour and fifteen minutes. I told Mike what was going on and asked if his daughter could sit in for me at the hospital and get him home later. Thankfully, his daughter was available.

I basically ran to the valet to retrieve my car, expressing a sense of urgency to the attendant. I told him to hurry, that I had a family emergency at home. In no more than five minutes, I was on the road toward home.

After about a half hour, I figured John would now be at the house and could relay to me if Matt had relapsed and what condition he was in. When he picked up, I knew immediately that it was much worse than that. He told me the police were already there on the scene when he arrived. They had kicked in the side garage door where our son lay in his Jeep, asphyxiated by carbon monoxide poisoning. The garage was full of fumes and very hot inside. The officers pulled him out of the car and placed him on the front lawn where the paramedics would spend fifteen minutes trying to revive him. John said there was still a mild heartbeat, and they would be transporting him to the local hospital emergency department. I listened to this and literally felt on the verge of throwing up. I felt so afraid and helpless, and was still forty minutes away. John said he would meet me there at the hospital.

It is amazing the strength that God gives us when faced with a crisis. I had enough wits about me to call my oldest daughter, Sarah, and tell her that her brother had attempted to take his life and was being transported to the hospital. She started screaming and asking me for details, but I cut her off, stating, "Sarah, I will fill you in later. What I need you to do as soon as I hang up is call the church and ask a priest to get to the hospital."

After I hung up, I started seeing stars and knew I was about to faint, so I pulled over to the right shoulder on the freeway. After a few seconds, I shook my head, refused to succumb, and headed back on the road. All the way to the hospital, I prayed loudly, "God, please don't let him die, don't let him die, don't let him die."

When I finally arrived at the emergency room, I still had hope. Surely, God would answer my fervent prayers. I walked up to the reception desk and told the gal I was there for my son, Matthew Anthony. She kept her cheery expression and said, "I'll be with you in just a moment," before exiting through the door right behind her. When she returned, she told me, "They'll be right out. You can have a seat if you'd like."

There I stood, almost falling to my knees in thanksgiving that my son and his dad would be right out. God had saved him. Before I even got to the chair, the door opened and two people walked toward me, two strangers. The man said, "Are you Matthew's mother?"

A hideous grip of terror struck me. I could barely breathe. In a perplexed tone, I answered, "Yes, I am." The man directed me toward the chairs and gently guided me to a sitting position. He then told me that sadly, Matthew didn't make it.

This will forever be defined as the very worst moment in my life. That instant when I was informed that my precious son, my Boy

Blue, was dead. I sat there in shock, like someone had eviscerated me. He then introduced the woman next to him as Ruth and told me that they volunteered to assist grieving parents because they, too, had lost a child this way. Then, he asked if I would like to see my son. "Yes," I said. I had to see my son one last time.

I was led into the room where my beautiful son lay. John was sobbing, seated toward the foot of the bed. The priest that my daughter had summoned stood at the head of the bed. I refused to believe that Matt was gone. I could not process it. I walked over to him, looked right at his face, and demanded him to open his eyes. I told him I was here now, here to save him. I started coming undone. I began trembling, my entire body started shaking; even my teeth were chattering. I stomped my foot and commanded him to wake up, to please wake up! When it was evident that I was about to collapse from sheer trauma, the grief volunteer offered me a chair.

I was seated about midway down the bed, where I could grab his hand. His hand was still warm, but it was lifeless. I held his hand and leaned over the bedrail to kiss his hand as my tears flowed over it. It was then that I had no option but to accept that my precious son was gone. Even though by now it was about 12:45 p.m., the official time of death was listed as 10:30 a.m. because the first responders were never able to revive him. And that explains my panic attack. I literally felt my son dying, his spirit leaving us.

The next few hours were a blur. I remember the extremely painful phone call I had to make to Amanda, telling her that Gracie's daddy was gone. I also called my mother and we both wailed on the phone, shock and grief overcoming us. I gave John the task of informing Emily, who was away at college, as I could not bear to tell her. Emily and Matt had always been so very close.

John and Sarah met me at the house. I asked John to check Matt's room, just to see if there were any clues as to why he chose to leave

TRAGEDY

us that morning. John came out saying that Matt had left a letter for Grace on his desk. So, Sarah walked with me upstairs and together we entered Matt's room. There on the floor was my small travel ironing board, the iron, and his black striped shirt that he was going to wear to look for work that day. Instead, he'd decided to end his life.

I will never comprehend the "why." I glanced at the calendar on his wall, and he had crossed off each day in anticipation of Gracie's visit, which was just six days off. Nothing about this day made sense to me, or to any of us.

I would not have survived the night had it not been for Mike at my side. His daughter dropped him off that evening, and I literally clung to him as the life force that would keep me breathing. He gently held me and cried right along with me, until we both finally fell asleep.

The next week and a half was a frantic blur. I was not mentally prepared to plan a funeral for my own child. I felt so confused and lost, but went through the motions and checked off the various items to be handled. I met with the priest, the same priest who had come to anoint him that fateful day, and then met with the mortuary to make the formal arrangements. John selected the casket and made some large posters for the church and the reception. My sister Elaine and her husband spent hours creating a slideshow for their godson's funeral, using the two hundred photos I had forwarded to them.

I asked his high school baseball coach to offer a eulogy, in addition to three other individuals who were very important in my son's life.

A week after my son's death, I realized that his friends at the seven a.m. A.A. meeting would be concerned about him, as Matt never missed a meeting. So, I drove over to the center and arrived just before they called the meeting to order. I approached the man who appeared to be leading the meeting and quietly told him the sad news. He then shared this with the group, and one by one, they walked over to me and hugged me. They had the most wonderful

195

things to say about my boy. One man later sent me an email stating that he had never seen anyone try so hard to succeed in recovery as Matt. I invited the guys to attend the funeral if they wished to pay their respects.

My son was a stand-up guy who was loved by so many in our community. The local newspaper ran a front-page story about him that happened to be published on the day of his funeral. I had someone pick up a stack of the papers to make them available at the church.

I barely held it together that day at the church. I can hardly remember who all was present, so I am very grateful for the guest book where the names are recorded. All the family was there, from our side and also Amanda's side. The most heartbreaking visual was seeing little Gracie there, having no idea what had happened. At one point, she started crying out for me, "Nana!" so Amanda brought her over to sit with me for the rest of the service.

In all, about three hundred people attended his memorial. Our dear friends hosted a beautiful reception at their home following the funeral. Mike was my constant source of strength throughout the ordeal, from the day we lost Matt to the day we buried him. I could not have managed any of this without his constant love and support.

Once my son was laid to rest, my focus returned to caring for Mike. He had just one week left of freedom before he would head back to the hospital where he'd remain for a very long period of time. During this last week, we took a day trip to Big Bear, of course including a drive by the family cabin, and we also enjoyed the local scenery at Dana Point Harbor and Laguna Beach. My goal to fatten him up before the transplant had come to fruition, as he had packed on twenty pounds by the time he returned to the hospital.

The day Mike was readmitted, I decided to go to the fifth floor to ask one more time if anyone had located my son's wooden Crucifix. Sadly, the nurses there were not familiar with this type of item, being of Asian descent, so I tried to describe it to them. They shuffled around the desk area and shook their heads. No such item was there. So, I thanked them, told them I would be down on the fourth floor, and gave them Mike's room number, just in case anyone happened to ever find it.

I had barely returned to his room when the phone on the side table rang. Mike answered, handed it to me, and said, "It's for you, Babe."

When I answered, I recognized the voice of the same nurse I had just spoken with upstairs. She asked me to come up and look at the item they found, to see if it was what I was looking for. I flew to the elevator and prayed a Hail Mary on the way up. When the elevator doors opened, the nurse stood there holding up my son's Crucifix. I burst into tears, hugging her and telling her that it had special meaning, as it had belonged to my son who had recently passed away. She got tears in her eyes, too. That Crucifix will never leave my sight again.

The stem cell transplant went very smoothly, for both the patient and the donor. Mike even acquired his brother's blood type, type 0, after spending fifty-five years with type A-positive blood. There were plenty of peaks and valleys over the next several weeks, but then in mid-December, he transitioned from the hospital to live in Hope Village, a cluster of bungalows for recovering patients there on site. How thrilled I was when he was assigned Bungalow #22, as #22 was my son's baseball jersey number for many years. It felt preordained.

Living at the bungalow was far and away preferable to the hospital. It was like a roomy studio apartment with a little front porch area. His brother, daughter, and I took turns staying with him and cooking for him. He was also allowed to enjoy restaurant fare, so we'd snag some Mexican food or whatever he happened to be craving.

All our sights were on Mike reaching the key benchmark of Day 100 post-transplant without the leukemia returning. He had to return to the hospital a couple of times for a surprise infection or setback, but generally, his stay at the bungalow was a very positive experience. Even just being able to get outside to put on the little putting green or to sip his coffee on the front stoop was such a treat. We spent a lot of evenings snuggled together in a twin bed watching movies. On New Year's Day, we watched *It's a Wonderful Life* together and bawled our eyes out. The theme of the movie was particularly suited for Mike, who was so grateful to be alive.

Mike's illness also impacted all of us who loved him. I spent many days outside on that little stoop at Bungalow #22 listening to the birds and watching the sunsets with a whole new appreciation. Seeing the children staying at Hope Village really put things into perspective. The little kids outside playing, their bald heads the telltale sign of their cancer battles, couldn't help but bring a tear to my eye. While wandering the grounds one day, I discovered a large statue of the Blessed Virgin Mary, the centerpiece in a lovely rose garden. Loved ones of patients had left little memorabilia at her feet—rosaries, flowers, wristbands, and other trinkets. This pretty garden became a refuge for me, somewhere I could go and pray my heart out while Mike napped.

We were thrilled when we were given permission to take a little day trip away from the hospital. Since we were in the San Gabriel foothills, I suggested I take him on a sightseeing trip of the places important to my family. He was on board, so off we went.

Our first stop was, of course, Gopher Hollow. I had not visited the place since that day in 1999 when I was homeschooling and brought the kids there. Now it was Mike's turn to see the renowned home of my grandparents. This time, fifteen years later, the house looked terrible. The owner was probably so old by now that she just couldn't keep up with the maintenance, and it showed. Mike, however, looked at it through the eyes of my stories of being a kid and finding refuge there with my loving grandparents. He never showed any hint of disappointment; instead, he asked me to stand on the front lawn so he could take my picture.

Next, we were off to see the community's Historical Society Museum where Grandpa's contributions were still on full display. Newspaper articles, photos, and other items from his community involvement made me feel so proud. We had lunch at Toohey's Burgers, which had been there for decades, the name being an inspiration for my sister's nickname "Tooie." We then drove to St. Therese Catholic Church, my mother's family parish, and then to La Canada to seek my cousins' old family home—which we were able to locate. It was a wonderful, nostalgic day.

After one month in the bungalow, on Day 52 post-transplant, Mike got the go-ahead to return home. Of course, he would have to make the trip to the clinic at City of Hope for labs and monitoring twice a week, but no worries, we were thrilled that he could come home. I was experiencing some anxiety, as this meant I would become his primary caregiver. This involved managing sixteen medications and whatever else should arise in the aftermath of a stem-cell transplant.

On Day 60, his new bone marrow biopsy was just perfect, no signs of leukemia and no graft-versus-host disease. GVH is an all-too-common adverse event that happens after stem cell transplants when the body rejects the donor cells. We were all very relieved to get such a glowing report.

I received a call in early January from Coach Dave, who was my son's baseball coach all through high school and who had given the eulogy at his funeral. Dave told me he was arranging an alumni tribute game on February 22 in honor of my son. He'd selected the date to correspond with Matt's jersey number #22. He told me that a couple of faculty members had donated funds to have a large eight-foot banner made with Matt's name and dates on it, which would be installed on the left field fence just prior to the tribute game. I was absolutely overwhelmed with gratitude that something so wonderful was being planned.

On that day, all the family, our closest friends, Gracie, and several of the baseball moms from the years our sons played ball together were present to honor Blue. Thirty-eight alumni players showed up to play against the current varsity team. I wore one of Blue's old vests, emblazoned with #22 on the back. Two news crews came to report on the event, and Gracie and I even ended up with our picture in the paper. Before the game, the banner was unveiled, a moment of silence was observed, and then I threw out—well, I attempted to anyway—the first pitch. Mike sat with his brother and my mom and looked so healthy and handsome. It was a beautiful yet bittersweet event, and I am forever grateful to Coach Dave for honoring my son in this way.

Just six days later, on February 28, I returned home at about five p.m. Mike and his daughter had gone to his clinic appointment that day, and he was there at home when I returned. I still could point to the exact tile on the floor in the kitchen where I was standing when I met him there and he reached out to put his arms around me. The doctor had told him that the latest bone marrow biopsy, for his 100-day mark, had revealed that the leukemia was back.

Just like that awful day when I had to face my deceased son, I came undone. I said, "No, no, no, no way is that right. It must be a mistake. Have them retake the biopsy!" Then, as it hit me, I started screaming and shaking and sobbing. I could not accept this earth-shattering news. We both knew that he had just one shot, that the transplant could not be repeated.

Somehow, and I deserved a best actress award, I managed to paste a fake smile on my face when Mike and I met up with some friends for a dinner event that evening that we couldn't get out of. The next day, I found the strength to host my granddaughter's fourth birthday party at my house. With a houseful of pink birthday decorations and party revelers, as well as an appearance by Princess Aurora who would dazzle Gracie and even paint her nails, I somehow pulled it off. Only my daughters knew of the fateful news Mike and I had just received.

So, in what felt like the blink of an eye, our focus shifted from treating and arresting the leukemia to accepting palliative care. We all felt sucker-punched. It was very surreal, as Mike looked so healthy and strong by this point in time.

Things got very bad the next month when he was stricken with GVH. It attacked his gut hard, so he was hospitalized for nearly a month. During that hospital stay, he was very down, surly even. He was pissed that he was wasting what little time he had left being stuck in a hospital.

It was getting harder and harder to keep up the positive front for my man. I was struggling to cope with the loss of my son, whom I never had the opportunity to grieve properly in the face of all that was going on with Mike. That grief, coupled with the anxiety that accompanied Mike's relapse back to leukemia, further complicated by GVH, had stretched my already shredded nerves to the breaking point.

With all this in mind, and with his future so unclear, we decided to create our own bucket list. We made plans to go to Augusta, Georgia, for the Masters golf tournament, to travel on Route 66 in a muscle car, to go to Yosemite in June for my daughter's wedding, and to Napa in July to celebrate my birthday. We were so excited to make the most of each and every day we had left together. We shared our bucket list on the Caring Bridge blog, the daily blog posts I'd been writing to keep friends and family up to date on his illness for nearly a year. We were completely blown away when his dear neighbor friends gifted us with a large sum of money to fund the bucket list. This came at a time when neither of us was able to work and earn a living, so these wonderful people made our dreams a reality.

Thankfully, in early April, Mike had a bit of a reprieve from his last speed bump. The GVH was under control and he was feeling a little better, so they discharged him from the long, treacherous stay at the hospital. He had lost forty pounds during that month. I acquired more caregiving tasks upon his release, which I admit caused a good deal of anxiety. In addition to keeping track of the sixteen medications, I was supposed to hook him up each night to an I.V. for fluids, flush his pic line daily, and administer a liquid protein solution called TPN through the port. To a non-nurse-type person like me, it was all rather daunting.

It was a huge disappointment that we had to scrap our trip to see the Masters Tournament in Augusta. No way was he well enough to make that flight. After a good cry, we adjusted to the idea of simply watching the tournament on TV like the majority of golf fans. We tuned into the event wearing the green Augusta t-shirts gifted to us and pretended we were there. We were learning how to lower our expectations and just enjoy what we had.

Together, we faced each day with hope and appreciation, fully taking advantage of each and every day that Mike still felt well. Each beautiful moment became sharpened into a laser-like focus as something to hold on to for dear life. To us, just the simple joy of sitting side by side together on the couch, holding hands and watching a movie, was nothing short of wonderful.

Still, there were some very bleak days. One such day was a trip to the hematologist. We sat there awaiting the new lab results, so full of hope that his numbers had improved, only to learn that his white blood cell count was scary low. This meant Mike was incredibly vulnerable to infection. Even a little jaunt to the Harbor, riding in a wheelchair and being entertained by his brother, left him worn out and grumpy. I so wished I could wave a magic wand to make it all go away. Watching someone I loved so much suffering day in and day out left me feeling so helpless that I just wanted to crumble.

Thanks to his fighting spirit, we continued to check off some of our bucket list items, starting with a weekend in Palm Springs. Mike had received an infusion of antibodies this time, which took about five hours, to protect his very weak immune system while we were out and about. This was the first time that we had to include an I.V. pole, wheelchair, and sixteen medications when packing, but we forged ahead and enjoyed three sunny days in the desert.

Oakley was wonderful to us throughout Mike's health crisis. One day in May, I received a call from his boss, asking me to plan on bringing Mike to the Oakley headquarters on a certain date and time. He told me to keep it a secret from him but to go ahead and invite family members to be present that day as well.

When we drove into the complex, me at the wheel, we were both completely blown away. Hundreds of Oakley employees lined both sides of the lengthy driveway leading to the main building, cheering for him as we inched through the crowd. I glanced over at Mike and he was already in tears. I maneuvered him out of the van and into the wheelchair and then pushed him up to the front entrance area where the C.E.O. greeted us.

In pure Oakley style, the C.E.O. made a heartfelt and sometimes humorous speech, telling Mike how much the company that he had worked for as a salesman for a total of twenty-eight years loved and supported him. The next thing his boss said was, "I heard a rumor that you were hoping to take a trip on Route 66 in a vintage muscle car. Well, our founder (Jim Jannard) is happy to make his car available to you to enjoy as much as you want."

At that moment, from behind a partition, a bright-red 1970 Chevy

Chevelle big block 454 came roaring out to greet us. It was unbelievable! Mike was just beside himself that he would have access to such a gorgeous car. But then, the C.E.O. popped the trunk and pulled out a giant faux check in the amount of $25,000 as a gift to their beloved salesman. The company had collected this sum in a matter of four days, simply by sending out a companywide email asking for donations for this beloved man. Oakley was much more than a billion-dollar company; it was a family that truly cared for its own.

After all the cheers and tears, it was Mike's turn to take the microphone. From his wheelchair, he spoke straight from his heart, acknowledging how much the company had meant to him all these years and thanking the amazing people he had been blessed to work with. He got choked up as he delivered this impromptu speech, trying his best to express to the crowd his pure feelings of gratitude. After he spoke, the driver took Mike and me for a spin in this incredible car, burning out as we exited the scene.

As much as Mike wished we could drive the '70 Chevelle on our Route 66 trip, we had to accept a truncated version of the trip. We had initially dreamed big, hoping to rent a classic Chevy (of course, Mike's preference was to buy one) and take the Route 66 trip to the Grand Canyon. The reality of his current physical condition, however, made it clear to us that he didn't have the strength to drive such a vehicle, and I knew I sure couldn't handle this beast. So, our Route 66 trip was reduced to a short two-day road trip to Needles, California, in his minivan. Oh, but there were some hilarious moments over that forty-eight-hour excursion, making it a very memorable getaway.

On a whim, we decided to return to Old Town, San Diego, the place we had stayed almost exactly three years prior. It was a lovely idea, to revisit the place where we had fallen in love. So, just as with the Palm Springs trip, we packed up all the meds, the I.V. pole, the bags of hydration, and the wheelchair and hit the road south.

When we arrived at the hotel, our goal was to somehow figure out which room we had stayed at the last time. The person helping us at the front desk was unable to access the information on her computer, so I decided to wander around the grounds to see if something would spark my memory while Mike rested in the lobby.

After no such recollection came forth, we implored the woman at the desk to find a way to get those old records. She made a phone call, and soon, a man appeared who said he could access the archives. To our amazement, he not only was able to discover the room number, but the room was actually available. When we arrived at the room, we were so happy to recognize the same beautiful acacia tree outside the door in robust bloom with brilliant yellow flowers.

By mid-June, as we approached our much-anticipated trip to Yosemite for my daughter's wedding, Mike was beginning to deteriorate. The now-familiar signs of infection reared up just as we were about to hit the road. His hematologist knew how much this trip meant to us, so he ordered two consecutive days of Nuprogin shots to boost his white blood cells, put him on an antibiotic, and had us restart the ten-hour hydration I.V. sessions at home.

We made it to Yosemite. I was in charge of decorating the large campsite where the reception would be held, so I busied myself with getting the spot all gussied up for a party. It really turned out adorable, thanks to lots of inspiration gleaned from Pinterest's "rustic wedding" boards.

As the hours wore on, it was becoming clear that poor Mike was not feeling well at all. He was such a trooper and hung out with all our friends to celebrate the wedding, but by day three, it was obvious he was ill and we needed to get home to see the doctor.

Once we got home, his doctor ordered some tests. These confirmed that he had pneumonia, so he was admitted to the hospital. Things were becoming dire by this point. After a couple of days in the hospital, the hard conversations were had. After conferring with the team at City of Hope, his local hematologist proceeded to place Mike in hospice. So, on June 30, 2014, Mike was transported by ambulance to our home. Hospice would take it from there.

Over the ensuing two weeks, we had a steady stream of his friends and family members come by to see him. It was a very emotional time, as everyone who came knew this was their final visit with him. I encouraged his friends, coworkers, and relatives to write a short letter or even just a text message that I could read to him. These letters were hugely important to his mental state now that he was in hospice, and the beautiful sentiments expressed left us both in tears. My daughters, sister, and close friends also penned beautiful letters to him, telling him what a gift he was to them, and also to me. Mike was the best thing that ever happened to me, outside of having my children.

As the days ticked by, I realized that there was a chance he might pass away on my birthday, July 13. I was terrified at the thought and even mentioned my fear to him. Being the sweetheart he was, he told me he would try not to die on my birthday. But then, a couple of days later, I had an epiphany. I realized that if he died on my birthday it would be a cause for celebration, because every year on my birthday, I would remember that it was the day he got to see Jesus in heaven. So, I told him on July 8 that I had changed my mind, that I would be honored if he passed away on my birthday. Again, he accommodated me saying, "Okay, Babe, I will try to die on your birthday."

That week was very, very difficult in every way. My nerves were shot, and it was so painful to witness his decline. Death was drawing near. One night, I was so anxious I could not fall asleep. So, at around midnight, I decided to write this post on the Caring Bridge journal:

He no longer lies next to me in our bed, but instead is situated about four feet away. I am propped up in my bed, mindless TV

TRAGEDY

on, background noise really. I watch him breathe, hard breathing, expending lots of energy to make the diseased lungs push oxygen in and out—something we all take for granted.

I love this man who lies there clinging to life. I love him more than I can ever try to describe to you. He is one of a kind. He gave me back my ability to trust again, to be willing to open up and share all the nooks and crannies that make me me. From day one, I felt peaceful in his presence. I knew he was a man to be trusted.

This man, who now has blood-scabbed arms that resemble mottled sticks, combined with a large, bloated belly, who struggles to push air into and out of his lungs...this man used to be a stud. He introduced me to his world starting in 2011, showing me the thrill of being at a drag race with earplugs pushed into my ears to drown out the roar of the high-octane, nitro-fueled cars.

He took me to the pits at Supercross to meet some of the racers, and taught me from the stands all about the nuances of motocross racing, and about the superstars who risk their lives to compete. He was one of them, an amateur motocross racer for almost twenty years. This man, lying in that bed struggling to breathe, used to soar ninety feet above the earth on a Kawasaki, just for the thrill of it.

By the time I met him, he was fifty-two years old and had switched to mountain bike racing. I remember how he practically begged me to come out to see him compete at Irvine Lake in the Over the Hump race series back in June 2011. There he was, in his neon-yellow helmet, amped and ready to tear it up. I was impressed that he had the guts to tackle the track and push himself that hard at age fifty-two. He trained and watched his diet and spent hours and hours on his bike, always pushing himself to be the best he could be.

When he took me out to PGA West that year to an Oakley Pro-Am tournament, I watched him hit a bucket of balls on the range that first evening. He had a beautiful golf swing, fluid and graceful, and the ball just soared. Over and over, he hit those golf *balls, with grace and patience. Again, I was impressed. He obviously didn't do anything half-assed. In all he tackled, golf, bike racing, moto, and work, he tackled full on, no holds barred. He set a high standard for himself and never looked back, even after he'd reached that standard.*

One Christmas, I got him a book about training for mountain bike racing. He seriously absorbed this book, page by page, and embarked on the entire plan outlined in it to be prepared for the upcoming race season. He was determined to always improve, to best himself, and had the self-discipline to actually achieve those self-imposed goals. In a word, he was a stud.

Correction... He is a stud. What this man has endured over the past fourteen months no regular guy could have ever survived. He steadfastly met all of the disease's challenges head-on, never complaining, never giving up. He marched on and on in a forward trajectory, with no option in mind outside of his goal of winning. He would win.

Through all his suffering, the chemicals and starvation, the infections and incapacities, he never lost sight of the goal: survival. We watched in awe of his strength, not only physical but of char-acter. And along the way, like the tortoise that eventually wins the race, his spiritual strength came up from behind to trump it all. He was finally aware of the source of all his many successes and blessings, and gave props to our heavenly Father. He fell in love with Jesus.

It's about midnight now. I have had a difficult time with sleep, waking with each bout of choking I hear from that twin-sized hos-pital bed. I cry in the dark watching him gag and cough. This man, once a stud who had a strong physique and boundless energy, is reduced to a bed-bound dying version of himself. He has zero mobil-ity and is one hundred percent dependent on his caregivers to keep him going each day with the most basic functions of life. I consider my life once he's gone and I can barely breathe, it feels so bleak.

But, alas, he is still a stud in my eyes. His strength may not be evident to a stranger, but anyone who has been following this story since last May knows the amazing capacity of strength he possesses. I am in awe. I am the luckiest girl in the world that I got to love, and be loved by, this man. May God please grant us a little more time together so I can spoil him and love him and care for him... just a little while longer.

On July 12, the doorbell rang and it was a flower delivery for me. Mike, even in his weakened state and unsure if he would live until my birthday, had, with the help of his daughter, ordered me two gorgeous flower arrangements and a pretty décor bottle with a lovely message of love inscribed on the front. Inside the bottle was a scroll that displayed a beautiful poem he'd selected, followed by a personalized birthday greeting. I just melted. That day, he was comatose, only being alert in the morning when my daughter stopped by to say her final goodbye. He awoke only two other times that day, both times asking, "What time is it, Babe?" I knew what he was doing. He was willing himself to survive until my birthday, so I simply answered, "You have six hours, honey" or "You have three hours, Baby."

The next day, Sunday, July 13, was my fifty-eighth birthday. I had hardly slept due to the difficulty Mike was having with his breathing, so first thing in the morning I called the hospice nurse requesting a visit. She arrived around noon to assess his condition and then sat downstairs with me to discuss her thoughts. She said she could bump up the morphine a bit to ease his breathing discomfort but that his heart was strong, so she wanted me to understand that he could linger a few more days. She stayed at the house with us, and the social worker also stopped by to check on us.

Mike's brother and daughter were there with me all day. We wanted to be with him as much as possible during these final days of transition. At around 3:30 p.m., Mike's breathing became sporadic, so I woke up his daughter, who was napping on my bed, and alerted his brother, who was on the phone in the front bedroom. I beckoned the nurse to weigh in on what I felt were imminent signs of death, and she concurred. He didn't have long.

As I sat there next to him, Mike suddenly regained consciousness. He looked over at me and said, "Okay, Babe, I'm gonna check out now." I assumed he was just delirious from the morphine and believed we were at a hotel. But no, he was letting go. He was saying goodbye. Twenty minutes later, with the three of us surrounding him with all our love, he took his last breath—on my birthday, just as I had wished.

Later that day, when Mike had been taken away and everyone had left, I was alone in my house. I sat there on the top step of the stairs, sobbing. I was in shock, even though I'd been well aware he was dying for months by then. It didn't seem to matter that I was mentally prepared because my heart was not ready to say goodbye. This beautiful man, the love of my life, was gone. The only bright spot, besides his suffering coming to an end, was the knowledge that he was right with Jesus.

As with my son's passing just nine months prior, I, along with his daughter and brother, became immersed in making plans for his memorial service. Each of us had a set of tasks to take care of, and it all fell into place nicely. Because Mike had made his preferences for the memorial known in advance, it was easy to make these decisions. He had even selected the speakers, the casket, and the venue, which was Saddleback Church.

It was Rick Warren's book, *The Purpose Driven Life*, that was most significant in his conversion over the past fourteen months. He had embraced Christianity and, until the last few weeks of his life, kept to a daily morning ritual. He'd read a chapter from one of Rick

Warren's books, listen to an audio supplement for additional ministering, read one of the devotions from Billy Graham's book, and read some Scripture. He had a notebook in which he made notes about his awakening, about what he was learning, and his thoughts during this final phase of his life.

Before he passed away, he ordered seven or eight copies of *The Purpose Driven Life*, jotting a message to each of the intended recipients inside the front cover. He then asked me to run these packages to the post office so he would be assured all of these loved ones would receive their copy.

During the last year of his life, he underwent a spiritual transformation. He changed everything; all the worldly things that he now viewed with disdain were replaced with wholesome television shows and movies and Christian praise music. He had become a new person in Christ, fully dedicated to living only for His glory.

I loved that, even though he was raised Lutheran, he often attended Mass with me at our local Catholic churches during our years together. In fact, that he wasn't a Catholic was the only item on that long list of wished-for traits in my future man that I had affixed to the picture of Saint Anthony back in 2008. When we went to Mass, he'd sing the songs with fervor and often get teary. He truly appreciated the two visits to our home by a priest from my church who was so kind in ministering to him during this difficult chapter of life, and anoint him.

Several hundred friends, family, and coworkers came to pay their final respects. The memorial service was poignant and beautiful. A longtime friend performed a song she'd composed entitled "Coming Home" at the end of the service as we filed out following his casket.

Our story is not just another typical tale of love and loss. This is a story of two human beings placed on a journey together, a trajectory that could have only been Divinely arranged. We are never quite prepared for that spontaneous instant when the stars align just so and God brings two souls into each other's orbit. God knew that we would need each other for reasons that our little human minds could have never anticipated. Ours was a union of pure and selfless love, and ultimately, Mike made me a better person.

CHAPTER 19

The Grief Journey Begins

EVEN WITH ALL THE LOVE AND SUPPORT I had received during the final weeks of Mike's illness, after his death, I found myself thoroughly depleted. I was in pain. The house felt like a tomb to me, and I suffered terribly from insomnia. While thrashing about, trying to find some peace in the aftermath of compound losses, I realized I needed to spend some time in nature where I could rebuild my spirit.

After all the commotion of the recent weeks, I craved quiet and solitude, so I embarked on a Google search and decided on a modest hilltop retreat in Ojai, California. My plan was to spend three days in Ojai, come home to regroup for a week, and then head to the local mountains for a couple of days.

I have kept personal journals for many, many years, as writing is very therapeutic for me. I realized these two short trips would provide plenty of time to record my thoughts and emotions, so I packed my laptop and hit the road. To get an idea of how hard Mike's death hit me, I will share one of my journal entries:

July 30, 2014

Today I arrived at a hilltop retreat in the Ojai Valley. My little bungalow is just darling, with panoramic views of the valley and a private deck. After dragging my sorry self here, a three-hour slog, I am realizing that I cannot escape my sad heart. That battered and tormented heart is still present and accounted for. I curled up on the chaise lounge outside for about an hour, napping, crying, and talking aloud to Mike. Though I am in a beautiful, tranquil spot far away from the drudgery of my own house, I am riddled with loneliness and sorrow. There is no escaping it.

I will go into town now and find some food. I want to distract myself for a while, to postpone returning to this lonely space where I have to confront the depths of my sadness. Still, I have hope, albeit futile, that these three days will refresh my spirit and loosen the grip of grief just a tad.

I decided to have dinner at a little Mexican restaurant. Few things are as uncomfortable as asking for a table for one. Trying to look occupied with my Ojai tourist brochure, I hoped no one would notice how forlorn I looked. I sat with my back to the door so my sad face wouldn't be seen. The whole time I sat there, eating my food as fast as I could, all I could think of was how much I missed sharing meals with Mike.

After the lonely dinner, I found a grocery store so I could stock up on some lunch items and snacks. Trying to shop at a store that is unfamiliar is hard enough, but throw in the fact that the entire time I was on the verge of tears and I couldn't get out of there fast enough. I find I have a very short tolerance for public settings. I get anxious and feel like I will burst out crying at any moment, just like after Blue died.

When I arrived back at my place, I was overcome with a sense of melancholy. The sadness that envelops me starting about this time every evening is the subconscious anticipation of facing yet another

THE GRIEF JOURNEY BEGINS

lonesome night. Most nights I wake up several times in a state of anxiety. The empty space next to me feels like a vast chasm in the middle of the night. I am definitely feeling the effects of so many restless nights. I am overly emotional and look haggard.

I sat outside on my private deck area as the sun began to set, spending about an hour just contemplating the vastness of this loss, really mourning it. I prayed a lot, too, and begged Mike to "visit" me somehow, to talk to me in my dreams. I miss his soothing voice. I miss his deep baritone laugh. I miss his twinkly blue eyes. I miss him.

After returning to my home, I had to face that sad, empty space that just fifteen days prior was bustling with people tending to or visiting my man. Now, with all the equipment gone and only my dog Jack to keep me company, it was time to seriously consider selling the house. I had allowed one week between the two mental health respites for just this purpose.

Even though I knew it was in my best interests to make a move and downsize, it still made me terribly sad. I admit, I am a sentimental fool when it comes to the people and things I get attached to. In some strange way, my house now possessed a sense of the sacred, at least to me it did. In this home, within a nine-month span of time, the two men in my life, my son and my love, had passed away. Each of these quality men battled a disease. My son fought a disease of the mind, and my man fought a disease of the body. Neither of them deserved their fate.

The thought of some stranger taking over the space where I had raised my family and lived for twenty-three years seemed somewhat sacrilegious to me on a mysteriously deep level. I reminded myself, however, that this house had also been a significant source of stress and angst for many years. A great spiritual battle had roared within these walls, tormenting us all, but especially targeting my poor son. Although all had been calm on the home front for over a year, thanks to a priest performing a home exorcism, the disturbing memories still loomed large.

Even in my sad and weakened state, I made the tough decision to put the house up for sale. Deep down, I realized that this was an important step in my healing. So, I invited my local real estate agents, a husband and wife team, to sit down with me to devise a plan.

This was a big first step and was all I had planned to squeeze in before heading up to the mountains for some more healing. Fortunately, my employer was willing to accommodate my need for extra bereavement time. So, I packed my bags, passed the dog off to my daughter once again, and left for the mountains, the place I always take my broken heart. Again, allow me to share a journal entry from that little excursion on the grief journey:

August 7, 2014

Today begins the next phase of my plan to restore my spirit and rest my weary bones. Since I was eight years old, I have enjoyed spending time in Big Bear, and have a treasure trove of sweet memories as a result. The drive up the mountain via Highway 38 is part of the experience, and I have a whole tradition around it. Right around 5,000-foot elevation, I roll down the window and smell the scents of sweet pine and musky earth. I sing along to my favorite CDs and for some reason always get emotional as I climb the mountain.

Once I arrive in Big Bear City, I have only one mission: to drive by the old cabin. Even though my stepdad sold our family cabin in the mid-70s, I always pass by the place every time I visit Big Bear. The little place is very sentimental to me and was in our family for

THE GRIEF JOURNEY BEGINS

almost thirty years. I stop across the street, close my eyes, and imagine sitting on the front porch with my mom and sister. I imagine the simple, Spartan furnishings inside, the rock fireplace, the Navajo rugs on the floor. Poignant childhood memories soothe me now in my sorrow. This cabin, Grandpa's cabin, represented a time in my life when I felt safe and secure and happy. I pay it homage and move on.

As I travel toward Big Bear Lake, thoughts shift to the present, to Mike. We came to Big Bear during his chemo break in November 2013. He was thin and weak, but we had a wonderful time up here. In all, Mike and I visited Big Bear four times during our time together—we both loved it. But as I drove along, I started to realize that I would be experiencing all the spots we enjoyed alone. Still, something inside me wanted to lay eyes on the restaurants where we dined, the stores we visited, where we bought ice cream cones. After driving around the lake, I headed down to Lake Arrowhead where I would be staying for two nights.

The Lake Arrowhead Resort is very beautiful, situated on the lakefront and surrounded by pines. I knew within minutes, however, that I had made a mistake by choosing this hotel. It was a very festive, busy resort filled with couples and families all enjoying their time together. To me, it felt like a big fat slap in the face.

Still, I checked in, took the key that was handed to me, and rode up the elevator to my floor. My room did not disappoint. Perched up here on my balcony, I could enjoy the best of both worlds—the natural surroundings that I am craving, as well as the kids splashing around in the pool. I was safely tucked away in my hermit's nest but still could witness human activity—included but separate.

I wondered how it happened that I, a woman who was so fiercely independent, had morphed into a woman who wanted to have this man next to me, to experience life with me. Pondering this, I realized my transition from Miss Independent to Mrs. Can't Live Without You stemmed from a slow but steady march toward trust.

Mike was an ethical man of virtue and honor in the old-school mold. He earned my trust and he deserved to be trusted.

I wasn't ready to sit in the restaurant alone, so I ordered takeout and came back to the room to eat it in solitude. That was a good call because I really needed to ponder and write and cry. Besides, it is very hard to paste a fake smile on my face and pretend to be normal, especially in a place where everyone is so happy and cheerful. My smile is a lie.

A glass of wine along with some chocolates provided the desired gentle stupor. The big, empty, king-sized bed feels cruel without someone to share it with. I looked over to my right and tried to conjure up an image of Mike in my imagination, propped up, remote in hand. I envision his profile. Sitting here in the strange bed, I draw the shape of his profile, his forehead, his nose, his lips, with my finger. Ah, but it is futile. The image of my lover's face vanishes from my mind, and I am left here in the empty darkness.

It was during this period in early August that my dad became very ill. This was a blow I hadn't seen coming. He and I had overcome so much in recent years and had forged a very close bond. He had been so very attentive during my recent trials, staying in touch with me several times a week and always offering his love and support. Now he was ailing, in and out of a couple of hospitals in a two-week period. When I drove out to visit him at the different hospitals, we had lovely conversations. I was able to thank him for all he did for my sister and me growing up, admitting to him that it must not have been easy taking on two pre-teen stepdaughters. I thanked him for being a wonderful provider and for forging in me a strong work ethic. He taught me to finish what I started and to never leave a task until it was done right.

I didn't have much in my tank to give my dad at this point. I was so spent from my recent trials that all I could do was pray for his recovery. Sadly, he was soon placed in hospice and then passed away at the age of eighty-three on August 16, about one month after Mike. Yet another loss. However, I am very grateful to have had the opportunity to tell him the things I wanted to say, to thank him for looking out for me during these past couple of years, and to tell him how much I loved him.

The house sold in just two weeks, much faster than I had hoped. The daunting task of packing up the house and moving loomed large. After having a garage sale, coordinating several donation pick-ups, selling most of my furniture, and filling a dumpster at my curb, it was time to pack.

Despite the many offers of help I received, I knew this process needed to be handled by me alone. No one was going to go through my son's belongings but me. Only I could decide which items to toss and which to keep. Had it been a routine move, of course I would have welcomed all the help I could get, but this was a very emotional move and needed to be mine to manage.

I knew how hard it would be to sift through all the material evidence of where a family had once lived, where milestones and holidays had been celebrated, where friends convened, where three kids were homeschooled, where tears were shed and laughter rang, where pet rats were buried in the yard. Yes, a family had lived here.

But it was time. I was alone now, just me and my dog Jack rattling around in that big house. The ceilings were too high. There was too much air. It was unbearably painful to be there in the house, in that empty, vacuous space. It was time to pare down my life to fit the new reality, the sad truth that I was going to have to forge ahead all on my own.

Torture is not too strong a word to describe the process of sorting through the items that belonged to Matt and Mike. It was, indeed, absolute torture.

I read through each and every card Mike gave me, cradled his shoes in my hands, and lovingly selected the clothing items of his that had special meaning to me. When it was time to go through my son's belongings, I geared up, knowing it would be very hard. Well, no amount of mental preparation could have prepared me for that kind of pain. I carefully packed three bins of my son's special keepsakes, plus a bin of his childhood toys that I wanted to someday pass to his daughter. I packed two bins of Mike's belongings, things I couldn't bear to part with, plus a box of all the cards and little gifts he'd given me.

The packing process took me three long weeks. I sat on the floor in each child's former room, going through their closets and all the memories they had kept in tubs and bins and bookshelves over the years. It was very emotional and very time-consuming because I had to read every card or letter, survey every Barbie doll and stuffed animal, and decide which items to hold onto for my daughters.

As I packed up the memories, I pondered my twenty-three years in the house. In 1992, when we moved in, I was a thirty-five-year-old mother of two beautiful children, a five-and-a-half-year-old daughter who was halfway through kindergarten and a little boy about to turn four. I was six months pregnant with my future daughter, whom we had decided to name Emma.

Over the weeks of emptying closets and tossing junk and savoring memories, I allowed myself to rewind that movie, those twenty-three years, while I was raising three wonderful kids. All the birthday parties, sleepovers, craft projects, holiday gatherings, and the home-schooling years flowed across the movie screen in my mind. And then I'd pass my reflection in the hallway mirror and see the current version of myself, beaten down by life's trials and tragedies. Still, no matter what challenges had befallen my family or me during our tenure here at the family house, those beautiful memories would take up permanent residency in my mind and heart.

What I needed most at this point was to see my four-year-old granddaughter, Grace. The multiple losses I'd experienced were weighing heavily on me. She was all I had left of my son, and I yearned to see her little face. Soon, I was on my way to Colorado to spend a few days with this precious grandchild.

I wasn't really prepared for how triggering that trip back to Summit County would turn out to be. The last time I was there was the day I'd packed up Matt's apartment while he was in the hospital in Denver. Before arriving at Grace's home, something made me drive over to the apartment. I wanted to see, just one more time, the place where I had spent that wonderful, hope-filled month, that September of 2012 when all the aspens had been cloaked in various shades of gold and yellow. It wasn't a great idea because seeing the apartment also meant returning to the scene where Matt had tried to take his life by jumping off the four-story building. I found myself hyperventilating and shaking in the car. It was too much, so on I drove to see Grace.

My time with her was exactly what I needed. The two of us enjoyed a special bond that I simply cherished. I got to see her school, meet her teacher, watch her play a soccer game, and go on some adventures with her. It was perfect. Soon, I was on a plane back to California.

One of the biggest challenges I faced after selling my home was to find a rental that would accept a large dog, my boxer, Jack. It seemed every desirable place I spotted in the ads had the "no pets allowed" banner attached. I searched high and low, but most of the dog-friendly rentals were in sketchy areas or shabby.

One morning I saw an ad for a condo in a nice section of my town that happened to accept pets. I was thrilled, but I also realized there would be a lot of competition for it. I met the owner at the property and she kindly waited outside while I walked through it. It was perfect but had an extra bedroom.

I walked back outside and told the owner how much I loved the place, but that the rent was a little outside my budget. I asked her if she might consider a slight reduction in rent. She said, "Sorry, but no, the price is firm." I was disappointed, but there was no harm in asking.

While standing there on the sidewalk, I asked if she had any leads to other rentals that accepted dogs that were a bit less expensive. As I spoke, I found myself getting choked up. My pain was so raw and fresh, and my anxiety about finding a place was so high that I was having trouble controlling my emotions. I apologized, explaining that I had just lost my man to leukemia a few weeks ago and was struggling.

The next thing I knew, this compassionate young woman was hugging me and crying with me. She said she really wanted me to be her renter, and she would reduce the rent by fifty dollars a month. It was still outside of my budget, but I went for it anyway. Jack and I moved into our pretty new abode on October 1, 2014.

What a perfect place this was for me. It was a friendly neighborhood with lots of dog owners, so it wasn't long before I made some new friends while out on walks. The quiet patio yard, which featured a pretty crape myrtle tree and a magnolia, backed up to a slope that was full of beautiful trees and foliage. The place was so peaceful and serene that I named it my Healing House.

Since moving to the other side of town, it made sense to make some basic changes to simplify my life, even though I don't really like change. I do understand that some people thrive on change and enjoy experiencing newness and mixing things up a bit. Not me. My preference is to cultivate a sense of familiarity and comfort through routine.

However, in my quest to embrace my new life, I decided to quit the gym I had been a member of for ten years and join a gym that was much more convenient, about a mile up the street. I also changed my bank and my grocery store. It felt good, like I was starting anew, even though I was only a couple of miles away from the old place as the crow flies. It was good for me to make small adjustments to my usual routine, and in a way, it helped me make a clean break.

Alas, even though I was making these positive changes, the grief journey had a life of its own and would take many twists and turns. As the full brunt of losing both my son and Mike in that short span of time started bearing down on me, I became very depressed. At work, I found it very hard to function like a normal person. I worked in a corporate setting as a staff writer, so it was busy and noisy and not conducive to attaining a peaceful state of mind. As my mood sank, a couple of my coworkers reached out to our superior to convey their concerns, and also to mention that my gloomy presence was starting to bring *them* down. When my boss shared this, I felt bad. Still, I just couldn't figure out how to sit there at my desk for eight hours a day looking happy and normal when all I really wanted to do was crawl under the desk and hide.

As my mood sank, so did my will to live. One evening that fall, while out walking the dog along the road adjacent to my condo complex, I literally prayed for God to send a truck careening off the road to take me out, to put me out of my misery. The grief was such a heavy burden that I honestly didn't want to live anymore.

About that time, I was guided toward a group of grieving mothers, a local group that also had a Facebook page. I began interacting with the women and eventually met them in person. It was very inspiring to see how these ladies had navigated their own grief journeys, and they gave me fresh hope that my life wasn't ready to end quite yet.

CHAPTER 20

Learning to Cope

IN THE FALL OF 2014, for the second time in my life, I started seeing a therapist. The first therapist I approached actually rejected me, saying she was not equipped to treat someone with multiple losses like I had suffered. I guess I didn't realize how unusual my story was until she sent me on my way that day. Fortunately, soon after this debacle, someone referred me to a grief therapist who specialized in helping people who'd lost a loved one to addiction. I met with her and instantly knew we were a good fit.

Even though the therapist was limited as to how much she could actually help with easing my pain, she was compassionate and patient, allowing me to sit there and cry as much as I needed. She provided some helpful reading material, some incredible and perfectly timed insights, and was able to gently guide me through the most crippling phase of my grief journey.

My dog, Jack, was getting old and was having health issues, so one day in December, while volunteering at a rescue adoption event,

I ended up adopting another dog. Rocky was also a boxer, a white boxer, and was six years old. I immediately fell in love with the guy, but realized soon after that he had intense separation anxiety. The days I had to go to work were very challenging. His anxiety caused him to destroy some items in the house, but when I left him out back, he barked the whole time. I decided to start coming home for lunch every day to break up the hours away, which helped a little. Still, the barking was a major problem, and my landlord called to tell me a complaint had been filed with the homeowner's association.

It was January 2015 and things at work were not good. I wished I was able to just snap back to normal, but I struggled to even focus at work. Even with the grief therapy, I was not doing well. I believe it was the suppressed grief for my son for all those months while I was caregiving for Mike that was finally demanding its due.

One day, while discussing this conundrum with my friend Franny, I told her I wished I could just work from home. I felt that trying to be in a cubicle setting eight hours a day was not healthy for me. I needed the freedom to grieve when it hit me. Franny didn't dismiss my idea about working from home as a freelance writer; in fact, she mentioned a friend who was doing just that and was successful.

Prompted by my friend's encouragement, my grandfather's genes embossed in my DNA were suddenly activated, and soon I was creating a plan to start my own content-writing business. As is my norm, trying too hard, I began researching this type of work to learn how to set my rates and where to find clients. I created profiles on a couple of freelancer platforms and set my hourly rate at twenty-five dollars an hour. In my view, that was a good starting point since I had to build up my portfolios and reviews on these platforms. The strategy worked, and soon I had a couple of clients.

Once I felt I had a viable business plan that would eventually provide a decent income, I gave my notice at work. My coworkers were happy for me, knowing that I would be much more content working for myself and having the freedom to cycle through my grief journey.

My content business grew over the next few months, mostly due to word-of-mouth referrals, as well as an opportunity to work with the former marketing director at the company I had just left. She decided to start her own marketing business, too, and invited me to provide content for her clients. We have cultivated a great working relationship and have now worked together for almost a decade.

It had been six months since I lost Mike and I was clearly still suffering, especially at night. I couldn't wait to crawl into bed, just to shut off my brain and forget about what I had lost. Some nights I would head to bed as early as eight p.m. because I just couldn't bear the loneliness.

One such evening, while I was trying to will myself to stay awake until at least nine o'clock, I suddenly had a thought. A few years prior, I had dabbled in making some crafts, little boxes and wall art décor pieces featuring a Catholic theme. I had recently come upon my grandmother's childhood missal that was stuffed with antique holy cards. These are family keepsakes, but it made me wonder if I could find some of these old cards on eBay.

I was thrilled to easily locate many vendors, mostly in Europe, who sold these beautiful vintage cards and was totally enthralled as I scrolled pages and pages of them. I wanted to buy them all, but I settled on buying ten. When they eventually arrived in the mail, I decided to keep the cool packages with return addresses and stamps from Italy, France, Portugal, Spain, and Belgium.

This was the beginning of a side hustle art and jewelry business that would fulfill my need to occupy my evenings doing something productive, instead of watching mind-numbing TV and heading for bed at eight. I opened an Etsy shop called Soul Stirrings Gifts, and am still in business today, with about eighty items for sale.

I believe that my grandfather's influence on my life, which is immeasurable, provided me with the moxy and positive thinking that actually served as coping tools during my grief journey. For me, as a single woman living alone, staying busy and productive was a way to fill up the space that would otherwise be filled with sorrow. Sure, I was still on the verge of tears every single hour of every single day, but staying distracted and busy with my two fledgling enterprises didn't leave as much time to ruminate.

In May 2015, Amanda reached out to tell me about an event happening in her town in Colorado called Out of the Darkness, hosted by the American Foundation for Suicide Prevention. Amanda asked if I would be interested in forming a team, fundraising for the event, and coming to Colorado to participate in the walk. I jumped at the opportunity. She wanted Gracie to also participate, so I ordered each of us a t-shirt with photos of Matt and his name and memorial date. It may seem like an event like this would be depressing, but it was actually quite uplifting and our team ended up being the number one fundraiser. Together we walked along the river, honoring this beautiful young man, a son, a husband, and a father.

However, not everything went well that year. One August day, I was working in my home office, both dogs keeping me company, when I decided to go downstairs to fix a cup of tea. Rocky, my Velcro dog, followed me down to the kitchen, while old Jack stayed snoozing in his bed. When I returned to the office, I noticed Jack was lying in an odd position, and seconds later realized the poor guy was dead. I freaked out. I called the vet screaming on the phone that my dog was dead. I was beside myself, wailing on the phone. They gave me the name of a service that would come to my house and transport poor Jack away. I had to hide out in the backyard while they removed my sweet dog because I couldn't bear to witness the sad sight. I also realized how thin my veneer of composure was, as this traumatic event really set me off. I had not healed as much as I had thought.

I was surprised to get an unforeseen tax refund that year, so after Jack died, I decided on a whim to book a trip to Italy. I selected dates that would coincide with the second memorial date, coming up in October, of the death of my son. For some reason, as time went on, the loss of my son became harder, not easier. The pain of missing your own flesh and blood child is something that only another grieving mother could possibly understand. Some days I could barely breathe. A trip to Italy, my first trip in fourteen years, would be the perfect distraction.

That October of 2015, I also reached a benchmark in my therapy process, as my grief counselor decided that I was ready to go it alone. I will never forget how she presented to me that it was time to close out our time together. She said, "I am amazed at your resilience, how you have continued to move forward and tackle new dreams. I have some clients who are still in their bathrobes three or four years after their child passed." Again, I can't take any credit for this ability to propel myself forward. I have to give props to Jesus Christ, who has filled me with such a strong faith and sense of trust, and to my grandpa who showed me how to be brave and create new opportunities—and to never quit.

In the spring of 2016, I was thrilled to learn that Gracie would be moving with her family back to California. Even though we had been able to see each other on her visits to California, it wasn't the same as having her living nearby.

God knew exactly what I needed. Having both of my grandchildren near me was just the medicine I needed to push me into a better place mentally. I regularly planned fun outings and adventures for Jake and Gracie, which were just as much for me as for them. We were off on excursions to the zoo, the Wild Animal Park, the movies, Chuck E. Cheese, the beach, the petting zoo, fairs, and the pool. We had sleepovers, picnics, and took train rides. When Gracie decided to play softball that spring, wearing her daddy's #22, I never missed a game. As a grandma, I was very active and involved, and so very grateful that I had both of my precious grandkids close to me when I needed them most.

A high point of that spring was when my daughter Emma graduated with a Bachelor of Fine Arts degree from Art Center College of Design, a top-notch art school in Pasadena. The whole family, plus close friends, joined there to watch Emma prance up the stage steps to receive her degree. From there, we went to the school where she had her senior exhibit, which was, of course, amazing. The program was extremely demanding and stressful, and I felt so proud of not only her talent but also what she had accomplished.

In July of 2016, just after my sixtieth birthday, my third grandchild, Caleb, was born, only adding to my joy. My daughter Sarah continued to amaze me, balancing her job as a teacher with matriculating through a master's program and being an attentive mother of two, including a newborn.

That fall, Gracie was playing soccer, yet another fun activity to participate in. However, it was her religious formation that became the highlight for me. I had asked Amanda if she would be okay with me heading up Gracie's faith formation and taking her to her catechism classes. Thankfully, she was very supportive of Grace receiving her sacraments and happily agreed to pass this on to me. Every single week, I looked forward to our dates. I drove to her city, picked her up from school, and then off we went to "church class."

We developed the sweetest tradition. As we crossed the lawn

heading toward the classrooms, Gracie would practice her cartwheels, and then we would stop off at the statue of the Blessed Virgin Mary to recite a Hail Mary. Every so often, we would bring flowers to place in the vases at the shrine. Then we'd head inside where all the students lined up for their class. I would stand in line with her and her class as we all recited the Our Father, Hail Mary, and Glory Be.

After her class, I'd come to collect Gracie and we would choose a local restaurant for dinner. Our favorite spot was Mimi's Café, where we always sat in the same red booth every time. I had been collecting these small animal toys for her, adding a new one each week. We would set the animals up like a classroom and act out their various characters. We had the teacher's pet, the troublemaker, the teacher's assistant, the mean principal, and so on. This was always fun and became our weekly routine.

When my daughter Sarah and I had visited Fatima, Portugal, on a pilgrimage in 2001, I vowed I would return for the one-hundred-year anniversary of the apparitions. It was in 1917 that the Blessed Virgin Mary appeared to three shepherd children for six consecutive months, so 2017 would mark one hundred years.

After returning to the Church in 1999, I learned about the events at Fatima and was fascinated by the story. I read four or five books on the subject, and then I decided to take Sarah with me, who was fifteen at the time. While we were in Portugal, my mom arranged for us to also visit the beautiful Sao Miguel Island in the Azores where my grandpa's roots were. Sarah and I visited the little town where Grandpa's family was from and got to meet a distant cousin who lived in the house that was once his parents' home. We saw the family parish church and also the graveyard where my great-grandparents were buried.

Now it was 2017, and my daughter Emma was also expressing a desire to visit Portugal. I arranged a trip with Emma, and we coordinated with Sarah's family who were also going to be in Portugal. Once all of us arrived in Fatima, we celebrated my sixty-first birthday. A huge crowd of about 60,000 pilgrims was gathered for the candlelight vigil, all praying the rosary in their native languages. My daughters and I lit large candles and offered up our prayers for our lost loved ones, Matt and Mike. It was a very special birthday.

From Fatima, Sarah and her family traveled to Italy, and Emma and I rented a car destined for the south coast known as the Algarve, and then drove back up the west coast to Lisbon. From there we caught a flight to Sao Miguel so she, too, could experience this island that resembles paradise, from which her distant relatives had descended. She loved it there as much as I did.

Meanwhile, back at home, the housing prices had been inching up and it was time for me to buy back in. It was kind of nice being a renter for a while, not having to worry about the costs of home repairs. But I preferred being a homeowner, so I started my search.

After several weeks of looking at properties in my budget, I was pretty discouraged. Most of them were in need of substantial renovations, something that I wasn't prepared to deal with. I had just about given up on the idea of buying a place when, as God would design things, a darling condo in my own complex came on the market. It was perfect. I became a homeowner again and got to stay close to my neighborhood friends at the same time.

In May of 2018, two years after starting our weekly church class dates, Grace made her First Communion. Her other grandma and I took her shopping and bought her a fancy white dress, a silk flower headpiece, and white patent leather shoes for the occasion. Just like me when I was a seven-year-old making my First Communion, Grace was obsessed with the shiny white shoes. After she had made her

First Communion, we headed right over to the Virgin Mary statue and prayed the Hail Mary together, side by side on the cement bench, exactly as we had done every week. It was a beautiful moment.

Later that month, Sarah announced she was expecting baby number three, due in early December. I was elated that another beautiful grandchild was on the way to love and spoil. This prompted Sarah to begin looking for a bigger apartment to accommodate their growing family. As fate would have it, the Healing House that I had rented for three years had just become available again, so Sarah's family moved in.

How blessed was I when my daughter and her family actually became my neighbors, a dream come true. Now, just four buildings separated us. I loved when the doorbell rang and I'd find Jake there asking to borrow a cup of sugar or whatever my daughter was in need of. And they helped me, too, by taking care of my dog Rocky whenever I left town. Mostly, it was like the olden days when families lived close to each other and had the ability to hang out together. That now described us, our clan, and I loved it.

When I first set out to write a book in the late spring of 2018, I set a goal to finish the first draft by my son's fifth memorial date, October 23, 2018. Embarking on my new journey as an author, I admit I was clueless. I spent months researching how to go about writing a book and getting it published. What those articles didn't prepare me for was the huge investment in time and energy that would be required. I often worked until ten p.m., juggling my book writing with meeting client deliverables. After all, I still needed to pay the bills.

The process of writing my first memoir, *My 13th Station*, was arduous. It required me to dig deep emotionally, which meant reopening the wounds that had barely healed in order to tell an authentic story that was often quite raw. There were certain points in my son's story that were so painful to revisit that I became physically unable to proceed and had to crawl into bed. I'm glad I didn't give up when those days threw me off track for a spell.

Writing the memoir, which involved parsing through all the details and emotions associated with some highly traumatic events, was actually therapeutic. It helped me process much of the residual trauma that lay just below the surface. My son was the victim of a spiritual attack, which I detail in the memoir. I believe this struggle with spiritual warfare contributed to his mental anguish and eventually led to his death.

As a person who is very deadline-driven, I was determined to meet my goal to finish the book by my son's memorial date. So, on October 22, just in the nick of time, I dropped off the file containing the first draft of the book to a local print shop and then headed to the Adoration chapel at my church. There, I offered God heartfelt thanks and praise that he had allowed me to persevere and complete my son's story, as painful as it was to write. Later, when I picked up the printed copy, I was surprised by how thick it was, much thicker than I had anticipated. My plan was to use the printed copy of the manuscript as a helpful tool to begin the editing process. As I paid the gal at the counter, I realized I was on the verge of tears. I was very moved to see the fruits of my labor sitting right there in front of me.

The next day, on October 23, I arrived at my son's grave, bringing five red roses, one for each year that he'd been gone, as had been my tradition every year. This year, the bound manuscript accompanied the five roses. I turned my tear-filled eyes to the sky and said, "Blue, I did it. I wrote your story."

While I'd been writing my boy's story, a nagging question regarding my biological father, George, who had also died by suicide, kept surfacing. Back in 1986, it was my aunt Bertie who had called to inform me of his death. Then years later, in 2003, I surprised myself when I suddenly felt a need to learn more about my dad. I searched and found the contact information for Aunt Bertie and Uncle Pat, and mailed them a quick note asking if they could please call me. My aunt soon called, and before I knew it, my mother and I were planning a trip to go visit them in Nevada.

Our short visit back in 2003 yielded a lot of information about my paternal side. I learned that my dad had remarried and had two sons, Sam and Joe. My aunt didn't know their whereabouts, but she gave me photos of my half-brothers. She also gave me an envelope stuffed with family photos of my dad, his six siblings, and his parents, which helped to provide me with a visual of the other half of my biology.

Now, in 2019, as I was preparing to publish my son's story, I had a strong desire to learn whether my father had also suffered from depression and/or alcoholism. Maybe there was a family genetic component that could help explain what had happened to my beautiful son.

So, I decided to search for my half-brothers. I found them quite easily online and penned a short note to each of them. I introduced myself as their older half-sister and asked them to get in touch with me. Both of my half-brothers responded within a couple of weeks. I was impressed while reading their letters, which were both well-written and thoughtful. They each provided their emails and encouraged me to contact them.

Thus an interesting new layer was added to my life. Both Joe and Sam were kindhearted, well-spoken guys, and were very forthcoming in answering the many questions I had about my father and his family. Some of the conversations were very difficult, mostly because I had decided to share with them the traumatic memories of my early childhood. Of course, I warned them first, since I needed to honor their memory of our dad. They both gave me the go-ahead.

When I shared about the disturbing acts that have haunted me my whole life, both of them were stunned. While our dad was emotionally unstable and never could keep a job, they had not been exposed to any cruelty. It was hard for them to reconcile their experience with mine, but they never doubted my claims for a minute. Both of them expressed sorrow that I had suffered so much as a child because of our father.

My half-brothers confirmed that my father had suffered from mental health challenges, telling me he'd been diagnosed with anxiety and post-traumatic stress syndrome, most likely diagnosed when he was hospitalized after kidnapping my sister and me. According to the boys, this trauma stemmed from his experiences in Korea during his tour in the early fifties.

I had wondered if my dad struggled with depression or alcoholism, and if that had played any part in him ending his life, but my half-brothers said he had not. However, both Joe and Sam did battle depression, which I found interesting. Apparently, my dad's second wife, their mother, had left him, and he never really got over that. Then, at some point in 1986, he received a medical diagnosis that he felt he couldn't live with. Sadly, Sam, who was just nineteen at the time, found him after the self-inflicted gunshot.

I also asked if anyone knew the cause of death of his father, Francis, our paternal grandfather, who died at age fifty-one, but they said their dad had never mentioned it to them. Although I wasn't able to connect any dots between my father or my paternal grandfather to my son's sufferings, these conversations with Joe and Sam were very blessed.

They wanted me to know that, as children growing up, our father always included my sister and me by name in their nightly prayers. They said that he was very sad when he learned, through a family member who'd reached out to him, that his daughter had passed away from cancer. They told me that he attended daily Mass at the local Catholic parish and also volunteered his handyman services to the church as needed. They also confirmed that my dad had played stand-up bass.

After having only negative input regarding my dad, hearing some endearing things about him was good for me. It didn't remove the terrible memories, but it softened them and painted a more balanced portrait of him. Sadly, my half-brother Sam passed away about a year ago, at the time I'm writing this, from prostate cancer. I was sad that I never met him in person but very grateful for the interactions we'd had.

My mom and I had both received our DNA ancestry reports. When comparing our reports, I was able to determine which Irish counties coincided with my maternal Irish ancestry and which ones were from my father's side. Of the four Irish counties that were highlighted in my report, those that didn't appear on my mom's report I could attribute to my paternal ancestry. When I later visited Ireland in the fall of 2019, I was able to discern whether the county we were visiting was where my maternal or paternal relatives were from.

I remember standing on a street in Waterford and thinking, wow, my father's grandparents may have walked on this very street. Then when in County Cork, I'd note that a great-grandparent from my maternal side had lived there. It was fascinating to me, traveling to the countries of my ancestral roots. I had traveled to Bavaria, Germany, back in 1979, never knowing that that was where my paternal grandmother was from. This fixation with my ancestry is possibly a common trait of people who come from broken homes or adoptive families. A subconscious yearning to put the puzzle pieces together, to assemble the facets of your whole being, surely drives this curiosity.

After spending several months unsuccessfully attempting to land a literary agent, I decided to self-publish my memoir. This entailed even more research, teaching myself how to be a self-published indie author, how to launch the book, and how to promote it. Finally, after completing the editing process, the book was published in July of 2019. I gathered my dear friends and relatives to my house for a launch party to give the book a solid boost right out of the gate. The book party gathering also provided me with an opportunity to thank all of these loved ones who have been so supportive in recent years.

Over the past five years, since I'd sold the family home following Mike's death in 2014, I had slowly, methodically rebuilt my life, brick by tear-stained brick. Looking back at my progress, I could see that I was now thriving. My freelance writing business was generating enough income to support me, I had published a book, and I was selling my art creations and jewelry at craft shows and on my Etsy shop. I had joined a women's group at my parish, delving deeper into my Catholic faith while developing close friendships with several of the ladies. I took daily walks with my dog, Rocky, and went to the gym twice a week for Zumba classes and workouts with weights. The abundant time I spent with my four grandchildren fed my soul beyond measure, as did cultivating strong bonds with my close girlfriends. All of this, plus some great trips—Italy, Portugal, and Ireland—had coalesced into a life filled to the brim with meaning and purpose. Bottom line—I had survived.

CHAPTER 21

Covid

THE YEAR 2020 STARTED OFF with some distressing news—my mother had been diagnosed with bladder cancer. The doctor informed us that before he could give us a plan or prognosis, she would have to undergo an outpatient procedure. This would involve removing tumors in the bladder as well as a biopsy. For the next couple of weeks, the family was on pins and needles awaiting the report.

My mom and her husband Bruce now resided in the Palm Springs condo that once belonged to her dad, my grandpa. When this news unfolded, I lived about two hours away and my sister Elaine resided in Arizona. When it was time to meet with the specialist to review the biopsy findings, I arranged to pick up my mom and her husband so I could be present, and my sister joined us via a conference call.

I sat next to my mom, holding my breath as the doctor explained the findings to the four of us. After losing so many loved ones to cancer, I was filled with anxiety when he entered the room to speak to us. We were incredibly relieved to hear that my mother's cancer was considered a slow-growing type of bladder cancer, and that the tumors would be managed by occasional outpatient procedures. I immediately threw my arms around my mother, pulling her close to me. I realized in that moment that I was not ready to lose her.

My mom, whom I lovingly called "Mamasita," and I had always had a strained relationship. In fact, throughout much of my life, I harbored a great deal of resentment toward her. Without going into the details, the bottom line was that my mom was just not the motherly type. I write this only to paint an accurate picture of our relationship. My mother had many gifts, but being a mom did not come naturally to her. Growing up with a mom who worked full-time and dated frequently meant my sister and I were often cared for by babysitters.

When I had my first child, Sarah, I remember holding her in my arms while standing in her nursery. I had never felt such deep love in all my life. Suddenly, I wondered why my mom never felt this surge of maternal love toward me. She was not an affectionate mother, and didn't tell us, "I love you." During my first twenty-nine years, I had reluctantly accepted this about my mom; it was just the way it was. But standing there that day holding Sarah, I felt ripped off, angry even, that my mother hadn't felt this way about me. Then and there, I vowed to not repeat that experience with my child. Instead, I would show her and tell her how much I loved her.

My cousins and I sometimes discussed this topic because they had grown up with a similar experience with their dad, my mom's brother. We would ponder this, wondering what had made them both so aloof toward their children. As hard as it was to admit, because we adored our grandparents, we surmised that they must not have received affection from their parents, and so they simply did not know how to express their feelings.

Even though I always felt sad that my mom wasn't able to show me that she loved me, I knew she did. Over the years, I learned how to enjoy my mom for who she was, not who I needed her to be. So, we enjoyed many wonderful times together, and especially our lunch dates to celebrate her birthday or Mother's Day. We'd chat and chat while finishing off a glass of wine or a margarita, always enjoying each other. We also enjoyed an ongoing conversation on Facebook Messenger. In other words, I came to accept her shortcomings in the mom department and shelved my anger and disappointment.

That day, sitting with her at the urologist's office, I cried tears of relief learning that her life was not in any imminent danger. I surprised myself with the powerful emotions that surfaced once we got this encouraging report.

We decided to stop at a favorite deli in town to celebrate. When we got out of the car in the parking lot, my mom did something she had never done before. She reached over and grabbed my hand. Together we walked, hand in hand, into the deli. Yes, my mom loved me.

The first couple of months of 2020 were pretty typical, with nothing out of the ordinary occurring. In February, I joined the family to applaud for Gracie in her latest play, *Shrek*, and a week later accompanied my church group to a wonderful event featuring Fr. Don Calloway. Life was humming along quite nicely…until it wasn't.

In March 2020, the world, in essence, was turned upside-down as news of a novel coronavirus called COVID-19 from China hit the media. By mid-March, fear had taken over and turned people into desperate hoarders of, what else, toilet paper. Aisles of empty bins in every store and videos on Twitter showing people fighting over toilet paper at Costco became commonplace in what seemed like overnight.

In my usual manner, in late March I decided to chronicle this event by keeping a journal. Unheard of events were unfolding in record time, and I wanted to capture them. I decided to combine photos with my journal entries to really convey life in 2020 for posterity.

The world was locking down, meaning we would be forced to isolate from others for what turned out to be weeks and months on end. Businesses, most stores, and churches were ordered to close down, an unheard-of response by our government. Of course, since everybody reading this will not need to be reminded about how awful that experience was, I will stick to my own personal experience during this particular year.

Living alone during the pandemic lockdowns was nothing short of torture. Thank goodness for my dog, Rocky, whose presence at least provided some modicum of social interaction. I'd have entire conversations with my dog, giving him his own voice when responding to me.

Easter was particularly sad. Never before had Christians, worldwide, been prevented from attending Easter services. It was strange and sad and terrible. I watched Andrea Bocelli perform via satellite feed, standing in front of the huge cathedral in Milan, Italy. During the performance, a montage of photos depicting the empty streets in New York, Paris, and Rome brought me to tears.

I was, however, very grateful to have already been working from home for five years by then. This meant that I was able to continue on with my daily work with no disruptions in logistics and only a slight reduction in clients. Many people faced layoffs or were forced to figure out how to do their jobs from home with little kids underfoot, so I considered myself lucky.

After the novelty wore off of gorging on unhealthy comfort foods, dancing to online Zumba classes, and watching the Mass on the internet instead of attending it in person, life became nothing short of miserable. As humans, our basic need for social interaction had been blocked to a great degree. Facial expressions were also hidden by the necessity of wearing facemasks, which stripped interactions of any personality or energy. The media stoked fear at every opportunity, so even while outdoors, we became nervous about standing too close to someone.

I noted in my journal how eerie it was when I ventured out for a drive with my dog in late April, about six weeks into the lockdowns.

There is such a strange feeling in the air that I notice whenever I venture out. Maybe it is because I have been sequestered for so long. I can't put my finger on it. Something just seems off, like we are not really in the moment—like we are in a secret movie. Can't explain it. I feel super self-conscious when I go anywhere, like I am sneaking around and about to be caught. It is very surreal out there.

I remember driving to Laguna Beach one Sunday, parking my car, and taking a little walk around. I noticed how loud the cars sounded on the highway as I walked along, which was in stark contrast to experiencing utter silence on the roads for many weeks by that point.

In May, Rocky and I surprised my mom and hubby in Palm Springs for Mother's Day. I showed up at her door with flowers and a Mother's Day balloon tied to Rocky's collar. I treated them to a home-cooked meal and even baked an apple pie. Of course, we had to sit outside on the deck to visit with each other, and they even wore their masks outside. As odd as this scenario was, at least I was able to see my mom and cheer her up. They were very isolated out there alone. As much as we all wanted to visit the folks, we were fearful of the prospect of potentially transmitting the invisible, asymptomatic virus to them. It was such a difficult time for families.

Later, when I got back home that day, my daughters Emma and

Sarah were there to greet me. The girls had arranged for an outdoor Mother's Day celebration, complete with flowers and treats, and best of all, precious time together. I felt very loved.

Then, a bombshell. Grace's mom and grandmother had decided to relocate to Utah where they had purchased a beautiful new home. They would be leaving in July. This was absolutely devastating news, as I had become so very attached to this precious grandchild. She was all I had left of my son, and I cherished all the time we had spent together over the past several years.

By July, Covid restrictions had eased a bit, but Americans still had to get creative for celebrating the Fourth of July this year. Our condo complex was filled with young families, so they organized a parade around the neighborhood. Dozens of kids whizzed by, including my three grandkids, on scooters and bikes festooned with red, white, and blue. They made the trek around the complex three or four times and then convened at an easy-up where a horde of millennial moms was hosting a chili cook-off.

I headed up to visit Grace and her family for their outdoor Fourth of July festivities. It was very bittersweet for me, since in a few days Grace would be moving away. Knowing this, I made the best of our time and just treasured those three hours we were able to spend together that day.

I had arranged to see Grace one last time before she moved. I had assembled a photo album filled with pictures of her childhood, her daddy, and all the wonderful memories we had shared together over the years. I also made her a box, with the letters "Notes from Nana" on the front and a collage of pictures of us on the inside, that would serve to contain all the letters and cards I knew I would be mailing her.

For weeks, I had cried myself to sleep thinking about her leaving. The day arrived when I had to say goodbye, so Rocky and I got in the car and headed up. Seeing her that day was very emotional for both of us. I gave her the gifts and she cried, so then I cried, and then there we were blubbering away in each other's arms. She was also sad to say goodbye to Rocky, whom she loved very much.

I continued to try to make the best of things during the pandemic. I took lots of hikes and little road trips to ease the feelings of going stir-crazy at home. Rocky and I drove to Big Bear, where of course I did the usual drive-by of our old family cabin. I dreamt of buying it back and restoring it as I drove past the place.

Later, down the hill a bit in Lake Arrowhead, I took Rocky out for a walk before hitting the road back home to Orange County. He didn't seem to want to get out of the car, which was odd, but I eventually coaxed him out and we strolled around the shops that line the lakefront.

Within days, I knew something was wrong with my dog. Suddenly, he was struggling with constipation. Then the next day, I noticed his urine was orangeish, so I called the vet. Because of Covid, I had to wait outside in my car while the vet examined him. The vet asked if he could take some X-rays, and I agreed. About twenty minutes later, the vet called to tell me the tragic news. Poor Rocky had advanced cancer. The large tumor had not been visible to me because it was tucked under his prostate. The vet said his condition was grave, but that he could send him home with pain medication so I could possibly get a couple more days with him. He also warned me that Rocky might pass away at home if I took this route.

I didn't hesitate to decline that option. I couldn't bear the thought of watching my sweet doggy suffer and then die in my house like Jack had. No, I had to face the brutal pain of putting my beloved Rocky to sleep.

The vet assistant met me at the door and accompanied me into the examination room where Rocky was comfortably lying on a quilt. I couldn't believe that just a few days ago Rocky had seemed fine, and here I was preparing to say goodbye to him. I instinctively wrapped my arms around my sweet boy as he drifted off to sleep, telling him, "Mommy's here. Mommy's here with you. I love you, Rocky."

Losing Rocky just two weeks after Grace moved away was too much for me. I suffered terribly over those next weeks. I was so very sad, languishing around the house with no sense of purpose. Rocky had kept my days structured with meal times and walk times. Now, I was utterly alone, which only made me yearn for Mike. How I needed Mike right now. We would have kept each other company during the lockdowns, and his shoulder would have been available for me to cry on at this sad time. I was so lonely.

Thankfully, I am not one to sink into total despair and stay there long. I have a strong survival instinct that kicks in when life becomes overwhelming or bleak. By the first of August, I was making plans to pay a surprise visit to Grace in Utah. I decided to combine this with a meet-up with my travel friend, Judy, whom I had enjoyed trips to both Italy and Ireland with. When I traveled with my daughter to Portugal back in 2017, it was Judy who volunteered to dog-sit Rocky for two weeks. This was exactly what my sad heart needed, to see a dear friend and then my granddaughter.

Grace was totally surprised when I showed up. She and her mom and grandma were on the porch because I had texted them saying I would be there shortly, although it was unbeknownst to Grace. When I pulled up, there was my beautiful granddaughter loping across the grass and running toward my car shouting, "Nana!" My three days in Utah were wonderful. We took walks, visited several parks, went shopping, went paddleboarding, and just had a great time hanging out together. We also sat on the bed and cried together over Rocky.

On my drive home, my happy state of mind started heading south again. Driving through the Las Vegas area, I started thinking about my life. How I had nothing to return to at home, just a box of empty air. I felt distraught about returning to that lonely place.

Maybe it was because of the ongoing sense of isolation and feelings of loss, but at about this time, I started a pros and cons list about moving somewhere that was cheaper and friendlier to people like me, a conservative Christian. California had about the harshest Covid restrictions in the country. The state legislators were proposing some draconian new bills that, frankly, terrified me. I found myself pining for a warm, inviting community where I'd feel welcomed.

I began to imagine moving somewhere and starting over, which prompted me to make a Word document with various scenarios and the pros and cons of each. I started to look at real estate in Utah near my granddaughter and in Arizona near my sister, where the cost of housing was about half of that in California. These also happened to be conservative states, which was alluring as well.

In September, I met with my mom at the doctor's in Palm Springs to discuss her condition. His tone was a bit more serious this time. He gave my mom a couple of treatment options, such as major surgery to create an external bladder and/or chemotherapy. She immediately dismissed both of these options. He asked her if she wanted to at least meet with the oncologist, and she flatly declined. Mom had decided to continue managing the tumors for as long as she could, and then let nature take its course. I supported her on this. She was almost eighty-eight years old and I believed we should honor her wishes.

The pandemic induced a strange state of perpetual fear that caused me to often feel frozen. In contrast to my usual productive nature, I just wanted to shut down and do nothing instead. On some deep level, I sensed that the world was experiencing something sinister and life-changing. This made me feel both anxious and depressed.

I found that the trick to surviving the many detrimental effects of the pandemic was to seek joy as much as possible. When Grace came for a visit in October 2020, I planned a full itinerary of fun outings for us. One of these was a beach day with her cousin, Jake. Now that she was ten years old, I decided she was big enough to ride her daddy's boogie board, which I had held on to for years. Jake brought his board, too, and they both had a fantastic time enjoying an Indian summer beach day in California.

During the holidays, Covid roared back up, so activities were once again highly restricted. This prompted me to become a little creative for our family Christmas Eve celebrations. Since we were advised not to hold family gatherings, I decided to throw a Christmas party in my garage. With the garage door wide open, we were able to enjoy each other's company in a most unusual party setting. In my festively decorated garage, I provided food, drinks, and Christmas music, while we enjoyed watching the kids playing in the little cul de sac in front of us. Yes, Covid had dealt us lemons, but we made lemonade.

CHAPTER 22

Mamasita

SOON AFTER WE RANG IN THE NEW YEAR, my mother experienced a health event that landed her in the hospital. She had taken a fall. Apparently, she had not been eating or drinking water for a few days, which made her so weak that she fell and hit her head on the bathroom vanity.

She was very ill, but because of Covid, we were not permitted to go into the hospital and see her. Finally, after five days, she was discharged, so I drove to Palm Springs to pick her up at the hospital. The person they wheeled out to me looked nothing like my mother. It was alarming to see how much my mom had aged in this short period. She could barely muster a smile, which was not at all like her.

After she met with her regular doctor that next week, he determined that she was in rapidly declining health and advised us to place her in hospice. He told us that she might have a couple of weeks to live. This was shocking news.

She was soon set up at home with a hospice care program, which provided two visits per week by a hospice-trained nurse plus someone to assist her with showering and such. She grew a little stronger each week, and by the end of January, she was out of bed and engaging in daily life again. We were all thrilled to see her rebound so quickly.

As the weeks passed, she became ever stronger and started looking more like her old self. We were thrilled, and I admit that I even hoped there might have been a miracle of some sort at work. Still, she was weak and, because of the bladder situation, needed to be close to her bathroom. This meant that it was next to impossible to convince her to go outside.

One day, sensing that she was in need of some fresh air and sunshine, I offered to take her for a little drive. She agreed, so I gingerly got her seated in my car and off we went. I took her on a drive in the gorgeous canyon that butts up against the San Jacinto Mountains. Knowing her musical preferences, which I share to a large extent, I set the radio dial to the local station that plays standards. There we were, mother and daughter, tooling around the desert listening to Frank Sinatra and other crooners. It was a lovely outing, although not a long one. After just twenty minutes, she announced that she needed to get home, which I realized meant she needed to use the restroom.

After a couple of weeks, her hubby Bruce was able to coax her out for some short walks in front of the condo complex, which was so encouraging. I even bought her a pair of pink tennies to keep her inspired. Things were looking up.

It was about this time that I set myself a new goal, to write a follow-up book that would provide guidance and inspiration for other grieving mothers. I needed a new project to snap me out of my malaise, and this was just the ticket. I invited ten women, all grieving mothers like me whom I had met over the past several years, to contribute their personal stories to the book. I envisioned a book that would contain input from a diverse group of women, each with their own voice and unique stories of loss. This way, any woman who had experienced the loss of a child would find someone in the book they would be able to relate to. I wanted my book to resonate with as wide a range of grieving mothers as possible.

I decided to devote this new book, *Hope Springs from a Mother's Broken Heart*, to my mother, herself a grieving mother. With my mom's health on the decline, I took this project on with a sense of urgency. My prayer was to have it published in time for her to see the dedication, and maybe even read the book.

In the early spring, I buckled down. I prioritized getting my part of the book written, which included the chapter about my own son, plus nine other chapters. That way I could focus on helping my beautiful Mamasita as much as possible while being available to offer guidance to the ten women who were contributing stories to the book.

Life in early 2021 was busy. In addition to writing a new book, I managed to attend both grandsons' Little League games, one of my favorite things to do as a grandma, and also keep up with my clients. Then in late March, I was thrilled to have Grace come for a visit. Whenever all four of the grandkids are reunited, it is always cause for celebration. So, we made the most out of Grace's time with us.

My sister Elaine, who resides in Arizona, owns a nice condo in Palm Springs. This became very helpful to us both during our time assisting Mamasita. Three weeks of the month, I'd drive out to Palm Springs to spend two days per week helping Mom in a variety of ways, and was able to stay the night at my sister's place. I offered to help the folks with the housework, shopping, cooking, running errands, and bill paying, which kept me hopping those two days each week. Then, one week per month, my sister would come to California to stay a week at her Palm Springs place and pitch in a great deal, too. Her forte was cooking huge meals and freezing some of the food for later. We were an excellent caregiving team, my sister and I, and we kept each other apprised of any updates on our mom during and after these visits.

When a special event or holiday came up, I did my best to make it very special for my mom and Bruce. For their anniversary, for example, I decided to create a romantic Italian feast, complete with candlelight and a music playlist of classic Italian songs. I cooked homemade lasagna served with Caesar salad, Chianti, and spumoni ice cream for dessert.

In June, I was dealt a terrible blow. My daughter Sarah and her husband Danny told me they were planning on moving to Tennessee in the fall. What? This could not be happening! I seriously couldn't handle the thought of all my grandchildren living out of state. It was too painful to even think about.

Of course, I did understand the reasons for them making this decision. They wanted to buy a home of their own, which was next to impossible for most young people in California. But…Tennessee? Why not choose a nearby state where I could drive to visit the kids? Idaho, Arizona, heck, even Texas were all great options. Nope, they had made up their minds that they were Tennessee-bound, and I was heartbroken.

Despite this bad news, the summer of 2021 offered me an opportunity to make many, many beautiful memories with my mom. During my weekly visits, I started a new tradition. Each week when I came to see her, I would not only cook a fabulous meal but also bring a movie or two for us to watch. She loved the sixties musicals and also Alfred Hitchcock movies. Her favorite movie, though, was an Elizabeth Taylor movie called *A Place in the Sun*, which we watched three times that summer.

Her appetite was amazing. She gobbled down anything I cooked and especially enjoyed the decadent desserts I made for them. My mom expressed her gratitude over and over for every little thing I did for her. The thing was, I truly loved being there with her. I would look forward to my weekly trip out to Palm Springs to help out as much as I could. It was an exhausting schedule for sure, but it was extremely edifying to be there, spending this precious time with her.

Around mid-summer, I mentioned something about praying the rosary. My mom surprised me when she asked if I would get her a rosary. She said she could not locate her old rosary and wanted one. I asked her what color she'd like, and she said she'd like a pink rosary. I was thrilled to shop for a rosary in the perfect shade of pink.

One of the most endearing developments that summer happened when I bent to kiss her cheek when I left to go back home. I always said, "I love you. You are my beautiful Mamasita." This time, she replied, "And you are my beautiful baby girl." This became our little routine as we said goodbye to each other every week. It just warmed my heart to hear her call me her baby girl.

As much as I needed a week off on those weeks when my sister took over, I honestly missed being with her. I realized how deeply I loved my mother, and I was finally experiencing her love being openly expressed to me. She even talked to me like a mom that summer, giving me advice when I had a problem to solve, or guiding me on this or that. I wasn't used to this at all! I had always been very self-sufficient because I had to be. All my life, I had to be a mother to *myself*, and had no option but to learn how to figure life out on my own.

Don't get me wrong. Throughout my adult life, my mom always commended me for my achievements. I lived for these nods of her approval. I had always strived for both her and my grandfather's approval because this gave me a sense of value and worthiness. My mother told me she was proud of me often, and it meant the world to me. These compliments were her way of communicating her love, and trust me, I lapped it up.

Thanks to Almighty God, I was able to get the new book published that July, allowing me to present it to her. I took a photo of her holding my book, and also one of her pointing to the dedication. She read the whole book and truly loved it. This was such a gift, an absolute blessing to be able to put the new book into my mother's hands.

Even though we were living in the Covid era, people still came out to visit Mamasita. Her brother John and his wife made the long road trip from Phoenix to spend a week nearby and visited her daily that week. They were very close siblings and often chatted on the phone, but these in-person visits were so very special.

My daughter Sarah brought the kids to spend some quality time with her, and my cousin Shannon spent a couple of lovely afternoons visiting with her. My sister's family also spent a good deal of time with Mom, especially her son, Jeff. He was very attentive to both grandparents on many occasions during the year, and I know how much that meant to her. Bruce has three sons, who also made trips out to visit the folks. Spending time with his sons provided him with a much-needed diversion. My daughter Emma stayed in touch with her grandma via regular phone calls, as did her longtime hairstylist and close friend, Jeanne.

And then, wouldn't you know it, I caught Covid. It was the delta variant that I caught while at church. Yes, we finally got to return to in-person Mass, and of course, I caught it. Ugh! This was terrible on many fronts, but mostly because I could not visit my mom for several weeks. I was only ill for about twelve days, but the virus stubbornly lingered in my system. I was very frustrated because I knew time with my mom was ticking by while I was stuck back home.

Finally, I returned to my post and restarted our wonderful tradition of watching movies and eating. However, about this time, in late August, it was evident her appetite was declining. The hospice nurse who weighed her each week confirmed that she was losing weight and that there was muscle wasting. These were bad signs. Still, her mood was upbeat and positive. My mom had a special ability to compartmentalize. She was able to block out things that upset her and almost live in a pretend world of make-believe.

Well, I am one who lives in reality, and I knew it was time to call for a priest to come and anoint her. No one knew how much time my mom had left, but we were all too aware that with cancer, we were on borrowed time. So, a priest from the local parish came to visit my mom and then gave her the anointing of the sick, a Catholic's final sacrament.

In September, I decided to throw my daughter's family a going-away party. She and Danny had grown up in our town and spent their entire lives here, so I felt it was only right to give them a proper send-off. Even though their departure date of October 3 was looming, I shelved my tears just enough to focus on making the party unforgettable. I also squeezed in as much time with my grandkids as humanly possible, considering my already packed schedule. I felt like I was lapping up every last little drop of time as a grandma.

Meanwhile, my beautiful Mamasita continued to decline. By late September, she slept most of the day and often didn't change out of her pajamas. Her declining appetite translated to continued weight loss. We sensed time was getting short. Still, when I arrived for my weekly visits, she would make the effort to get dressed and sit in her chair, waiting for my arrival. She always had a smile for me, even if she wasn't able to stay in her chair for very long. While she slept, I would catch up on the housework and grocery shopping and keep Bruce company. He was such an attentive husband, and we were all very grateful for his loving care. He went out of his way every single day to make her breakfast, coax her to drink water, and generally watch over her. It was beautiful to witness their love.

The going-away party was a big hit. About thirty-five of their friends and family members joined me in wishing the adorable little family much joy and happiness in their new lives in Tennessee. I fought tears during most of the party but did my best to keep a smile on my face. A week later, they were gone on their big adventure, moving two thousand miles away from everyone and everything they'd ever known to bravely chase their dreams.

And then, the unthinkable happened. I received a call from my mom's husband saying that she had taken another fall. The paramedics who arrived to assess her condition believed it was a hip fracture, and they transported her to the hospital. My mother, suffering from end-stage cancer, was in excruciating pain. I just sobbed.

The hospital did not permit visitors, so I was only able to get information through Bruce, which could be challenging. It was confirmed that Mom had broken her hip and needed to have immediate surgery to stabilize the bone. My heart just broke for her. The added suffering and stress were too much to bear.

After the surgery and a few days to recuperate, she was transferred to a local nursing home. Due to Covid, we were limited to a certain number of visits to see her there. Of course, her husband would get top priority, so my sister and I coordinated our visits to sprinkle in between his. When I first saw her lying there in the bed, I was so sad. She looked so small and frail, and even though she was taking medication to control the pain, she was clearly suffering. The nurses were not even able to adjust her position without eliciting a scream from my mom.

The three of us did our best to keep her spirits up. We encouraged her to give her best effort during physical therapy, but she wasn't able to walk. She took a couple of steps one day early on but never walked again. My sister, a former school teacher, took charge of decorating her bulletin board, giving it a festive fall theme and pinning photos of her kids on it. I followed suit, adding a few photos of my children to the bulletin board. At least Mamasita could gaze at her beautiful grandchildren from the bed.

With our mother's eighty-ninth birthday coming up, my sis and I decided to give her a Hawaiian-themed party. The thought of her sitting in that dismal place on her birthday was too sad to bear, so we got busy planning. We went all out, adding colorful Hawaiian decorations around her half of the room, making a festive scene. We were thrilled that she was able to sit in the wheelchair and enjoy her little party. We all wore Hawaiian leis, and her husband sported a big straw hat. We enjoyed lunch together while my sister played a beautiful video she had assembled with the help of her son, Jeff. She had asked all the family members to record a birthday greeting, which was just so uplifting for my mom to watch on her birthday.

When it was determined that she was not going to be rehabilitated after the hip surgery, plans were made to send her home to resume hospice. This time, we were all very aware that she didn't have much time left.

Those final days at home with her were both difficult and beautiful. Pain management was escalated to a whole new level, and we were trained on how to apply the fentanyl patch and administer the various pain medications. Even with all these powerful drugs, poor Mamasita would cry out in pain if the caregivers tried to move her. Finally, the doctor determined that the cancer had metastasized to her bones.

On Tuesday evening, November 9, 2021, after spending three days with her, I was preparing to leave. Before I did, I read aloud all the cards that loved ones had sent her and showed her, once again, the photos of all her grandchildren. Lying there in the hospice bed that was set up in the den, she looked frail but still radiated such natural beauty.

As I went to leave her, I said my usual, "You are my little Mamasita. I love you," to which she replied, "And you are my precious baby girl.

I love you, too." In that moment, I had a strong feeling that I was saying my final goodbye to her. Suddenly, I blurted out, "You were the best mom, the best," while fighting back tears. Upon hearing this, she rolled her eyes, as if to say, "Yeah, right." But to me, now that I had opened my heart to who she was and been willing to forgive her shortcomings, I truly meant it. She was the best mom for me. Exactly what God had planned for me, and He is never wrong.

On my short walk to the car, I burst into tears. I was certain she wouldn't make it through the night. But alas, the next day, her grandson Jeff came to visit her and revived her spirit. As weak as she was, she surely enjoyed his attention and love. On Friday, my sister arrived from Arizona. By this point, my mom was on a heavy dose of morphine, which my sis had to administer at specific times. It was all very stressful. I stayed in touch with my sister all evening, continually asking if she felt I should hightail it back to Palm Springs. She put me at ease, saying no, she was stable and there were no changes in her condition to speak of.

The next morning, I decided to drive out there even though my sister wasn't sensing any urgency. I did have a strong sense of urgency, so I hit the road at 8:30 a.m. after first locating my sister Ann's scapular, a traditional sacramental, that I was in possession of. I knew that if you pass away while wearing a scapular, it has protective powers. I wanted to give my mom the best send-off possible, and this had belonged to her daughter, Ann, which made it very special.

As I was driving out to the desert, my sister called. She wanted to update me about my mom's condition and admitted things were looking less stable. As we were chatting, I was distracted and missed the turnoff I needed to take. Ugh! Of course, trying to reroute by getting off the freeway and reversing course, I found no northbound entrance, so I had to drive another mile to turn around and then catch that turnoff I had missed earlier. I lost about fifteen minutes.

When I pulled up to the condo, my sister was there to greet me at the car. I suddenly felt sick. She threw her arms around me, telling me that our beautiful mother had passed away peacefully fifteen minutes prior. I was devastated that I had missed her taking her last breath.

I went up to the condo and crawled onto the little hospice bed with her. I placed Ann's scapular around her neck and, knowing she was gone, turned my eyes toward the ceiling where I was sure her spirit was lingering, waiting for me, and told her just how much I loved her.

Later that day, after things had settled down, I drove home in silence. Two hours of quiet time. I pondered the way the day had gone, and how by missing that exit I also barely missed her dying moment. I decided that this was the way it was supposed to unfold. That I had my moment with her on Tuesday while she was fully lucid and able to hear me tell her how much I loved her. Maybe God felt I just couldn't bear to witness another dear loved one die, and He spared me.

We laid Mamasita to rest right next to her precious daughter, Ann. She had purchased the plot when we buried Ann in 1985, so we always knew that was the destination for Mom's earthly remains. It was a beautiful graveside ceremony, with an especially wonderful priest. He gave us all a sense of deep peace in the words he spoke.

As we walked up to place a pink rose on the casket, I noticed Uncle John struggling. He was grieving deeply for his beloved sister and was sobbing as he shuffled toward the casket. I stepped over to him and gently guided him up to the casket to help him place the rose on top. It was a tender and very moving moment that I will never forget.

My heart just ached. I realized we are never ready to lose our mother, never.

My sister Elaine and I pulled together a truly wonderful celebration of life to honor her. We decided on a Mexican restaurant, her favorite cuisine, that had a nice roomy patio. Yes, Covid was still an issue, so fresh air was a smart setting for the gathering. We asked the guests to wear bright colors, as that was our mom's signature look. We incorporated into the table décor all the things she loved that made her so unique—Betty Boop, romance novels, owls, wolves, DVDs of sixties musicals, her favorite Mexican pottery, and tons of framed photos at every stage of her life. Bright Gerber daisies and bold-colored tablecloths provided the perfect accents to this colorful affair.

My sister and I got up and gave our little speeches about our mother, but it was the sweet, impromptu words spoken by her loving husband, Bruce, as he stood up there, a bit unsteady on his feet, that were so very heartwarming. In all, the well-attended celebration of our mother's life was very special and meaningful, and I truly felt she would have approved.

At about this time, some of the gals from my high school Vocal Ensemble, the singing and dancing group, reached out to me. One of them, Sally, had, with the help of her husband, put together a video of footage taken by her father back in 1972 and 1973.

There on the screen I saw the seventeen-year-old version of me —long flowing hair and big smile—dancing and singing like the world was my oyster. I reflected on that young Theresa who had not a care in the world, totally unaware of all the losses that would incur in future years: my sister, my grandpa, my son, my love, my stepdad, and now my mother. I am glad I didn't know. So, I watched that video again, and this time just enjoyed it for what it represented, a vibrant, exciting time of my life when I believed that, yes, the world was indeed my oyster.

CHAPTER 23

Finding Gopher Hollow

MY MOTHER'S PASSING was very hard on me. I found myself crying out in the shower, like a little kid, "I miss you, Mommy!" The painful effects of the loss of my mom so soon after my daughter's family had moved away left me with only one solution, one singular medicine that would cure me—a visit to see my grandkids in Tennessee.

I arrived in Middle Tennessee in early December, when the air was crisp and the weather unpredictable. I welcomed this change of scenery for that very reason; it was totally different from Southern California, which seemed to perpetually register a perfect seventy-two degrees. As my son-in-law drove us southbound from Nashville, I marveled at the huge swaths of greenery that still commanded the landscape, even with the naked trees sporting bare branches. It was a beautiful scene.

After settling in with the family, my daughter mentioned that the town they lived in, Columbia, had a cute little town square. She didn't really describe it, other than to call it quaint, with very old buildings.

She mentioned that on Friday, there was a community event being held on the square that I might be interested in attending. It would feature a Christmas-themed parade and a tree-lighting ceremony. So, of course, I said, "Sure, let's go!"

When we drove to the town square, I envisioned a ramshackle town with a sprinkling of families there to witness the tree lighting. Boy, was I wrong. As we walked up the parade route, I was thoroughly charmed by a succession of adorable and creative holiday floats passing by, and by the large, enthusiastic crowd cheering them on.

We made our way to the square to find a spot on the crowded street, which was packed with families. I was enchanted the minute I saw the town square. Something about it just clicked in my soul. We popped into a cute little store called The Balloon Shop where I ordered popcorn for all of us. We stood huddled together out on the sidewalk in our parkas, munching popcorn while observing the wholesome scene unfolding in front of me, when it suddenly dawned on me. This was Mayberry.

The city of Columbia, located in Southern Middle Tennessee, was historically an agricultural town. It was given the nickname "Mule Town" because for many years it was the go-to place to purchase mules. Columbia is also the site of the ancestral home of President James Polk. The town square is as cute as you can imagine, featuring beautiful old brick buildings dating back to the 1850s that have been lovingly restored. The square is the hub of the town, the place where the community goes for live music, great meals, classic car shows, live theatre, and excellent shopping. In a word, the town is delightful.

My children would tell you that I often pined for a life like the one portrayed in the Andy Griffith Show. Mayberry was a fictional town in the Northeast, set in the early 1960s. The simplicity of life depicted in the episodes set in Mayberry was always so attractive to me. And there I was, in December 2021, standing in a little town that felt exactly like Mayberry. I glanced at my daughter and didn't even need to say the words out loud. She knew. I had finally found Mayberry—in Tennessee.

Although my daughter and her hubby showed me all around the Middle Tennessee region, there was no contest. Columbia had stolen my heart. After four days of making a whole batch of new memories with my adorable grandkids, I headed back to face real life in California. At the time, I wasn't planning on moving to Tennessee, or anywhere. My hope was to be able to visit the kids every three months.

Sadly, this realization meant I had to face the fact that my days as an actively involved grandma were over. That chapter was closed. All my grandkids now lived out of state, so there was no reason to designate half a kitchen pantry, a hall closet, and half the guest room closet for storing kid's toys any longer. The grandkids were gone.

That January day, I gritted my teeth and faced the hall closet first. I was sitting on the floor, surrounded by the contents of the closet, sobbing. It broke my heart to get rid of all these toys. I sat there revisiting the memories made when baby Gracie and Jake, and then my two youngest grandkids, played with these toys and books. I wept as I packed them up. Still, I pushed forward, tackling the pantry, the bedroom closet, and finally, the garage shelves that were filled with Nerf guns, balls, pool toys, sidewalk chalk, and sand toys. This process, this closing of a wonderful chapter of my life, was akin to grieving a loss.

In mid-February, my mom's husband, Bruce, who was still living in the Palm Springs condo by himself, had taken two consecutive falls, each time hitting his head. Thanks to the assertive actions of a close friend who wondered why he hadn't seen any sign of him, my mom's widower was alive. After Paul entered the condo, he found my mom's husband lying unconscious on the bedroom floor and quickly had him transported to the hospital. When chatting with Paul on the phone later, he mentioned the paramedics that day telling him it was unsafe for Bruce to be living there alone at his age. His recovery was slow, so he spent a full month at the hospital.

Meanwhile, the contents of my mother's will revealed that I would be the beneficiary of the condo. This presented me with several stressful decisions. Her husband called me from the hospital in early March to say he'd be moving in with one of his sons and suggested I start looking for a renter. I was glad to know he would be well cared for and not be living there alone where he could possibly suffer another, worse, accident. However, this also meant I had some big decisions to make.

As usual, I made a pros and cons list to parse through the various options to consider. The place was admittedly in very shabby condition, having never had the kitchen or bathrooms renovated in fifty-five years. Everything was run-down and needed to be replaced. After doing the math, I calculated the minimum expense to make it rentable at $70,000. Since I didn't have that kind of money lying around, I began to consider the idea of selling it.

In reality, the thought of selling the place was heartbreaking. While raising my children, through their entire lives, this little condo in the desert was our go-to vacation home. Although it was a very modest place, built on Indian lease land, it was located in a beautiful canyon corridor. Countless memories had been made from the time I was a pre-teen until the present day in that condo. Long-ago memories of being there with my grandparents, my mom and sister, and later my blended family, were so special to me. Even more so were the memories of all the wonderful times spent there with my own family over the years.

Since my grandmother's death in 1971, the condo actually came to represent Grandpa to me. From the late seventies through the eighties, I made many trips out to spend time with Grandpa there in Palm Springs. In all the years, until his passing in 1994, when the condo was passed to my mother, Grandpa never changed a thing. To him, it was where he and Grandma had made their own memories over that short four-year period until she lost her battle with cancer.

When I'd come for a visit, he loved to take me downtown where we would explore the hotel lobbies and peek into the shops, and always stop for an ice cream cone at 31 Flavors. We also walked the canyon corridor together, always the same route that ended at a hotel that was on the corner about a mile away. He loved going inside hotels and wandering around. I could hardly keep up with him, as Grandpa was a fast walker. He was fit and active until his late eighties, staying in shape by playing tennis, golf, and dancing at the senior center on Thursday nights. I loved hanging out with him at the condo in Palm Springs.

Later, when my children were older, I had more time to sit down and read the pages he had typed, and I was in awe of his life story. I confess that I never got past the fourth book, though. However, my younger daughter Emma had an affinity for learning about her great-grandfather, which was the purpose of him writing the books. He dedicated the books to his grandchildren and his great-grandchildren, feeling strongly that we would benefit from knowing the details of our family history. So, the books were stored in the Palm Springs den closet, lined up inside a large wooden cabinet that my mom's husband had built to house them.

After Grandpa died and the place belonged to my mom, I still felt his presence whenever I visited the condo. Sometimes, I'd dig out his old pipes stored there and smell them because the scent reminded me of him. One year in particular, while going through my marital problems, I was in a bad place and spent a couple of days there alone. I sat on the edge of the bed and talked to him, like he was standing right in front of me. Being at the condo always made me feel physically close to my grandpa.

This explains why I struggled so much with making a decision about the condo once I inherited it. My heart wanted to keep it, but my pocketbook saw it as a financial liability. There were monthly expenses and property taxes, which I couldn't afford to take on. I certainly couldn't rent it out in its current condition. I agonized over the quandary I was in.

Then one day, after discussing it with my sister, it became clear to me that it would be wise to sell it while the real estate market was on fire. I called each of my daughters to get their feelings about selling the place. Although they were both sad that we needed to let it go, they understood.

And then an idea suddenly popped into my head: I would use the proceeds to help my daughters buy their own homes. This was perfect. By using the inheritance this way, Grandpa would still be helping his family, just as he had often done while he was alive, but through his daughter. This aligned with his patriarchal tendency as a long-term planner to take care of his family for generations to come.

I returned to Tennessee for a second visit in March and was blessed with beautiful spring weather. Flowers were blooming and the trees were greening up again. Just like during my last visit, I drank in the small-town atmosphere of Columbia, finding even more to love about it this time around.

My daughter was slowly overcoming her homesickness, as she'd made some new friends and embraced the southern country lifestyle she had craved, which had brought them here. For years, Sarah was obsessed with Laura Ingalls' *Little House on the Prairie* books and television episodes. She had worn cotton frocks sporting tiny floral prints almost exclusively for the last few years and even had a *Little House on the Prairie* cookbook. She baked her own bread and dreamt of someday raising chickens and growing a garden. It warmed my heart to see her adjusting to her new lifestyle. Her husband and the kids seemed to have no problem adjusting at all to their new environment, which surprised me since Danny was an avid surfer who now lived more than six hours from the closest beach.

The day before I left, we were in the square shopping and enjoying an ice cream cone. We wandered into the darling Duck River Bookstore, and while we were browsing, I asked the owner to recommend a book for my flight home. He suggested a book written by local writer and songwriter, Rory Feek, entitled *This Life We Lead*. It was a memoir about his life, but mostly about losing his beautiful wife to cancer shortly after their daughter was born. I took his suggestion and purchased the book.

On the flight home, while reading his story, I realized right away that Rory Feek had a way with words. He was a gifted storyteller who possessed a genuine and relatable writing style. When I got to chapter four, something he wrote really resonated with me, yet at the time I didn't really know why. In this chapter, he described a small town where he'd lived for about three years when he was a kid, and how special that time was to him. When describing the impact it had had on him, he'd written:

Without realizing it, deep roots had grown into that soil, and though in the years to come, I might have been living in Avoca, Michigan, or stationed in El Toro, California, a part of me was still back there in that little town. Why do you think I live in an old 1870s farmhouse now? OR drive a 1956 Chevy or play guitar and write songs and stories about small-town life? It's all part of getting back there. Finding my way back to that place in my head when everything was good, everything was right.... I woke up one day and realized that I have subconsciously spent my entire adult life trying to get back to that one moment in my childhood that I loved most.

I returned home to California and worked hard on getting my mother's condo in as good a shape as I possibly could, considering its beleaguered appearance. My sister joined me so we could go through our mom's belongings together. Even though it was sad to handle her personal items of clothing and other possessions, it turned out to be a sentimental experience.

In late April, after much ruminating, I made the big decision to sell my own home and then relocate to Tennessee. In weighing everything out, especially considering how hard it would be to leave Emma and all my treasured friends, it was the thought of missing out on being a grandma to my young grandchildren that trumped everything else. This was the decision-maker for me because I wasn't ready to quit my role as an involved grandmother. Was I ever relieved that I had kept the Legos and some favorite books to take with me to start on this new grandma chapter in Tennessee.

Now that I had made this decision, it was time to get my house spruced up and put on the market. Properties were still moving quickly, but I was hoping for my condo to take a while to sell so I'd have ample time to find a suitable place in Tennessee. Wouldn't you know it, the condo sold in three days for the full asking price. I panicked, but fortunately, the new owners agreed to a rent back, which bought me an additional month.

I sure had my hands full. My mother's place sold at about that same time, meaning I had to return to Palm Springs to empty its contents and say my final goodbye to the condo. It was a huge job. Once the discards had been hauled off, it was time to pack up the mementos. Among the prized acquisitions were some items that

Grandpa had brought to the condo after selling Gopher Hollow in the mid-seventies.

How thrilled I was to be the new owner of two frosted glass mugs with thick wooden handles that I fondly remember from the "bar-beque" area at the Gopher Hollow property. These mugs were kept in a hutch down in the barbeque with the other dinnerware and glass-ware, and my sister and I would pretend to have parties at the big table using the dishes and these mugs. Not only were they cool, but they had sentimental value to me.

Most meaningful of all was taking possession of Grandpa's mem-oirs. As I gently packed up the treasure trove of family lore left by my grandpa, I made a vow to dig into them and read each and every book once I got settled in Tennessee. I also filled several boxes of family memorabilia to share with my two cousins. Before leaving, I walked through the little condo one last time, the place where my family would forever leave its deep imprint and much of its soul, and quietly walked away.

Later, when my cousin Johnny came to my home to retrieve these family treasures, he was visibly moved to be in possession of so much family history, including Grandpa's pipes. I handed off a box filled with slides of our grandparents' many travels and a half-dozen old photograph albums with some amazing family photos. There were also some cool Native American artifacts he and Grandma had purchased at the Navajo reservation in the late forties and fifties. Although our grandpa had clearly stipulated before his death that the books were to remain together as a set, I happily disobeyed and handed off a couple of the books to my cousins.

Now that I was getting down to the wire, my focus turned to finding a little home in Columbia, Tennessee. Wouldn't you know it, the market was red hot and inventory was low, so the first couple of places were swept right out from under me with much higher offers.

As the time grew short, I started to panic and accepted that I may just have to rent for a while if I couldn't find what I was looking for in my budget.

This revelation led to a quandary—what to do about my grandma's 1934 Baldwin spinet piano? As I scoured the floor plans of apartments and condos for rent, for the life of me I couldn't find a spot for it. So, I asked my family members if anyone wanted to take the piano, with the hope of at least keeping it in the family. When I had no takers, I had to face an upsetting possibility…that I would have to sell it. The cost of shipping belongings across the country was calculated based on weight and distance, and I was told my piano weighed seven hundred pounds. I was very torn but reluctantly decided to put it up for sale on Facebook Marketplace.

As part of my process of saying goodbye to California, I made plans to visit my favorite places one last time. This particular day, I had invited Franny to join me on a day trip to Big Bear. As we hit the road, I almost broke down in tears telling her I had placed the piano up for sale, and that three people had already reached out asking to see it. Without a moment's hesitation, Franny told me sternly, "Do not sell the piano. If you sell it, you will always regret it." Franny has the woo-woo thing, she just knows stuff, so when she said this to me, I took it seriously. After our wonderful day in Big Bear where, yes, I took her to see the family cabin, I removed the listing for the piano.

Wouldn't you know it? The very next day, as I made my daily visit to Redfin to check for new listings, there was an absolutely darling little cottage up for sale. Because properties were selling within hours of being listed, I immediately reached out to my realtor in Tennessee, and also my daughter Sarah, asking them to please, please, please go view the house. As a team, this was how I shopped for a home from the opposite end of the country. My daughter would connect with me on FaceTime and show me the house as she and the realtor toured it. Luckily, they were both available.

As Sarah and the agent showed me the place, which was built in 1934, I fell in love with it. My realtor exclaimed, "Theresa, this is a writer's house!" Sarah, who was also shopping for a home, said, "Mom, I will be jealous if you get this house—it's my dream house! But it's too small for my brood, so I hope you get it."

As they filed out the front door, the elderly owner of the home, Don, was standing on the front porch, so my daughter introduced me to him on FaceTime. I told him I loved the place, and, after noticing he had an American flag up on the porch, I said, "And Don, if you accept my offer, I promise to have a flag flying, too." He said, "Those are some well-behaved grandkids you have." I replied, "Thank you, I agree, and they are the reason I am looking to buy your home, so we can be reunited." An hour later, my realtor put together our offer.

That night, as I was getting ready for bed, I pulled up the photos of the house one more time. With tears in my eyes, I prayed, "Jesus, I know it is just a box, a rotting object just like me, but if it is your will, *please* let Don accept my offer."

At about seven a.m. the next morning, my agent called to congratulate me. Don had accepted my offer. I was blown away. And the best part was, there was an absolutely perfect spot for my grandma's piano.

Once reality kicked in, that I was really going to uproot and move two thousand miles across the country, I was filled with equal parts excitement and sorrow. As a person who doesn't like change, I was nervous to leave the only place I have ever really known. I had cultivated beautiful relationships with so many special people over the last six decades, some of whom are my best friends to this day.

Leaving my thirty-year-old daughter Emma, who lived in Long Beach, was going to be very difficult for me. She and I have always enjoyed a close relationship and never went longer than three months without seeing each other. Although we held very different opinions about some pretty big issues, there were plenty of things we shared a deep love for. One of them was a passion for sifting through vintage shops, where we both seemed to be attracted to the same items. I decided Emma was an old soul born decades late, as vintage kitchen and décor items from the forties, fifties, and sixties were of as much interest to her as to me. I would spot items that I recognized from the Gopher Hollow era and point them out to her with glee. She always knew when we went antiquing together that her mom would be in a blissful state of nostalgia. So, as I processed the upcoming move, it made me sad to think I would be so far away from her.

I had hoped to visit Palm Springs before leaving but wasn't sure if there'd be time. Emma surprised me with concert tickets for my birthday to see The Zombies out in Joshua Tree, a funky desert enclave located a short distance from Palm Springs. I was thrilled! Three original members still played in the band, and they were just amazing. Emma has a deep appreciation for old-school music, so she thoroughly enjoyed the show, too.

We stayed the night at my sister's condo in Palm Springs, and the next morning, Emma and I had breakfast at Elmer's, a tradition in our family, one last time. For decades, we always went to Elmer's every single time we visited Palm Springs. Emma, being just as nostalgic and sentimental as me, suggested we say goodbye to the condo one last time. Even though we no longer had access to the unit, we just went into the pool area, where our beloved orange metal 1960s poolside umbrellas still provided their much-needed shade.

Standing there, I closed my eyes and imagined the beautiful scene in May 2013 when all three of my children were there in Palm Springs with me, hanging out in the pool. It was the last time we would ever visit the Palm Springs condo together. My son looked strong and healthy and happy, and I was so full of hope. Sadly, he was gone just five months later.

I gazed up at the four towering palms one more time, the palms I had watched grow taller and taller over the decades from my vantage point lying on a raft in the pool. I remember being out on the raft about five years prior, looking at the quartet of majestic palms, and deciding to attribute them to represent my grandpa, my sister, my son, and my man…my angels.

My heart was so full from the outpouring of love over those final weeks in California. I was the guest of honor at a lovely gathering hosted by my church friends, these beautiful and inspiring women I had grown to care deeply for along my spiritual journey. Another group, the dear friends who'd walked alongside me for decades while raising our children, and who'd held me close to their hearts through the sorrowful loss of my son, threw me an amazing going-away party. I felt so very blessed, and so grateful for the souls God had placed in my life.

As I went through the motions of packing up one room after another, my mood shifted to excitement. I began to look forward to starting my new life in Tennessee. Yes, packing up and moving across the country as a single woman in her mid-sixties was stressful, scary, and exhausting. But I knew in my heart that a whole new adventure awaited me, and I found this exhilarating.

I arrived in Tennessee on August 13, 2022. All the important events in my life seem to occur on the thirteenth. I was born on a Friday the 13th, after all. But mostly, I attributed the high volume of thirteens in my life to my devotion to Our Lady of Fatima. So here I was, on the thirteenth day of August, to begin my new life as a southern gal.

I drove up my new street, a gorgeous old street with huge trees and quaint homes, to finally lay eyes on my little house for the first time. I couldn't have smiled any bigger. It was adorable, inside and out, and best of all, it had a cute front porch.

There was something special about this place where I had landed. I couldn't define it yet, but I could feel it. Maybe it was because I was so thrilled to once again live near my daughter and her family, but I felt like I was floating on cloud nine. Everyone I encountered, in the shops, the DMV, the contractors I hired, my neighbors, everyone was so welcoming and friendly.

Because of the stigma currently attached to my home state of California, I had been forewarned to be sure to replace my license plates as soon as possible. I quickly learned, when asked where I was from, to tell the locals the truth, that I was a California refugee. This strategy helped put to rest any worries that I'd be voting liberal, as Tennesseans are very protective of their freedom.

I took walks around my neighborhood to get a feel for where I was now planted. It is a lovely neighborhood only a smidge over a mile away from the town square. The area was first settled nearly two hundred years ago. In fact, just three houses down from me is a beautiful historic home built in 1840.

I was thrilled to discover pine trees lining some of the streets, which immediately reminded me of Big Bear. I closed my eyes and breathed in the pungent scent of pine as my feet crunched the fallen pine needles and dried pinecones. Then it dawned on me that this place, Columbia, represented the *new* Gold Mountain, the landmark in Big Bear that my grandpa had shown me to guide my way home.

While walking down the road, I soon discovered that folks passing by would wave at me. This truly made my heart sing, being seen and acknowledged like that, like I mattered. In fact, it turned out to be very easy to make new friends in Tennessee. I'd sit outside on my front porch while sipping my morning tea, and passersby would stop and introduce themselves. Everybody seemed to have a dog, which was on my list of goals once I got settled. Rocky was irreplaceable, but that didn't mean I didn't have plenty of love and affection to give to another dog someday. Once I did get a new dog, it would fulfil my years-long dream of living in a charming cottage with a porch and a dog.

One day, while standing on my porch chatting with a contractor, I spotted a yellow butterfly floating across my property. This sight made me catch my breath and triggered immediate tears. For years now, yellow butterflies had come to represent my beloved son, so seeing one in Tennessee was a sign that he was still watching over me. The carpenter noticed my tears and so I shared about my son and the significance of yellow butterflies. The next day, he gave me a little yellow butterfly made of wood and said to "put where you will see it often through the day."

It was time to unpack my life from California and give it a whole new purpose here in Tennessee. As I carefully placed my décor items around my little cottage, I soon realized that I was surrounded by memories of Gopher Hollow. The cute little whimsical salt and pepper shakers and cookie jar that had once adorned the kitchen shelves at my grandparents' home were now proudly displayed in my own vintage kitchen, a perfect backdrop for these beloved keepsakes. The marble-topped side table I'd inherited accented a wall in my living room, the hexagon-shaped, rustic, copper-topped table sat in my entry, and Grandma's piano took pride of place on a prominent wall near the kitchen.

Just as in California, I hung the framed photograph of my grandfather on the wall next to the desk in my new office. I discovered a beautiful cherry-stained desk with craftsman-era design elements inside the shed that sits in a corner in my backyard. I dragged it out of the shed and, after scrubbing off the thick dirt and abundant number of bugs, I realized it would be a perfect writer's desk.

The following Sunday, I joined the family at what would be my new parish church, Saint Catherine of Siena. There are no words to describe how wonderful it felt to be sitting there at Mass with my loved ones. Jake, the oldest, was an altar server and looked so handsome in his vestments.

After Mass, a very friendly, wholesome energy filled the narthex, the gathering space in front. I had attended Mass here two other times when I was visiting and noticed then all the young families and cute kids filling the space with exuberance and positive energy.

As is the norm, the kids like to go outside and climb on the big magnolia tree out back. As we stood out front watching them, in my peripheral vision a man caught my eye. I looked over and, by gosh, it was Rory Feek, the songwriter/author who had written the memoir I'd bought back in March. I recognized him from the book cover. I confirmed with my daughter that he was indeed Rory; she said that he and his daughter sometimes attend our church with his friend Matt.

I excused myself and walked over to Rory to introduce myself. I told him I had purchased his book in March to read on my flight home to California, and how much I enjoyed his writing style. I offered my sincere condolences for the loss of his lovely wife and told him I, too, had suffered some heavy losses, so I knew how hard it was. The next thing I knew, Rory embraced me in a big hug, telling me he was sorry for my losses, too. He asked me if we'd like to be guests of his at his next concert out at his homestead, to which I of course said, "Yes."

Over the next few weeks, we ran into Rory a couple more times, including at First Friday. First Friday is a monthly event held in Columbia when the community descends on the town square to enjoy abundant live music, food trucks, vendors, and family fun. That time, just as the other times we'd run into Rory, he gave us a round of his hugs and reminded us about his upcoming concert.

When we arrived at the beautiful Hardison Mill compound, the hundred-acre farm he'd once shared with his late wife, Joey, we found Rory had reserved the best seats in the house for us. That night, it was easy to grasp the appeal of Rory Feek. He intricately wove together a string of his well-known songs, recorded by famous artists, with tender stories about his darling little daughter and his beautiful wife. It was clear to anyone present that he was a quality man, a godly man, and I felt grateful that my grandchildren were present to enjoy such inspiring and wholesome entertainment. After the show, we met up with Rory in the lobby where I asked him to sign my copy of his book, and then the six of us posed for a photo with him.

When the fall arrived, I truly felt I had died and gone to heaven. Leaves took on the rich hues of amber, gold, and maroon, recoloring the trees in jaw-dropping beauty. After enjoying a Thanksgiving feast with the grandkids, it was time to start thinking about doing some Christmas decorating.

Since I now lived in a cute little cottage, built in the thirties, I decided to head to the town square where there is a large vintage store. My goal was to find some old-fashioned Christmas decorations to give my tree a nostalgic flair. It was a chilly late afternoon on a Sunday when I entered the store on the square.

Inside, I smiled as the sounds of old-school Christmas songs were piped through the store, sung by crooners like Nat King Cole, Dean Martin, and Bing Crosby. I found myself even feeling a little emotional as I soaked up the nostalgic ambiance of this scene. All around me were reminders of yesteryear, with antique kitchenware, toys, and aprons. This was definitely my kind of store.

As I was walking through the store, to my amazement, right there on a shelf was the same vintage Nativity set I had pined for since the sixties, when my grandparents had such a set on their front lawn at Gopher Hollow. I could not believe my eyes; it was exactly the same set.

After selecting a half-dozen vintage-inspired ornaments, I carried them to the counter and told the sales gal I also wanted to purchase the plastic Nativity set. I asked her, just to make sure, what year the set was made, and she answered, "The 1960s." Bingo. So, there I went, proudly walking down the street with the Virgin Mary tucked under one arm and Joseph under the other. After gingerly placing them inside my car, I went back to retrieve Baby Jesus. On my way home, I cried tears of joy.

About this time, I learned that a high school friend and her sister had also recently moved from California to put down stakes in Tennessee. After meeting for a nice long lunch to become reacquainted, we decided to get tickets to Rory Feek's Christmas Show out at his farm. The show was just as wonderful as the prior show I had seen in September, and right about in the middle of his set, he opened the floor up for a question-and-answer session. During this segment, he encouraged anyone with a question to raise their hand. A woman asked, "What is the significance of the many signs reading Highland, Kansas, that are on the walls at Marcy Jo's?" Marcy Jo's is the Feek family's café, just down the road.

Rory began to retell that passage from his book that I had noted while on the plane flying home to California. He explained that Highland, Kansas, was a small town where he and his family had lived in an old white farmhouse for three years when he was a kid. He told the audience that the years they lived in Highland were the best years of his life, that it represented everything good to him. He said that ever since, he has attempted to recreate that magic by surrounding himself with the things that remind him of being there and being happy.

Hearing him say these words aloud registered, loud and strong. Being there that night, listening to him share this story, felt serendipitous. I acknowledged the powerful impact his words had on me and realized in that moment that he, in some inexplicable way, was talking straight to me. In reality, he didn't even know I was in the audience, but his words that night held a special significance for me—I just didn't know why.

This California gal received a special gift when a light layer of snow accompanied my first Christmas in Tennessee. On Christmas Eve, my house was alive with the joyful sounds of Christmas music and kids playing. I invited my next-door neighbor and her nephew to join us, two Louisiana transplants. What a hoot it was to listen to Kelly recite the hilarious *The Cajun Night Before Christmas* in her thick Louisiana accent.

One day that week, while there was still snow on the ground, I glanced out my office window and spotted a brilliant red cardinal perched on my white picket fence. What a glorious sight, seeing the bold red bird against the stark white snow. It seemed like he was looking at me through the window, so I decided that day that cardinals would represent my grandfather. From then on, each time I saw a cardinal, I'd say, "Hi Grandpa."

I rang in the New Year by singing and dancing my heart out at the local Puckett's, which is a chain of barbeque joints in Tennessee. I joined some neighbors and a packed house to enjoy the amazing sounds of an oldies band called Boomerang. As I returned to my car that New Year's Eve, I wanted to pinch myself I was so happy, and I was proud of myself for having had the guts to make such a huge change in my life.

Because I am a chip off my grandfather's block, every single January, like clockwork, I experience a huge rush of motivation to set some goals for myself in the New Year. It is my norm to be filled to the brim with ideas and plans in the early weeks of January. For some odd reason, this year I was completely flat. I felt absolutely zero motivation and had no gumption whatsoever. It was very strange.

Then, on Wednesday night, January 11, I had a dream about

Gopher Hollow. Having a dream about the house was not unusual, as over the decades I've had many, many dreams about Gopher Hollow. What is interesting about these dreams is how my subconscious imagination inflates the house into a grandiose palace while I sleep. For example, once I dreamt there was a big carnival going on in the backyard area. Apparently, our family owned this carnival, and in the dream, I was walking around enjoying all the guests and rides, and of course, my grandpa was there running things. In reality, all that was in the backyard area at the real Gopher Hollow was a modest little fenced yard with grass.

In this latest dream, again my imagination embellished the details of the house. I knocked on the door and introduced myself to the new owner. I told her the house was built by my grandparents in 1941, and I was hoping I could take a look around. The woman graciously invited me inside to show me the amazing renovations she had done to the place. In my dream, I tried to commit to memory all the cool architectural design elements she was showing me.

We walked through the house, and the lady opened the back door, and there before me was an enormous cliff-side ocean view. As we sat there, taking in the ocean vista, the owner asked if I had seen my grandfather of late. I told her, yes, that I had visited him recently. This is another feature of the Gopher Hollow dreams, that Grandpa is still alive. But as I awakened from the dream state, I snickered because he would actually be 122 years of age by now if he were still alive. I lay there thinking about the dream and even tried to summon up the visuals of the beautiful décor renovations shown to me in the dream.

Suddenly, like being struck by a lightning bolt, it dawned on me that the same observations Rory Feek had described in his book, and to his audience just a month ago, also applied to my own life. In that moment, lying there in my pajamas on a chilly January morning, I realized that I, too, had been on a subconscious search for my happy place, for Gopher Hollow. That was the place where as a child, I'd felt safe and secure, loved and cared for. Where mourning birds cooed and gardenias bloomed. Where the days were filled with exploration and discovery.

Suddenly, everything made sense. From my search for a house with a porch to my recently planted gardenia plant, I had been trying to recreate a time when I felt alive and happy.

The day I heard the song of the mourning dove while out on a walk immediately invoked thoughts of my little sister and that front bedroom at Gopher Hollow.

And the surprises and blessings that I experience here in Columbia, Tennessee, continue to enthrall me. I had promised my grandkids this summer that I would make them root beer floats. It later dawned on me that I have three grandkids and only two of the frosted glass mugs I inherited via Gopher Hollow. A couple of weeks later, while shopping in the square, I entered my favorite vintage store and literally could not believe my eyes. There, nestled in a stall near the staircase was one lonely mug, exactly the same as mine but in orange. Not a set but one single mug. In all my years of antiquing and flea market excursions, I had never spotted a mug like the ones my grandparents had…until I moved here. So, I plunked down the eight dollars and made good on my promise. I served my three adorable grandkids delicious root beer floats in matching vintage mugs.

Over a three-month period this year, I have been blessed with several houseguests, loved ones who have seen for themselves now what the attraction is in my new hometown. My front porch, to me, represents a magnet, drawing these friends and family members from far and wide. I make sure to take a photo of each visitor while they sit on my porch, which I later print and attach to my fridge.

My beautiful granddaughter Grace, now thirteen years old and five foot four, came for a visit in late June. I was thrilled to have all the grandkids reunited for the first time in two years, and we made sure to pack each day with fun activities—bowling, the water park, shopping in Nashville, a family barbeque, and an eventful five-mile kayaking trip down the Duck River.

Having the grandchildren gathered together in one place again struck me as the work of God, who'd lovingly reassembled the puzzle pieces of my life and completed the picture.

One day during her visit, Grace and I visited the town square and explored yet another vintage store. While I was browsing, she came over to me, saying she wanted to show me something. It was a Ninja Turtle t-shirt. This caught her attention because of how much her daddy loved the Turtles. So, unbeknownst to her, I went back to the store the next day to buy it, surprising her with it. And now I have an adorable photo of Grace on my porch wearing that Ninja Turtle t-shirt.

Now, as I walk around my house, my heart swells seeing the little artifacts left for me by loved ones who've come to visit. These sweet gifts each have their own special energy that reminds me each day how much we mean to each other, no matter how many miles may separate us.

It is not by random happenstance that certain people appear in your life at a particular time. Back in March 2022, James, the owner of Duck River Books, of all the books in his bookstore, suggested I read Rory's story on my plane ride home. Five months later, I ended up moving to Columbia, Tennessee, a place to which my heart and soul were drawn. A week later, I spotted Rory Feek at our church. A month after that, we were guests at his concert, after which he signed my copy of his book. Three months after that, at his Christmas show, a random woman in the audience raised her hand and asked him to explain about Highland, Kansas. He explained the significance of the place to him, and I hung on every word. Then, one month after that, I had a dream of Gopher Hollow, and the concept for this book was born. Rory Feek, someone I had never heard of prior to 2022, was the person who inspired me to write this book—a book about finding my way home.

My lifelong love of Gopher Hollow was not solely based on the physical place, the house, or the land it sat on. No, Gopher Hollow was in reality a *state of mind*—what living there had come to represent in the deepest folds of my heart. That childhood experience, of finding refuge with my grandparents, was life-changing and left an indelible mark on my soul.

What resulted was a subconscious quest, a search I wasn't even cognizant of, but one that propelled me forward each and every day as I looked for that place, that ethereal sanctuary where my brokenness would be mended and my soul restored.

As I travel along my life's journey, the powerful influence of those short months on a little girl back in the summer of 1964 is now clearly evident. Now I can see how that magical time and the lasting love of my larger-than-life grandfather have continued to shape me—my goals, preferences, desires, and expectations.

I am forever grateful to my daughter and her husband, who blazed the trail that would lead me to my *new* Gopher Hollow, not just a place, but a state of mind, one that was immediately familiar, yet new…right here in Columbia, Tennessee.

AFTERWORD
The Books

WHEN I FIRST EMBARKED on this book project, I needed a little clarification about my grandfather's birthplace, to learn whether he was born in Portugal or Massachusetts, U.S.A. I pulled the first volume of his memoir collection, i.e., The Books, off the shelf to look up this important detail. Thus began my journey into Grandpa's memoirs.

Using his vintage 1940s Underwood manual typewriter, Grandpa began typing his life story at the age of eighty-one and completed the project at age ninety-one. There are very few typos, which is pretty amazing for a person of that age. Grandpa typed an astounding 416,000 words, single-spaced, which translates to 1,600 pages in a standard book. For perspective, it is equivalent in size to *Atlas Shrugged* and *Moby Dick* combined.

In all, my grandpa filled sixteen albums, which contained these typewritten pages, composed of historical information about his ancestry, his family life, and his career, as well as chronicling current happenings in his life, his family, and world events. Interspersed with the typewritten pages, Grandpa added photos, both vintage and current, newspaper clippings of the many articles that had been written about his career and community involvement, and, my personal favorite, his colorful travel brochures.

My grandpa had a way with words and expressed his thoughts in a lively, conversational style. I found myself unable to put them down, spending hours and hours out on the front porch in recent months immersed in his writings. Although this tangent set me behind on my own writing schedule, I believe it was God's way of bringing awareness to all the layers of the man who held the titles of son, father, grandfather, and great-grandfather.

In the books, I discovered many long-forgotten family moments once captured in photos that instantly summoned up memories of the occasions, events, or gatherings depicted in them. Ancestral family photos captivated me, as I searched the faces of his parents in their youth for features that I might have, too. I especially appreciated the many photos taken of my grandparents, mother, and uncle at the Big Bear cabin in the 1940s, pictures of Grandpa in the Palm Springs condo, and of course, all the photos of Gopher Hollow.

Grandpa was very sentimental, which was quite evident as I looked through his memoirs. He saved every letter and greeting card his loved ones had sent him over the years. These included letters from me, my sister, my cousins, my mom, and my uncle, and other family members. He also saved his grandkids' resumes and business cards, and yes, even that business plan for my future store that I had asked him to review back in 1981.

Some of the letters he received had been translated from Portuguese with the help of a friend of my cousin Shannon's who was fluent. These letters were from correspondence he had with the priest at the Sao Vicente parish on Sao Miguel, which had been the family church for a century. My great-grandfather had bequeathed four parcels of property to his two sons, who then donated them to the Sao Vicente church. The priest sent renderings of the two chapels they'd been able to add to the church, creating a cruciform shape from what had been rectangular. He also described the housing units that had been built on the other donated parcels that were occupied by the elderly and infirm. This was such a blessing for my grandpa, to see how, because of his father's hard work and ability to save money, the locals in the little town were now benefiting.

My grandfather was born to two Portuguese immigrants in Fall River, Massachusetts, on August 15, 1900, which is also the Feast Day of the Assumption of the Blessed Virgin Mary. He had a brother, Sylvian, who was two years older than him and was born in Sao Miguel, Azores, the homeland. Each of Grandpa's parents had recently immigrated to the United States from the Azores, a Portuguese archipelago off the coast of North Africa. His mother had come from Sao Jorje and his father from Sao Miguel, and then they met in Fall River, Massachusetts, at the cotton mill where they worked.

Before my grandpa was two years old, the family returned to Sao Miguel because his father, Joao, was very sick with tuberculosis and wanted to be home near his family members. His father passed away soon after at age thirty when Grandpa was only two years old. Once back in the States, his mother, Maria, eventually was remarried to a man named Manuel Charola, and soon the little family moved to the Stockton, California, area where they lived on a working farm.

By his story, you'd never guess that my grandfather was not born a go-getter. In fact, Grandpa often describes himself in his youth as "lazy" in the pages of his memoirs. He attributes this to his distaste for the farm life and also to having weak lungs due to asthma. He admits that his brother Sylvian was a very hard worker, while Grandpa preferred to lie in the haystacks and get lost in a good book. In 1917, at age seventeen, he joined the Army, mostly to escape farm life.

He served five honorable years in the Army until they downsized the troops after World War I and discharged him. After the Army, he put himself through business school, met and married my grandma at age twenty-three, bought their first house at age twenty-four, and got a job as a trader in the mining business. Soon after, at age twenty-seven, he designed a board game called the American Derby, a horse race-themed game, and sold over 10,000 units. That same year, my grandparents experienced a tragedy when their full-term baby boy died in childbirth. Grandpa mentions his son several times throughout the memoirs.

Later, he and Grandma moved to New York, where he worked as a journeyman under a certified public accountant, and Grandma worked at Gimbel's department store. A year later, they decided to put down roots in California.

In Los Angeles, Grandpa took a job as a traveling auditor for Greyhound, the bus line, and found that one of the offices he was overseeing was underperforming. Grandpa spotted an opportunity and asked to take it over.

This was right at the outset of the Great Depression, so to prosper, or just survive, Grandpa had to get very creative. He accepted items like watches and other jewelry in exchange for tickets, and focused on accommodating sailors looking for cheap transportation to the Midwest. He managed to keep the business afloat during the Depression, and as soon as it lifted, he began opening more offices.

When my grandparents were expecting my mother, they decided to build a home in Manhattan Beach. The total cost, including the land, was $2,500. While living there, Grandpa surprised my grandma with a brand-new piano, which I am the lucky beneficiary of today. Two years later, my uncle was born.

During this period, my grandfather also built a motel in Redondo Beach that he called the Grandview Motel. It had just fourteen units, but he added a small grocery store and restaurant to the property. He owned the motel for many years. In a page in Book 14, he laments not holding on to the property, and attached an article from 1989 announcing it had just sold for $2.53 million, where an eighty-room hotel was to be built.

After living in Manhattan Beach for nine years, my grandparents decided the family needed more space. They purchased the acre-sized lot and built the family home they lovingly nicknamed Gopher Hollow.

Grandpa's travel business grew to include nine travel offices in the Los Angeles region. During his illustrious forty-year career in the travel business, as the President of the American Society of Travel Advisors, he often visited countries that were seeking to open up to tourism, like Cuba and Argentina. I found a photo of my grandpa sitting right there in a meeting with Fidel Castro, and another photo of him standing with Eva Peron.

As I plowed through the books in his collection, I found many pictures of my grandpa photographed with celebrities. These were the photos that had once been framed and hanging on the wall in the den at Gopher Hollow. As a child, I'd sit on the twin bed there in the den, wondering who all those people were standing with my grandpa. Now, browsing through the books, I found photos of him with Anthony Quinn, Piper Laurie, Louis Armstrong, Ava Gardner, Cornell Wilde, and many other notables of the era.

When I spotted the brightly colored Funtour travel brochures, the trifolds I so clearly remembered being fascinated by as a kid snooping around in the den, I just smiled. Seeing them again now, nearly six decades later, brought back that same wave of pride I felt when I rifled through them as a child. The Funtours brand was his brainchild, born of a desire to provide people with fun and joy following the end of WWII. And his idea was a smash hit. The Funtours were annual train trips from Los Angeles to New Orleans timed around Mardi Gras. Passengers enjoyed a party atmosphere to and from the Mardi Gras celebration, with live Dixieland and Big Band music and even clowns adding to the festive ambiance.

In the books, Grandpa included dozens of professional black-and-white photos of the party trains and all the happy travelers, the

large, opulent balls, and amazing vintage photos of the Mardi Gras parades in the forties and fifties. He was granted the keys to the city of New Orleans on three occasions. As a career topper, in 1959, he was elected King of the Mardi Gras for the Krewe of Iris. Grandpa is listed in six volumes of Who's Who in America, of which I am in possession of three, while my cousins have the other three volumes.

After completing the review of all sixteen books, it was very clear to me that my grandfather loved nothing more than to make people happy. He walked around Gopher Hollow whistling, and his big, beautiful smile lit up any room. You could spot this joie de vivre in the fun, whimsical mid-century marketing materials and travel itineraries he'd created for his business that are sprinkled through the books.

Grandpa's presence was larger than life. He had an outsized ego and was a shameless ham who loved to dance and truly enjoy life. In fact, at eighty years old my very unique grandpa appeared on *The Gong Show*, a silly amateur talent show on TV at the time. His skit was very clever. In it, he shuffles out to the stage like a decrepit old man. He sits down on a bench to rest. Suddenly, he hears music playing (cue the song), and with that, Grandpa stands up straight and tall and begins dancing around on the stage like a thirty-year-old. As the music ends, he shuffles back and returns to the bench as an old man. And hey, he didn't get gonged!

Another admirable trait about Grandpa was his fierce loyalty to God and country. He was extremely patriotic and headed up the local WWII veteran's chapter. His crowning achievement was to have a memorial flagpole erected in his community. In several of the books, he chronicled the five-year red tape process, which was frustrating and tedious. But that day in 1991, when he stood proudly with his buddies in the veterans group, he finally got to see his dream come to fruition. As they raised the flag, honoring local

Medal of Honor recipient Thomas Pope, all his family got to witness the deep sense of accomplishment and love of country that shone on my grandfather's face.

I also discovered a revelation tucked into his memoirs, an admission made in multiple entries that he, too, "tried too hard." This brought a big smile to my face, as I recalled him telling me back in the early eighties that my problem was, "You try too hard." He had recognized in me the same exact tendency he'd had throughout his own life, and probably wanted to spare me from the ulcers he later suffered because of it.

Although I had always found my grandfather's successful career to be incredibly inspiring, his memoirs were equally balanced with sentimental writings about his beloved wife and family. I had to gear up emotionally when I got to the book written in 1985, as that was the year my sister died of cancer. Reading his words recounting the suffering and eventual death of his precious granddaughter revealed the depth of his love. He had happily supported her for nearly two years as she battled that monster, and he felt immensely blessed that he had the resources to do so. He adored us all and was a source of financial help to each of us at one time or another during our lives.

Was he perfect? Absolutely not. In fact, based on the frequent mentions of his Guardian Angel and God having guided him through life, I have no doubt that his Guardian Angel prompted him to seek out a priest in 1971, while his wife, my grandma, was dying of cancer in the hospital. That day he was on a mission to get to confession, to seek absolution for his sins.

This was a turning point for him, as it prompted his return to the church of his childhood, the Catholic Church, and with zeal. In the memoirs, he recalled sweet moments in his family home as his mother lit candles in front of a statue of the Blessed Virgin Mary and led them in the rosary. After his return to the Church, he never

THE BOOKS

missed Mass and often attended daily mass at the chapel adjacent to the Carmelite convent down the street from his apartment.

I wouldn't learn of my grandfather's shortcomings until many years later, and when I did, yes, I felt disappointed and sad. These human frailties were not supposed to happen to someone I had placed up on a pedestal my whole life. But with time, I forgave my grandpa. I figured if God had forgiven him, then I should, too. Plus, looking at my own past, who was I to throw that stone?

I eventually overcame those disappointments and have come to love and respect him for who he is, a wonderful yet flawed human being. His weaknesses did not overshadow all the good he'd done throughout his life. I am able to love and adore my grandfather for what he contributed to all of our lives, mine in particular. He had such a positive impact on me, through the things he taught me and demonstrated by example while I was young. In fact, once my cousin noted that I even whistled just like Grandpa. Hopefully, I have been demonstrating all he taught me to my own children and grand-children, to be a positive force in *their* lives, thanks to his example.

My grandfather prepared me for my life. While God has been right here with me, guiding me and protecting me throughout my life, my grandpa gave me the tools that would help me to face my many trials. And for that, I am forever grateful.

From Book #14 (circa 1990):

Theresa, like Grandpa, is a go-getter with a brain that never stops. She was doing a real good job with the Pacific Golf Club and they liked her work managing the golf shop. Now she was an expert in buying golf wearables that did not stay on the shelves very long. She, as she has done before, wrote Grandpa and outlined her plan to manage golf shops—2 or 3 to start, at a set figure per year. She would have a contract signed stipulating the yearly figure and explaining just what her expert talent would provide.

Just a few days ago, on April 17, she telephoned Grandpa elated, enthusiastically explaining that she had signed the third golf course. And to top everything, she said that she had given a contract price a little higher than the last golf course. This made Grandpa jump up and down on the couch that he was resting upon because he was so happy with the good news. Yes, Grandpa felt she was making a wise decision and he told Theresa so, but, frankly, she needed no encouragement. That is why Theresa is now Entrepreneur no. 1 in our family. Grandpa's rating has dropped to 1-b, and he is happy about that.

Indeed, I was a chip off the ole block—and how blessed was I.

About the Author

THERESA ANTHONY is the author of three nonfiction books, including *My 13th Station* (2019), *Hope Springs from a Mother's Broken Heart* (2021), and *In Search of Gopher Hollow* (2023).

After a twenty-year stint as a freelance writer, Ms. Anthony started her own business offering content writing services. As a content writer, she provides clients with inspiring and informative content within the mental health and addiction recovery fields and assorted other industries. In her personal quest for her happy place, Ms. Anthony has recently relocated to Columbia, Tennessee, where she finds every single day filled with new discoveries and abundant beauty. Ms. Anthony continues to find intense joy in her relationships with family and friends, her four beautiful grandchildren, creating artwork and jewelry for her Etsy shop Soul Stirrings Gifts, and her Catholic faith.

Website: www.TheresaAnthony.com
Facebook: www.facebook.com/theresaanthonyauthor
Instagram: @theresaanthonyauthor

Please kindly leave a book review on Amazon, Barnes & Noble, or on any of my social media platforms!

Made in the USA
Columbia, SC
24 November 2023